Strategy Execution

Strategy execution is one of the most important and exciting topics in management. Implementing strategy in today's complex organizations is an enormous challenge but one that all leaders must tackle. This lively book is an essential guide to strategy execution for practising managers and those in advanced management education. It combines the rigour of advanced research with the accessibility of practical experience and application to lead readers through the subject.

Drawing together existing knowledge and reporting findings from his own research, Andrew MacLennan brings this often neglected topic sharply into focus. After introducing and defining strategy execution, the book presents a series of systematic frameworks to help managers and leaders:

- identify common strategy execution barriers and diagnose performance problems in particular situations;
- translate conceptual strategies into concrete activities;
- align emergent activities and projects with strategic objectives;
- support critical activities by aligning organizational designs and systems.

Strategy Execution is an insightful, engaging and practical book. The models are supplemented throughout with real world examples, summaries of key issues and signposts to further readings. It is a comprehensive, easy to use book offering practitioners and advanced students a systematic approach to strategy implementation.

Andrew MacLennan is a facilitator, educator, researcher and leading expert on strategy execution. He is Managing Director of Strategy Execution Ltd, a member of Duke Corporate Education's global faculty and lectures at Edinburgh Business School in the UK. He has written widely on strategy execution and is a sought-after speaker on the subject.

"This is a masterful book about an important subject. *Strategy execution* is the missing link, without which even the best of plans is rendered impotent. Yet it is so often inadequately addressed or overlooked completely. This is why Dr MacLennan's book is so welcome. It is both eminently practical and intellectually rigorous, with a wealth of sensible and rational advice, and extremely useable models. It will hold the attention of anyone who is interested in how strategy can really be made to work in practice."

Professor Nigel Slack,
Professor of Operations Management & Strategy,
Warwick Business School, UK

"This is an excellent book highlighting the common disconnect between what organisations think they should do and what they are actually doing. All too often, organisations find making the right things happens very difficult. This book explains why this is and what you can do to change it – it is relevant for all companies trying to make change happen."

Neil Roden,
Group Director, Human Resources,
The Royal Bank of Scotland plc, UK

"Andrew MacLennan manages to blend his extensive experience and deep knowledge of underlying theory into a marvellously readable, accessible and practical manual on strategy execution that that belongs within easy reach of every strategist – whether manager or student, practicing or aspiring."

Professor Neil Kay,
Emeritus Professor of Business Economics,
University of Strathclyde, UK

"The art of the possible made a reality. This book is a must read for budding strategists, full of great frameworks and techniques, all of which can be applied in real situations. It provides the reader with a practical perspective and confidence to make things happen. A rare read in the area of strategy, indeed."

Tony Brown,
Managing Director – People & Change,
Friends Provident plc, UK

"Deeply thoughtful and well researched. Provides clear, practical ways to ensure that strategic plans really do achieve their intended business results."

Tracey Ashworth-Davies,
HR Director,
Molson Coors Brewing Company, UK

Strategy Execution

Translating strategy into action in complex organizations

Andrew MacLennan

Routledge
Taylor & Francis Group

LONDON AND NEW YORK

First published 2011
by Routledge
2 Park Square, Milton Park, Abingdon, Oxon OX14 4RN

Simultaneously published in the USA and Canada
by Routledge
270 Madison Ave, New York, NY 10016

Routledge is an imprint of the Taylor & Francis Group, an informa business

© 2011 Andrew MacLennan

The right of Andrew MacLennan to be identified as the Author of this work
has been asserted by him in accordance with sections 77 and 78 of the
Copyright, Designs and Patents Act 1988.

Typeset in Times by
HWA Text and Data Management, London
Printed and bound in Great Britain by
CPI Antony Rowe, Chippenham, Wiltshire

British Library Cataloguing in Publication Data
A catalogue record for this book is available from the British Library

Library of Congress Cataloguing in Publication Data
Strategy execution: translating strategy into action in complex organizations /
edited by Andrew MacLennan.
     p. cm.
  Includes bibliographical references and index.
  1. Strategic planning. 2. Management. I. MacLennan, Andrew.
HD30.28.S739679 2010
658.4'012–dc22   2010002286

ISBN: 978–0–415–38055–3 (hbk)
ISBN: 978–0–415–38056–0 (pbk)
ISBN: 978–0–203–84733–6 (ebk)

Contents

Illustrations

Figures

Tables

Boxes

Acknowledgements

I could not have written this book without the help and support of a great many people. It is the result of many years of interactions with colleagues, clients, and friends.

Through publications, presentations, and personal conversations, other writers and researchers across the world have heavily shaped and influenced my thinking. My peers have generously shared their insights to develop this difficult field, and I hope they will value this contribution to the team effort. I have endeavoured diligently to trace the sources of facts and ideas and, if I have failed in any way, welcome information that fills in gaps.

Practitioners in their thousands have contributed to the development of this book through my field research and work with organizations, and I hope I have given their input faithful voice. It is no small thing to allow researchers access to organizations and their dirty linen (which one invariably comes across in the strategy execution field). I thank them for their generosity, patience, and trust. I am also grateful to my business school students and executive education programme delegates who often furnished me with as many insights as I did them.

There are some people and organizations I would like to thank especially:

To Alex Roberts for first igniting my interest in strategy execution, generously sharing his insights and spending lots of time debating the fine details of the subject.

To Alex Scott and Iain Henderson for supervising my doctorate in the area – and in doing so, imparting great wisdom and encouragement in equal measure to build my research and writing skills – and for their kind support since.

To other colleagues and friends who have given their advice and time without hesitation, including Iain Harrison, Graham Lee, Ian McIntosh, John Sanders, Bill Wallace, and many others.

To the teams at Duke Corporate Education and Edinburgh Business School for providing opportunities for me to connect with so many fine minds.

To Edinburgh Business School and Pearson Education for kindly permitting the use of some material I wrote for *Making Strategies Work* and to Strategy Execution Ltd. for kindly permitting the use of various diagrams and other material.

To the team at Routledge, especially Jacqueline Curthoys, Nancy Hale, Terry Clague, and Sharon Golan, all of whom demonstrated the patience of saints and were steadfastly supportive as the book emerged.

And finally to my wife, Jane, and children – Callum, Duncan and Isla – all of whom accept the stream of projects that steal me away from them without complaint and give me all the energy I could ask for to implement my plans. I dedicate this book to them.

Andrew MacLennan
January 2010

Chapter 1

Introduction

Words are easy and many, while great deeds are difficult and rare.

Winston Churchill

The strategy execution challenge

This book is about one of the most important and exciting fields in management – strategy execution. The challenge of implementing strategy successfully is one that faces managers across the globe and in organizations of every kind. However, few organizations have discovered how to make strategy work reliably – the failure rate of planned strategies remains remarkably high.

A survey conducted by the *Economist Intelligence Unit* revealed that barely 40 per cent of executives rated their companies as being successful at execution.[1] Another survey suggested that companies typically realize only about 60 per cent of their strategies' potential values because of breakdowns in both planning and execution.[2] *Fortune* magazine estimated that 70 per cent of chief executive officer departures are the consequences of strategy execution failures.[3] Yet another study found that half of all strategic decisions fail to get implemented.[4] Others have suggested that upward of 70 per cent of strategies fail to achieve intended objectives upon implementation.[5] Each of these studies has limitations, but together they paint a picture that reflects the impression of experts in the field – an alarmingly small proportion of strategies are implemented successfully.

There are many causes of strategy execution failure but, intriguingly, even the largest and most resourceful organizations have generally failed to overcome them. Given they can attract the most talented executives and access the world's finest consulting and business school minds, one might expect they should be able to navigate the challenges successfully. However, incredibly little guidance on strategy execution is available to managers from these sources. Only a handful of books have been written on the topic, many of which are out of print. A review of articles in academic journals paints a similar picture. This is in stark contrast to the field of strategic planning, where numerous theories and tools are available to managers. A quick Internet search illustrates this discrepancy – at the time of writing, a Google search using the term *strategic planning* retrieves nearly 13.9

million hits, whereas searches for the terms *strategy implementation* and *strategy execution* retrieve only 520,000 and 283,000, respectively.[6]

This book aims to help plug that gap, and the rest of this introductory chapter outlines how.

A focus on 'real' strategy execution

The boundaries of *strategy execution* (a term used interchangeably with strategy implementation) are hazy, and there is no doubt the subject has important links to other areas of management. However, for clarity it is worth distinguishing strategy execution from two other important fields that are often misleadingly confused with this area.

Strategic change is a similarly important and ill-defined topic but relates mainly to changes in the *content* of strategy and how decision makers decide upon these.[7] These issues, though relevant to strategy execution, are obviously not its focus. Correspondingly, the substantial body of knowledge on strategic change generally does not address the issues important to strategy execution.

Change management has long been an important area of interest to managers. An increasing number of business authors are tackling this topic, focused on the challenge of 'execution' and 'making things happen'.[8] These are worthwhile endeavours, but not all organizational changes are 'strategic', and most of what is written in the change management field does not address the issue of strategy. Managing change successfully is, of course, important, but it logically *follows* the challenge of translating conceptual strategic objectives into sets of concrete actions that can actually be implemented. That challenge is strategy execution's principle role and the focus of this book.

In my view, these subtle distinctions are the reason that many organizations have apparently sound strategies and well-managed operations but cannot demonstrate any real connections between the two. Some books, titled as if focused on strategy execution, actually discuss changes to planned strategy at the cost of how to implement it. Others explore general organizational change without that critical link to strategy. This book seeks to bridge the gap between strategy and action and, hence, it really is about strategy execution!

A rigorous but practical guide

This book is specifically intended to be of high practical value to managers and serve those pursuing academic qualifications and undertaking research. It combines existing knowledge and the findings of rigorous empirical research with wide practical experience to produce insights that should take practitioners' thinking well beyond where it would be with experience alone but aims to avoid the pitfall of irrelevance encountered in some research-based literature. Some interesting material has been published on strategy implementation in recent years[9] but, generally, it does not explore the detail necessary to inform concrete decisions for practicing managers under pressure to deliver; this book aims to do that. It is partly for this reason that many of the learning materials generally associated with a textbook have been migrated to the companion website rather than letting them impede the flow of the book itself. Writing a book for audiences that are often treated separately requires a delicate balance, but I am passionate that we need to draw management practice, education, and research closer together to make valuable progress in these arenas. The medical profession benefits from tightly integrated practice, teaching, and research – and I believe management can gain from a similarly rounded approach.

A focus on rigorous thinking

Management ideas and theories often have an alluring quality that makes them hugely popular – for a while. It is perhaps the implication that complex management challenges can be distilled into short, sharp programmes of change delivered according to a simple template that is so attractive to overwhelmed managers. For authors, it is tempting to stack books full of popular management ideas that keep them 'up-to-date'. However, a glance back through management history confirms that most management ideas fall out of favour before long, only to be replaced by something new. The speed with which this cycle passes is increasing as publishers, consulting firms, and conference organizers devour each sellable idea as it appears. Actually, few of the popular 'fashions' are new ideas, and even fewer live up to the promises made about them.[10] Many of them suffer from significant problems, and organizations can create more problems than they solve when attempting to implement them.

The focus of this book is the *clear-headed thinking* necessary to tackle management challenges. A small number of key frameworks are presented – some of which are new, others of which have pre-existing roots – but no claim is made that they can be used successfully on 'autopilot'. Strategy execution is difficult, and the techniques discussed need intelligent and diligent application.

A strong research underpinning

Strategy execution is a seriously under-researched area without an established theoretical basis, so this book has to do more than pull together what is already known about the challenge. The findings from original research are also presented. This research, conducted over the last 10 years, includes a number of in-depth case studies, some lasting many years, making it the largest study ever undertaken in the strategy execution field. A range of data collection methods has been used within these studies, including the following:

- document and archival analysis
- semi-structured, multi-level interviews

- passive and participant observation
- action research via interventions to test structured techniques

Sophisticated qualitative data analysis techniques have been employed to distill these data and tease out the findings presented in this book. For those with an interest in them, further details of the research methodologies used for the studies that underpin this book are set out in the appendices. In addition to the case studies, the presentation of ideas here draws on strategy execution consultancy and executive education work with dozens of organizations and thousands of managers. Effort has been made to complement each idea – whether original or not – with a calibration of how valid and reliable the evidence base for it is. As discussed, strategy execution science is at best patchy – and it's important to recognize this when making decisions based upon the ideas emerging from it. For example, where considerable uncertainties remain, managers are wise to use pilot exercises to test and refine ideas before full-scale implementation.

The identities of many of the organizations involved in these case studies have been veiled. The issues explored are commercially sensitive, and data were collected under agreements to protect the identities of the individuals and organizations involved. However, general information about each organization is provided insofar as is possible and necessary to provide a rich context.

The audiences and format of this book

This book is aimed at several audiences – practicing managers, those in advanced management education and, to a lesser extent, researchers. Correspondingly, the format of the book has been designed to suit the needs of these groups.

Ultimately, this book is intended to help practicing managers tackle the challenge of executing strategy. Hence, the book sets out to demystify some conceptual issues and provide a structured and elegant framework for strategy execution that is oriented toward enabling *decisions* and *action*. Managers seeking clear guidance can read the text flexibly without necessarily troubling themselves with the endnotes, appendices, and companion website.

However, as noted earlier, strategy execution is an extremely difficult area. 'Airport' books do not do it justice. They are often crammed with the names of well-known corporations but barely scratch the surface of complex topics and can leave intelligent managers feeling short-changed when they return to the realities of their work. Many of those interested in moving beyond this superficiality will have chosen to study strategy execution at a business school or through another learning route. Hence, this book focuses more on the necessary detail than the tales of corporate heroes and their conquests and seeks to assist these scholars to *apply* the ideas presented and hence learn by doing. These students can work through the book methodically, dip into the endnotes and appendices for further information, and explore the references and suggested further reading. They can also make use of the additional resources available on the companion website at www.strategy-execution.net. All of the learning aids useful in a good textbook, such as learning summaries, case studies, videos, and multiple-choice questions, are available. So, too, are interactive learning tools that will usefully aid study.

Finally, within the context of management science, the subject of strategy execution is in its infancy. Much of what we think we know must be held contingently – subject to revision and refinement in years to come. Hence, this book has to balance the need to inform practitioners with the duty to stimulate thinking and support the work of other researchers in this area. They will wish not only to read the main text but to explore the endnotes and appendices in detail, where these deal with topics of interest. The book is intended to signpost existing strategy execution literature and present original research. Those with the additional responsibility (and challenge!) of teaching strategy execution will be interested in the companion website at www.strategy-execution.net, which includes material for teachers and students of the subject.

The companion website also provides all interested readers with a constantly updated source of information about strategy execution. This includes news about developments in the subject and a list of references to other publications.

The structure of the book

The remainder of the book is structured as outlined in Table 1.1, which explains the purpose, and underlying rationale, behind the structure of the book.

Summary of key points

- Strategy execution is difficult. Research suggests that around half of strategic decisions are not executed at all and that a substantially higher proportion of strategies fail to achieve their objectives upon implementation. Executives seem to recognize this – a significant majority of them do not rate their organizations as being successful at strategy execution.
- There is little guidance on strategy execution to help these executives – we know far more about how to plan strategy than how to execute it. Strategy execution and strategy implementation are terms used interchangeably.
- Strategic change is not the same as strategy execution – it relates to changes in the *content* of strategy. Change management is not the same as strategy execution – even changes that improve performance do not *necessarily* execute strategy. Many organizations have sound strategies and efficient operations but only a vague relationship between the two – strategy execution deals with this gap.
- This book is aimed at both practitioners and advanced management students – it is intended to be both a practical and rigorous guide that encourages disciplined thinking about what is a complex topic. This book weaves together existing ideas and new insights from original empirical research.

Table 1.1 Structure of the book

Chapter	Purpose
1 Introduction	Introduces the book, what it seeks to achieve and how it is set out.
2 What is strategy execution?	Locates strategy execution within the field of strategy and provides a clear definition of the term and related concepts.
3 The strategy execution challenge	Explores how the environment is changing and making strategy execution more important but also more difficult.
4 Diagnosing strategy execution problems	Explores how strategy execution problems in organizations can best be diagnosed and identifies the most common ones, to ensure that strategy execution efforts are properly directed.
5 A framework for strategy execution	Introduces a set of core principles and a framework to manage the strategy execution process, covering how it should be applied and important caveats. The following three chapters explore the elements of this model in depth.
6 Translating strategy into action	Tackles probably the greatest strategy execution challenge – identifying what actions to undertake in order to achieve strategic objectives. Introduces strategy execution maps and shows how they can be used to explore competitive advantage generated by strategy execution capability.
7 Aligning action with strategy	Introduces a series of techniques to complement and validate 'top-down' planning with a systematic approach to ensure activities planned 'bottom-up' are aligned with strategic objectives.
8 Aligning organizational designs and systems	Explores the key organizational components which affect strategy execution, including the allocation of accountability and responsibility, organization structure, performance measurement, targets, and reward systems.
9 Conclusion	Summarizes the key points made in the book and reflects on the strategy execution challenge set out.

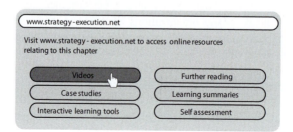

Chapter 2

What is strategy execution?

Theory without practice is pointless, practice without theory is mindless.

Lenin

As already noted, strategy execution is a subject without clear boundaries. In fact it has no widely accepted definition and very few writers have yet attempted to pin down what it really means. However, doing so is really important to enable a useful exploration of the topic. Rather than leaping straight to a definition, it's worth locating the strategy execution concept within the wider realm of strategy to give it context.

Organizational fundamentals

At a fundamental level, an organization is a simple entity:

- Its formation is driven by **objectives** – such as producing a financial return, providing a public service or tackling a social problem.
- The organization needs funding (be it investor capital, taxpayers' funds or charitable donations) for **resource interactions** such as purchasing raw materials, equipment, services, and paying for employees' time and commitment.
- These resources are secured in order to undertake **activities.**
- These activities directly or indirectly cause **market interactions.**
- Over time, the pattern of these interactions constitute a level of **performance** In relation to the organization's objectives.
- If performance is inadequate, the objectives are not achieved and the organization's existence is threatened.

Figure 2.1 summarizes this logically sequential framework.

Those managing an organization must therefore make crucial decisions that answer fundamental questions. For example:

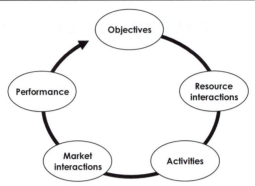

Figure 2.1 Organizational fundamentals

- What are the organization's objectives?
- What resources must be secured, and how might resources best be allocated?
- What are the critical activities managers must ensure are undertaken?
- What pattern of market interactions must the organization aim to create?
- How will performance be measured, to determine if the organization is sustainably achieving its objectives?

Strategy as a pattern of market and resource interactions

The element 'market interactions' requires elaboration. Organizations interact with their environments in thousands of ways[1] but the interactions with by far the most widespread and ongoing importance relate to:

- products (and services) offered
- channels used (to market, sell and deliver products)
- markets (and the segments within them) with which interactions occur.

Any organization provides examples of this mix in action. A street newspaper seller offers newspapers (the product) through direct personal selling (the channel) to news-seeking pedestrians (the market). Multinational software businesses sell ranges of software applications (the products) through retailers, partners, directly online and by mail (the channels) to appropriate hardware users (the market). Figure 2.2 depicts these decision areas graphically. The scope and the mix of products offered, channels used and markets targeted should of course be selected on the basis of objectives – it should be plausible that these interactions will cause desired performance.

Organizations also need to bear in mind the resources available to them and the strengths built up internally as a result, when selecting optimal products to offer, channels to use and markets to target. The continual flow of the right kinds

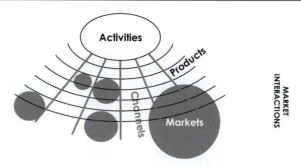

Figure 2.2 The pattern of market interactions fundamental to strategy

of supplies and staff into an organization develop strengths and enable continual exploitation of assets. Resource strengths simultaneously constitute opportunities and constraints that affect product, channel, and market decisions. In fact, we can think of performance as the *value* the organization creates through its decisions about what resources to secure, activities to undertake with them and the pattern of market interactions that follow. Figure 2.3 builds upon Figure 2.2 by adding these resource pattern considerations.

Of course, most organizations must make all these decisions in anticipation of and in response to competitor activity. Profit-seeking businesses almost always have some rivals (even if only indirect ones) and not-for-profit organizations inevitably compete for the opportunity to influence stakeholders, be they citizens served by a government agency or potential donors to charities. Rivals complicate decisions about resource and market interactions considerably.

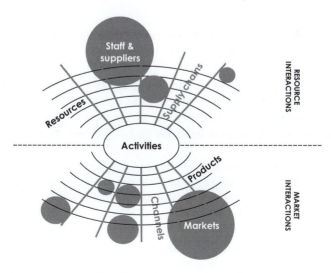

Figure 2.3 Strategy as a pattern of market and resource interactions

This quick exploration of fundamental ideas has helped illuminate the nature of strategy. The *pattern* of resource and market interactions (incorporating major product, channel and market decisions) is core to what strategy means in an organizational context. The next couple of sections define strategy and then strategy execution clearly. Pinning down these meanings is important, not just to explain the title of this book. The field of strategy execution has been evolving without a clear definition of what it is really about for far too many years!

Defining strategy

The exact nature of the strategy concept has been a matter of some debate.[2] At an abstract level, there is little room for disagreements about definitions. However, definitions of strategy that relate to specific entities (such as corporations or business units) vary considerably and this has clouded the meaning of the term. Just think how many different answers would you get if you asked managers you know to define what strategy means. Despite its ambiguity, it is a term that is typically used liberally. An analysis of formal definitions of strategy from a selection of leading thinkers over the years is displayed in Table A1 in the appendices. A number of common themes emerge from these definitions, suggesting that strategy incorporates:

- long-term objectives/mission/purpose/goals
- plans/policies for achieving these, relating to:
  - managing interactions with the environment
  - market/product scope of business activity
  - resources allocation.

For the purposes of this book, we can distinguish long-term organizational objective/goal/mission/purpose from strategy and call it an origination's *overall objective* for simplicity.[3] The rationale here is that organizations have a fundamental purpose and can devise a strategy that articulates how (within the environment in which they operate) this overall objective can be achieved. We can then therefore define *strategy* as the pattern of resource and market interactions an organization has with its environment in order to achieve its overall objective.

Most large organizations now attempt some form of strategic planning. 67 per cent of those responding to Bain & Company's Management Tools survey in 2008 reported using it. Executives also reported high levels of satisfaction using strategic planning as a tool.[4] However, as discussed in Chapter 1, there is little evidence that investments in strategic planning are complemented by successful efforts to implement the strategies developed.

With strategy defined, it is now possible to cleanly tease apart planned strategy and strategy execution. For the purposes of this distinction between formulation and implementation, we can define *planned strategy* as the pattern of resource and market interactions an organization intends to have with its environment in order to achieve its overall objective.

We ought also to define strategic planning to clearly differentiate it from the strategy execution. Building on the logic outlined so far, we can define *strategic planning* as the process of determining the pattern of resource and market interactions an organization intends to have with its environment in order to achieve its overall objective.

Of course, not all strategy is systematically planned. Patterns of interactions emerge as a result of planned and more evolutionary activities that are nevertheless legitimate responses to the environment. Hence for completeness, we can define *emergent strategy* simply as the pattern of resource and market interactions an organization is having with its environment.

Defining strategy execution

The discussion thus far about the meaning of strategy has been an essential preamble to defining strategy execution (or, if you prefer, strategy implementation). Sharp-eyed readers will have noted that the definition of strategy did not deal with the 'activities' component of the model introduced in Figure 2.1. This is because strategy is conceptual – it relates to *patterns* of interactions. However, organizations need to manipulate these patterns, and can only do so (albeit indirectly), through concrete activities. It is the link between strategy and activities that is the domain of strategy execution.

As noted already, strategy execution has not been clearly defined by other writers, despite there being several books on the subject. Some thinkers, such as Paul Stonich have distinguished strategy formulation and implementation by suggesting planning is about *where* the firm is going, whereas implementation is about *how* to get there.[5] Such distinctions are a useful start but fall short of giving the definition needed for practical application of the ideas. Tony Eccles provides perhaps the most useful description of strategy implementation in the management literature to date:

> ... strategy implementation is the action that moves the organization along its choice of route towards its goal – the fulfilment of its mission, the achievement of its vision[6] ... strategy implementation is **the realization of intentions**.[7]

This is helpful, and we can go even further and offer a clear definition of strategy execution that builds upon the definitions of strategy, planned strategy and emergent strategy laid out above. We can define strategy execution as the process of indirectly manipulating the pattern of interactions an organization has with its environment in order to achieve its overall objective. Box 2.1 summarizes this and all the definitions we have developed in this chapter.

> *Box 2.1* Key definitions
>
> *Strategy* is the pattern of resource and market interactions an organization has with its environment in order to achieve its overall objective.
>
> *Planned strategy* is the pattern of resource and market interactions an organization intends to have with its environment in order to achieve its overall objective.
>
> *Strategic planning* is the process of determining the pattern of resource and market interactions an organization intends to have with its environment in order to achieve its overall objective.
>
> *Emergent strategy* is the pattern of resource and market interactions an organization is having with its environment.
>
> *Strategy execution* is the process of indirectly manipulating the pattern of resource and market interactions an organization has with its environment in order to achieve its overall objective.

Strategy execution relates to how planned strategy is translated into the concrete activities that will actually cause its realization and how more emergent activities can be aligned with overall objectives.

The caveat in this definition that manipulations are indirect is of particular importance. Michael Porter, amongst others, has noted that strategy is essentially a solution to the Principal-Agent problem, because senior managers simply cannot undertake every activity required in organizations.[8] Strategy deals by definition with *patterns* of interactions, which means execution of it must be tackled via frameworks that seek to manipulate these patterns, rather than via isolated direct actions. This reinforces the distinction made in Chapter 1 between strategy execution and managing change. Lots of changes can be made to improve organizational performance, but unless they are integrated and together can plausibly deliberately change the *pattern* of resource and market interactions an organization has with its environment, these changes are not necessarily 'strategic' and not within the primary focus of strategy execution. At a practical level, they might also be low-value distractions that miss the bigger strategic picture.

The evolution of strategy execution

It's useful to give a quick overview of how strategy execution thinking has emerged to locate this discussion within the field. As is perhaps unsurprising, given the lack of a clear definition of the term, strategy execution theory is patchy. So too is the empirical research in the area.

The subject of strategic management originally incorporated strategy implementation as one of its elements.[9] Early theorists focused on organizational structure and resource allocation in particular. Less attention was paid to people management issues that might be important for the successful execution of strategy. Progressively, those studying strategic management focused increasingly on strategic planning at the expense of strategy execution.

In the 1970s and 1980s, several management thinkers began taking a dedicated interest in strategy execution.[10] However, they remain small in number right up to the present day. Today, only around fifteen books focused on strategy execution have been published. Only a few of these are underpinned by any empirical research and a similar picture emerges from the modest number of academic papers and articles on the topic. As a result, much of the existing literature must be viewed as early-stage and explorative.

This does not mean that there is little guidance on how to execute strategy. On the contrary, there is a great deal of advice available, however it is spread throughout dozens of different disciplines and areas of study.[11] It is possible to draw useful ideas about implementation from fields as diverse as strategic planning, change management, organization theory, human resources, marketing, organization behaviour, psychology, industrial economics, and systems thinking. Unfortunately, little of the material that can be useful is neatly labelled as being of value to those seeking to understand strategy execution, so a significant challenge is presented.

Summary of key points

- Strategy execution has been an ill-defined term and the boundaries of the subject are fuzzy.
- Organizations are fundamentally simple, having objectives, using funding to secure resources, undertaking activities, interacting with markets and thus performing – ideally, but not always, in ways that achieve their objectives.
- Market interactions are critical and centre around three key choices – products/services to offer, markets/segments to serve and channels to use.
- Resource interactions are also critical to develop internal strengths and undertake the activities that will cause these market interactions.
- Organizations create value through their decisions about resources interactions, activities and market interactions – and compete with rivals creating value with similar resource and market interactions.
- An organization's *overall objective* is its ultimate purpose and reason for existence.
- *Strategy* is the pattern of resource and market interactions an organization has with its environment in order to achieve its overall objective.
- *Strategy execution* is the process of indirectly manipulating the pattern of resource and market interactions an organization has with its environment in order to achieve its overall objective.
- Strategy and strategy execution deal with *patterns of interactions* because managers cannot directly manipulate every action an organization has with its environment – they must use frameworks to achieve an organization's overall objective.
- To date, there has been little empirical research into strategy execution, but useful ideas do exist in other areas of management science.

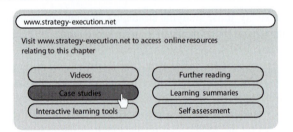

www.strategy-execution.net

Visit www.strategy-execution.net to access online resources relating to this chapter

Videos

Case studies

Interactive learning tools

Further reading

Learning summaries

Self assessment

Chapter 3

The strategy execution challenge

In theory, there is no difference between theory and practice.
But, in practice, there is.

Jan L. A. van de Snepscheut[1]

Chapter 1 summarized the findings of several research studies that together confirm what managers know intuitively – strategy execution is difficult and often unsuccessful. However, overcoming these difficulties is an essential challenge. Logically, organizations that execute strategy better, faster, at lower cost, and taking less risk will outperform competitors. This chapter explains what makes strategy execution difficult and why overcoming these challenges matters and lays the foundations for how to execute strategy effectively.

The dual challenges of scale and complexity

As Chapter 2 highlighted, at a fundamental level, organizations are simple entities – formulating objectives, securing funding and resources, undertaking activities, interacting with markets and, thus, performing. Stated in plain language, this process sounds rather simple and easy to think through – and for small, uncomplicated organizations, it generally is. However, successful organizations have two important tendencies. First, they grow and start serving more customers, employing more people and producing more products or services. Second, they expand the range of interactions they have with their environments by doing things such as introducing new products, expanding into new geographic areas, and using new channels. These things complicate organizations and make managers' tasks much more difficult.

Size and complexity are the principal reasons why managers in most organizations need to concern themselves with the idea of strategy – the conceptual framework that helps them think about resource and market interactions. The limitations of human thinking mean that large and complex organizations cannot be micromanaged. Those leading these organizations cannot collect and process information about every activity or monitor all environmental interactions, for example. They are forced to use 'frameworks' that deal with *patterns* of these activities and interactions and provide a *way of thinking* about them that supports decision making. Even managers wholly uninterested in the idea of strategy have to make many potentially strategic decisions – such as introducing new products, selecting organization structures, and making budgetary allocations.

Making planning useful

It seems self-evident that any organization that invests in strategic planning should also pay particular attention to strategy execution. For the benefits of strategic planning to be realized, the plans that result from it must be converted into action. However, in practice, this rarely happens in a coordinated way. Strategic planning might often be seen as an indulgence on the part of senior managers. Anyone with experience in large organizations will be all too familiar with 'away days' where a select few managers go off to enjoy some intellectual stimulation and produce a 'strategy'. A great deal of time is dedicated to finding the 'right' wording for mission statements and strategic objectives. Often, someone is tasked with writing a document that summarizes the plan, which might be used to justify budget requests but then is filed on a shelf or in a drawer until next year when the process restarts.

It is typically difficult to see how the thousands of day-to-day activities of organizations are actually impacted by leaders' strategizing. Many planning participants will return to the office with some bland re-articulations of high-level objectives such as 'income growth' and 'increasing operational effectiveness' but not articulate in any detail how these goals will be achieved.

Despite this, strategic planning is highly popular. In practice, organizations use strategic planning in different ways and, in spite of managers' enthusiasm for the process, the fundamental quality of strategic plans is highly variable. Many 'economically sound' strategies are generated, but a key criterion in assessing any strategy must be its potential to actually be implemented. My own research suggests that such strategies are rather rare – and this seems to fit with common anecdotal complaints from managers.

The environmental pressures

Although these problems persist, there is evidence that more managers are paying attention to the strategy execution challenge. This resurgence of interest is reflected in a modest increase in the number of books and articles on the topic – albeit from a very small base. Almost certainly, this new interest is being driven by specific changes in the environment that are putting managers under much increased pressure to ensure their organizations perform.

Regulation

Regulation of industries by governments has changed dramatically over the last couple of decades. Regulations historically created monopolies and oligopolies or defended them. In many countries, the likes of banking, telecommunications, energy supply, broadcasting, rail transport, mail delivery, health care, and civil aviation have traditionally been either provided by government or tightly controlled by them. These controls minimized competition in these industries, and whether organizations were profit seekers or public sector bodies, those managing these organizations were protected by this lack of rivalry. They had enormous freedom to run their organizations as they saw fit, sometimes with little regard for stakeholders such as customers and employees. Many organizations were undoubtedly run poorly but, without comparators or an efficient market to weed out underperformers, ineffective managers and organizations survived.

The nature of regulation has changed. Many of these industries have been 'deregulated', insofar as they have been opened up to market competition. In the United Kingdom, for example, Margaret Thatcher's government led a massive privatization of public sector companies. Frustrated with perceived poor service and inefficiencies in organizations such as British Rail, they saw competition as the force that would drive greater customer orientation and efficiency. Efforts to open markets up to competition continue to this day, with the continuing deregulation of the postal system in the United Kingdom, for example.

The result of these privatizations and the introduction of mandatory competitive tendering of a great deal of public sector work mean a great deal of activity has been transferred away from monopolies to the more ruthless arena of commercial enterprise, where poor performers – including those who cannot execute strategy – are more likely to struggle to survive. Commercial organizations in oligopolistic industries have also seen deregulation open up their industries to new entrants. For example, retail banks now compete with building societies, life assurance companies, supermarkets, and a much wider range of rivals than they previously did.

Government regulations can still create barriers to entry in industries. For example, in financial services, regulations to counter money laundering, mis-selling, and financial instability have the side effect of protecting existing incumbents. The 2008/2009 'credit crisis' that triggered the collapse of several major global financial services companies is sure to necessitate further regulation that restricts how firms behave and makes industry participation more costly. However, the long-term trend is still toward enabling competition. Powerful legislation has been introduced in many countries to prevent the misuse of dominant market power by companies. Microsoft is perhaps one of the best-known targets of such regulation, defending 'antitrust' lawsuits brought by the U. S. Department of Justice and the European Commission, after bundling its own Internet browser and media player with its operating systems, allegedly to the disadvantage of less-dominant competing software providers.

New corporate governance regulations have further reduced the scope for underperforming managers and their companies to shroud poor performance. Increased competition, transparency, and scrutiny are going some way to force managers to pay attention to their strategy implementation responsibilities.

Consumer power

There is no doubt that in most industries, consumer power is rising. In part, this is caused by increased education and awareness. Consumers in developed countries are familiar with sophisticated advertising, sales promotions, sponsorship, personal sales techniques, money-back guarantees, offers of free credit, and so on. The increased use of these is in fact some evidence of reducing supplier power. However, what is fascinating is the speed with which consumers can gain the upper hand even in new industries and with novel and complex products. This step-change is one of the most salient implications of Internet technology and the new media sources that have developed around it. Consumers now have access not only to newspaper 'best buy' tables and occasional consumer television programmes. They can systematically search literally billions of Web pages or go directly to one of the hundreds of price-comparison websites available (many of which specialize in one product area or another). So-called smartphones promise to continue this trend. For example, a software application is now available for Apple's iPhone that uses the phone's camera to scan product barcodes and the phone's Internet connection to retrieve price listings for scanned items in multiple retailers. This enables shoppers to instantly check competitor prices without even leaving a store.

The transparency of product availability, features and, in particular, price has increased consumer power enormously. The result is that businesses have to fight harder to maintain competitive advantage.

Knowledge transfer

Globalization has been talked about for a long time now, and there is no doubt that it is becoming a reality for an increasingly wide range of industries. Increasing numbers of multinational companies and the emergence of truly global brands confirm this. A huge proportion of the world's population recognize not only the classic global brands such as Coca-Cola, McDonalds and Sony but much newer names such as Amazon, Google, iTunes, Facebook, and Twitter.

The implications of globalization for business are many, but of particular relevance to strategy execution is the speed with which competitive business are – often unintentionally – sharing important ideas, technology, and expertise. This inadvertent sharing of knowledge operates at many levels.

Huge media have built up around publishing business ideas. Newspapers, magazines, trade journals, academic journals, and book publishers all specialize in serving managers with information about organizations. Much of that information

Box 3.1 Mini case study – Cheap insurance

The general insurance industry is changing rapidly. Following the example of Direct Line, launched in the United Kingdom in 1985, there was a steady trend toward insurers' dealing with customers directly rather than acting through insurance brokers. The rationale was clear – using new technology to run call centres, quotation systems, and then websites, insurers could 'cut out the middlemen' and secure a much higher margin for themselves when selling car, home, and other general insurance products.

However, things changed again. As the number of insurance brands grew, consumers were presented with a problem. There were simply too many options to systematically compare. Being sure of getting the best deal might have entailed getting quotes from two-dozen insurers or more – a time-consuming process. A solution appeared in the form of a new type of intermediary. Over the last 10 years, firms such as confused.com, moneysupermarket.com, comparethemarket.com, and many others have launched online services to enable quick comparison of insurance quotes (and many other services besides). Thus, consumers once again can rely upon an intermediary to search the market for them, albeit thereafter progressing to a direct relationship with the insurer.

These new intermediaries have, through exploiting the structure of the market, captured a profitable role for themselves, acting as sales and marketing servicers of insurers and reducing insurers' margins commensurately by taking a referral fee for each customer passed on to the insurers.

At the same time, a second type of intermediary has emerged. 'Cashback' websites such as topcashback.co.uk and quidco.com also refer customers to insurers and other retailers but pay all or some of the referral fees they collect back to their customers, often relying upon advertising instead for revenues. For products such as home or car insurance, this cashback can be in the region of £100 – often a substantial proportion of the product cost and an attractive reward for a few extra clicks. There are even websites that compare cashback sites to determine which is best to use for a particular provider.

Knowledgeable consumers can exploit the situation. By using price comparison websites to find the best deals but – rather than progressing through their sites to purchase the product (whereby the comparison website gains a referral fee) – using a cashback site to purchase the product and thus collect the referral fee themselves. There are even cases of customers securing so much cashback that they have effectively been paid by an insurer to have their homes insured.

is based on what competitors and other businesses are doing. Numerous tools have grown up to do this: case studies, special features, profiles of senior managers, annual rankings, and so on. All of this information – some of which is highly detailed – is made available to competitors, in addition to corporate websites, annual reports, accounts, analysts' reports, and so on.

Conferences perform a similar role as a medium through which business ideas are systematically spread from one organization to another. They have to some extent become platforms for senior managers keen to raise their profiles among peers (and potential new employers). These managers often provide detailed descriptions of what their organizations have achieved and how. It is ironic that many organizations are paying these employees – and doubtless their travel and accommodation costs too – to systematically give away competitive advantage through these events.

Consultants, software providers, and other suppliers also speed up knowledge transfer. Many of them offer the same products to multiple clients, effectively making them reliant on the same ideas and technology. When a method to enhance the use of these assets in one organization is found, this practice is likely to be assimilated into the supplier's offering to others.

An increasing number of supplier firms are going even further and offering clients the opportunity to outsource entire functions. In IT, companies such as IBM, EDS, and CSC manage enormous amounts of activity on behalf of their clients under long-term contracts. Even in sensitive government-controlled areas such as the military and intelligence gathering, such contracts are becoming commonplace. Outsourcing means that large numbers of activities are conducted in the same way across rival firms.

Finally, the movement of employees between organizations is more intense than ever before. Employees leaving organizations take with them unparalleled knowledge about strategies, technologies, customers, and so on. Controlling this leakage of intelligence is a serious challenge for businesses.

The impact of all this knowledge sharing is that good ideas are copied quickly. Firm homogeneity is the inevitable result. Increasing numbers of businesses – and other kinds of organization – use similar information, approaches, technology, and so on. Few firms hold on to unique advantages for long, suffering from the rapid replication enabled by knowledge sharing.

Investor pressures and shortening CEO tenure

As the foregoing discussion explains, historically many organizations were in industries protected from competitive forces. If, despite this, these organizations performed poorly, their chief executive officers (CEOs) might have passed their regrets to investors or other stakeholders, citing 'difficult times'. Others might have pleaded for more time to turn their businesses around. The competition (if there was any) was unlikely to be performing much differently. Generally, CEOs

Box 3.2 New CEO, same strategy

There is evidence that investors are seeking CEOs with the ability to execute strategy effectively rather than those with novel strategies. Bob Mendelsohn was ousted as chief executive of insurance giant *Royal SunAlliance* by institutional investors. He had spent months trying to revive the company's fortunes but – in the eyes of investors – was making little headway. He was replaced by Bob Gunn, who outlined essentially the same recovery programme Mendelsohn had proposed a year earlier. However, city analysts sensed Gunn could deliver it and rallied behind him. *Royal SunAlliance* thereafter made a strong recovery.

A similar pattern emerged at HP, where Carly Fiorina resigned as CEO after the company failed to produce strong results in the wake of its merger with Compaq. Her replacement, Mark Hurd, made few changes to the planned strategy of the business, focusing more on strategy execution. He is now widely credited with turning HP around.

would have to demonstrate spectacular incompetence before their jobs were threatened. However, with growing pressures in the environment, this is changing.

Fortune magazine reported that the tenure of CEOs had reduced significantly over the previous 15 years.[2] Their investigations into why CEOs fail and are replaced revealed that in as many as 70 per cent of cases, these CEOs had failed on execution. It is likely that the environmental pressures explored earlier have begun to take their toll on CEOs – and are underlying causes of this increased turnover.

Fortune made the interesting observation that investors relatively rarely have problems with companies' strategies – they are looking for successful execution. Of course, these increasingly demanding investors, more prone to dismiss CEOs of struggling companies, in turn create another source of pressure upon organizations. Investors are demanding consistently acceptable returns and, in the absence of industry-wide pressures that depress returns for all players, quickly blame CEOs for poor company performance. CEOs need to be confidant that performance promises they make to investors can be kept and thus that their strategic intent can be realized.

Problems with success attribution

It is important to consider further *why* practitioners seem to have such difficulty with strategy execution, as this illuminates the task facing us. Strategy execution's multi-disciplinary nature is doubtless a problem, but most organizations contain teams of people with diverse skills and expertise who can come together successfully to accomplish tasks. Why is strategy execution different?

It seems likely that one problem is *success attribution*. This is a fundamental challenge in most organizations. Organizations are complex entities and undertake so many activities that the impact of any single activity on overall performance is often difficult to isolate. Many activities have consequences that will *somehow* affect the achievement of overall objectives, but they do so indirectly, and there may be quite long time lags between an activity happening and its impact occurring.

In summary, though managers across organizations may be charged with determining, managing, and controlling hundreds or thousands of activities, connecting them with overall objectives is difficult. We need to be careful about claims made either before or after the successful achievement of organizational objectives.

Box 3.3 All down to me

At a management seminar some years ago, the chief executive of an FTSE 100 UK company gave a presentation. He displayed a graph showing the profits of his company and how they "had increased since he became chief executive". The profit increases were indeed impressive, and the CEO proudly explained how this success was due to his leadership and approach to strategy.

There can be little doubt that the chief executive had contributed positively to the organization for which he worked. He had demonstrated entrepreneurial flare, with the company launching several new businesses at considerable risk, all of which had flourished. He had taken difficult decisions that appeared to have paid off. He was widely respected by colleagues, competitors, and city analysts. However, it is also obvious that his contribution was one of many things that caused the success. To start with, the organization was operating in an industry that had generated superior returns for decades. These returns were to an extent protected, because the industry's barriers to entry were high. The period to which the CEO referred had been one of strong economic growth and favourable market conditions. Almost all competitor organizations had fared as well as the company in question. Internally, the CEO had been supported by a strong management team (most of whom were appointed before he appeared). Customer sophistication in the sector was typically limited, as was switching between alternative suppliers. Pricing was stable, and supply-side costs were moving downward.

In short, it would have taken some bad luck to fail in this sector, and success was attributable to many factors. The chief executive may well have been deserving of significant credit, but if he were, he failed to explain in satisfactory detail how he created the success, thereby specifying his contribution and disentangling it from that of others. It is possible that he was just lucky.

Box 3.4 Success attribution challenges

Success can be wrongly attributed even in simple situations. Consider the example of a small greeting card shop, which invested in a new brand identity, incorporating a new logo, signage, and repainting of the shop front. The shop owner is delighted with the changes, as trade picks up over the next two weeks and she sells 15 per cent more cards than in the previous fortnight.

Was the shop owner correct to assume that the redesign work was what attracted more customers into the shop? It is difficult to say without some careful research. Consider some alternative explanations for the sales increase:

- A new range of cards was particularly successful because a new TV art series (which the shop owner didn't see) showcased the range.
- A diversion in a pedestrian area increased the number of people passing the shop by 25 per cent.
- One morning when the owner was away, a large coach full of elderly tourists broke down right outside the shop. Many of them came in to shelter from the cold and bought cards.

Obviously, attributing success to the design work without doing some rather detailed analysis is unwise. Many different factors may have caused the sales uplift.

Now consider the example of a large corporation's IT function. The IT director is considering a reorganization of the IT support teams, moving them from being organized according to their technical expertise into 'consulting' teams, each serving a division of the business. He thinks IT needs to be more customer-focused and better aligned with the organization's strategic objectives.

The IT director is, presumably, implying that reorganizing his support teams will increase the company's profit (its overall objective). Otherwise, there would be no reason to expend time and money on this complex task. Even were profits to increase after this change, it would of course be unreasonable for the IT director to claim that his reorganization contributed to the increase without conducting some sophisticated analysis.

These problems with success attribution complicate strategy execution decisions. Consider the following issues.

- It is essential that organizations' overall objectives are not only clearly defined but can be articulated so as to enable planning of those activities that can enable their achievement. Few organizations have overall objectives articulated in this way.

- Business environments change constantly. Though this is an obvious point, its implication is critical: Even where managers have correctly constructed notions about what activities should best be performed to produce desired outcomes, these working assumptions can become invalid. The environment creates barriers to the achievement of objectives and can make intended plans redundant. (Of course, it is also environmental change that creates opportunities, but exploiting them faster and better than competitors is non-trivial!)
- As organizations become larger, they become difficult to manage. The sheer number of activities required to achieve overall objectives is usually so high that owners and managers must rely upon others to undertake activities that they cannot reasonably attend to themselves. This delegation extends to planning, management, measurement, feedback, and oversight tasks. Of course, with greater reliance on others, the attribution of success becomes more difficult. The fact that employees may or may not share owner/manager objectives further complicates this issue (the 'principal/agent problem'). Owners/managers must recruit and motivate staff to undertake activities on their behalf – a perennial challenge for organizations.
- Effective success attribution relies upon effective feedback. The quality of feedback is contingent upon measuring the right variables, measuring these effectively, communication of this information to the right decision makers, and the ability to interpret it accurately. Most organizations have developed complex measurement, reporting and communications systems. However, most organizations also recognize these tasks as among the most challenging there are.
- Assuming that all of the foregoing challenges can be overcome, managers are then faced with the challenge of actually making strategic decisions. Most managers find them difficult, and rarely can they be confident they make good decisions.

It will come as no surprise, given the foregoing discussion, that there does not seem to be a 'magic bullet' when it comes to executing strategy. There are no simple answers or easy recipes upon which managers can rely.

Strategy execution matters

In 1999, an article in *McKinsey Quarterly* made the point that the best strategy a company can adopt is one that it can implement, but strategy execution is often ignored during discussions about strategy.[3] This observation tallies with the findings from my own research. There are some interesting theories about why senior executives have sometimes seen strategy execution as a secondary issue.

Fortune magazine suggested that the fascination with strategic planning is built on the mistaken belief that if the strategy is right, exceptional performance will automatically follow.[4] Some research has found that senior leaders have a tendency to assume that middle managers will handle the details of implementation adequately, however, middle managers do not always act as their leaders might hope.[5] Other researchers have noted that some senior executives seem to see strategy execution as a tactical matter that is 'beneath them'.[6] Implementation can be seen as relating to the 'dirty detail', and those who are good at it make great 'second-in-commands'. Strategic planning is often perceived as needing intellectual skill, whereas strategy execution demands hard work and persistence. This is curious, as strategy execution is understood far less than strategic planning – and it certainly appears far harder to do well.

Larry Hrebiniak makes the point that managers are trained to plan rather than execute and thus know more about planning than execution.[7] Certainly, as managers are promoted, their formal training is likely to be oriented toward strategic planning. For example, virtually every MBA programme in the world incorporates strategic planning in some way, but only a tiny handful run courses on strategy execution. Although most managers gain knowledge of execution through experience, this knowledge is unstructured and is much more likely to relate to managing change rather than strategy execution specifically (Chapters 1 and 2 note this distinction).

Strategy execution is not only difficult; it is poorly understood, intertwined with many organizational processes, takes a long time, involves lots of stakeholders, and often must reflect the decisions made by others (e.g. executives and strategic planners). It requires discipline, persistence, and patience. Unfortunately, in many organizations in which this is not recognized, there are quicker and easier ways to achieve personal recognition and success. Being effective at strategy execution also might require an unusual set of skills and personality traits. It requires managers to be able to connect concepts and concrete actions – to see both the big picture and the detail. It necessitates enthusiasm for the creative novelty of planning, the discipline of delivery, and attention to detail for completion. It is probably the case that few people possess the personality traits and learning styles that cover this diverse range of requirements.

As this chapter has shown, the strategy execution challenge is enormous. However, it is one we cannot duck. Effective strategy execution is about more than outperforming competitors in industry. It is also central to the success of public sector bodies and other not-for-profit organizations. Whether spending taxpayers' money or donated funds, these organizations have a duty to implement strategy effectively and efficiently. Sometimes, their objectives are more important than those of the private sector, affecting our quality of life more directly (see Box 3.5).

Box 3.5 Mini case study – Life-threatening strategy execution failures
A BBC television documentary investigated the impact of target setting in the United Kingdom's National Health Service (NHS).[8] It reported numerous dysfunctional outcomes of the government's enthusiastic use of targets to drive performance and future resource allocation.

The investigation alleged that some surgeons elected to operate on long-waiting patients rather than those needing operations urgently because this enabled them to reduce their patients' average waiting time – an important performance indicator in surgery. This practice was certain to cause the conditions of seriously ill patients to deteriorate further.

The investigation also discovered patients being admitted to hospital several days before scheduled operations, purely to ensure these patients were admitted within target waiting times. This practice was extremely costly and blocked beds from patients who needed them.

The investigation further discovered hospital Accident and Emergency wards refusing to receive patients brought in by paramedics until doctors were available to see them, to avoid increasing recorded waiting times. This practice detained paramedics unnecessarily, preventing them from attending emergency incidents.

In a more recent live television broadcast, the then UK Prime Minister was shocked when several members of a studio audience informed him of another dysfunctional effect of targets in the NHS.[9] They complained that their local doctors' surgeries would not allow appointments to be made more than a day in advance, as this allowed their waiting times for appointments to be kept artificially low.

In 2007, the auditor for the former Wiltshire Ambulance Service NHS Trust issued a public interest report, detailing how staff had routinely made alterations to records of ambulance response times. An audit found that control room staff manually altered response times for hundreds of incidents to bring them within the targets set by government.[10]

Each of these problems is a failure of strategy execution. Government ministers and health chiefs sought to improve the service provided by the NHS, but the interplay of performance measures, targets, resource allocation systems, and reward/punishment systems derailed important elements of their strategy upon implementation. The result for some patients could not have been more serious.

Summary of key points

- Organizational size and complexity force senior decision makers to make use of frameworks – ways of thinking – to tackle patterns of activities and resource/market interactions.
- Most large organizations undertake strategic planning, but many do little with the strategic plans produced.
- Much of the potential value of strategic planning is lost through developing strategies that cannot realistically be executed.
- Several environmental trends are placing organizational leaders under greater pressure to ensure high performance – relating to regulation, consumer power, and knowledge transfer.
- Regulatory changes have generally increased levels of competition in many industries that were previously protected and introduced commercial competition into areas of the public sector.
- Consumer power is increasing rapidly, mainly owing to advances in information technology that provide greater access to suppliers and transparency of price and other product characteristics.
- Knowledge transfer between organizations is increasing through the media, conferences, consultancies, outsourcing, and employee turnover – speeding up replication of strategies, tactics, technologies, and products – and intensifying competition.
- Investor pressures upon organizations are growing, particularly in relation to the ability of chief officers to execute strategy – while CEO tenure is shortening, with more leaders being dismissed because of performance failures.
- A major challenge for successful strategy execution is success attribution – it is difficult to predict and evaluate how activities impact organizations' overall objectives – and even harder to guide and motivate employees to align their actions with overall objectives.
- Some leaders are reluctant to spend time and effort on strategy execution, seeing it as a messy business that more junior employees should deal with.
- Many senior leaders mistakenly believe that the organizational realignments required to execute new planned strategies will be initiated by middle managers without their active input and oversight.
- Relatively few managers seem to possess the learning and thinking styles required for strategy execution – to link conceptual ideas with concrete actions.
- Effective strategy execution really matters – not just so that private sector firms perform for their shareholders but so that public sector and not-for-profit organizations deliver for their stakeholders.

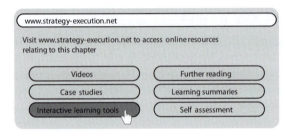

www.strategy-execution.net

Visit www.strategy-execution.net to access online resources relating to this chapter

Videos

Further reading

Case studies

Learning summaries

Interactive learning tools

Self assessment

Chapter 4

Diagnosing strategy execution problems

Between the idea
And the reality …
Between the conception
And the creation …
Falls the shadow

T. S. Eliot

Overview

With the strategy execution challenge laid out, we can consider how it might best be tackled. It is tempting to leap straight to some principles and a framework for successful strategy execution, however these must wait until Chapter 5. Beforehand, it's crucial to understand what typically gets in the way of successful strategy execution in practice and how to identify barriers in specific situations. Therefore, this chapter explores how to diagnose strategy execution problems.

In Chapter 1, a Google search provided a rough idea of how thoroughly strategy execution has been explored by humankind, and doing the same is useful for this topic. At the time of writing, "diagnosing business problems" produces only 219 hits, including duplicates (by comparison, a term like "talent management" returns 2.5 million hits).[1] This quick search speaks volumes – we don't yet know much about how to diagnose business problems. However diagnosis is a critical challenge in strategy execution for several reasons.

Strategy execution can be thought of as the process that seeks to close the gap between planned and emergent strategy. There will inevitably be a discernable pattern to the resource and market interactions an organization has with its environment that have implications for the achievement of its overall objective. However the organization can plan to alter this pattern and try to realize its intentions through strategy execution. There are two common scenarios where this arises:

- for a new strategy – where plans and implementation efforts must anticipate likely and foreseeable barriers and be designed in such a way as to overcome them

- for unchanged strategies – where any gaps between plans and current reality reflect difficulties executing the strategy, barriers having prevented implementation occurring as intended.

Given the statistics outlined in Chapter 1, we know that the majority of attempts to implement strategy do not succeed as intended, so both anticipating and responding to strategy execution barriers is vital. It thus makes sense to discuss barriers to strategy execution at this juncture, before we look at designing strategy execution efforts, rather than tackling the problems *post hoc*.

Symptom-oriented problem solving

It's useful to start by looking at how organizations tend to tackle business performance problems to better implement their strategies. My own research has detected a clear pattern in many cases. Often, managers assessed problems superficially, focusing mainly on their symptoms and failing to conduct systematic diagnosis of problems and their underlying causes. This finding will not surprise those alert to distinctions it implies. My study dug deeper to uncover the implications of this superficial approach.

Table 4.1 provides three real examples of solution-oriented problem solving, along with the findings from proper diagnostic exercises.

It's important to note that in each case, any number of underlying causes might have created the apparent problem. The true cause uncovered by good diagnosis often bears no relationship to the proposed solution.

Table 4.1 Examples of symptom-oriented problem solving

Perceived problem	Proposed solution	Diagnostic findings
Poor sales performance	Management training for salespeople	Unrealistically high targets are de-motivating staff. Skills are adequate and not the source of the problem, so training would have no material impact on sales performance.
Low morale amongst middle managers	Conduct pay review for middle management roles	Morale is low because of poor leadership and communication. Pay levels are not the source of the problem, so increasing them would have no sustained effect on morale.
Poor coordination between functions is damaging customer service	Restructure from functional into customer segment-based structure	Poor coordination is caused by conflicting management team objectives and lack of structured communication between functions. There is nothing inherently wrong with the structure and proposed changes to it would not overcome the reported problems.

My research suggests that this symptom-focused problem solving approach is often embedded in and reinforced by organizational routines. For example, managers tend to enlist support functions to deliver solutions that they think will neutralize a problem. Human resources (HR) functions provide a good example because apparent performance failures are often attributed to people matters. Many HR practitioners intellectually recognize that there is a danger in 'doing whatever managers want' – because requested interventions might not be optimal ones. Harassed managers without razor-sharp analytical skills are liable to request solutions that address symptoms of problems – not their underlying causes. However despite recognition by some practitioners of its risks, solution-orientated problem solving remains commonplace. One of the reasons for this is that the pressures that reinforce it are subtle and tricky to unpick. For example, a reinforcing cycle tends to develop when line managers request solutions from support functions, rather than assistance to diagnose problems. When managers get speedy reactions from support functions that are perceived to 'put out the fire', their satisfaction naturally fuels further similar requests – often of those colleagues who are most 'co-operative'. This cycle is further reinforced informally by praise and 'back-slapping', which encourage more of the same behaviour. The cycle is also further reinforced systematically if support functions use poorly designed performance appraisals or internal customer surveys that essentially test only whether line managers approve of their colleagues' behaviour. Tying such misaligned measures to reward virtually guarantees a solution-oriented mindset. All of this can also lead to the most reactionary people being selected for key senior roles, who then reinforce an approach that ignores or downplays the need for diagnosis.

It's important to acknowledge the severe risks created by solution-orientated problem solving. If no diagnosis of business problems is conducted, the probability of introducing inappropriate solutions is huge. If this happens, underlying problems constraining business performance are not solved, investments are wasted and new problems are often introduced (as the systems being changed are not properly understood). This complex and subtle pattern is depicted in Figure 4.1.

In organizations where solution-oriented problem solving is endemic, there are usually some telltale signs, and managers should be alert to these. Box 4.1 provides a quick test for some of the most common signs, enabling readers

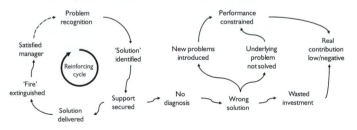

Figure 4.1 The reinforcing cycle of symptom-focused problem solving

Box 4.1 Quick test – Solution-orientation
How solution-oriented is your organization? Take the quick test to check for warning signs …

1 What best describes typical interactions with support functions in the organization?

   a. They are tasked when initiatives need to be implemented to fix problems – 'fire fighting' is the norm.
   b. They are consulted on how initiatives should be implemented.
   c. They help generate and assess options for organizational initiatives.
   d. They draw management attention to issues needing to be diagnosed and involve others in this work.

2 What best describes support functions' provision of management information to stakeholders?

   a. They provide management information *ad hoc*, following stakeholder requests.
   b. They provide basic management information to key stakeholders on a regular basis.
   c. They provide management information and associated analysis and commentary to key stakeholders on a regular basis.
   d. They provide sophisticated management information explicitly linked to key business objectives and facilitate examination of trends with key stakeholders.

3 What best describes the effects of changes made?

   a. Change is always rushed and creates conflict, confusion, or duplication.
   b. Change often takes longer and costs more than expected and creates some conflict, confusion, or duplication.
   c. Change occasionally takes longer and costs more than expected, and only minor adjustments to plans are required.
   d. Change usually progresses as planned and results in simplification of organizational activity – things happen more smoothly.

4 Which of the following best describes structural change?

   a. The structure is always changing, especially with senior management changes, often returning to similar forms as used in the past.
   b. The structure changes fairly often when it isn't working optimally (e.g. when there is conflict, confusion, or duplication).

    c. Changes are made to structure when there's a fundamental change to the organization's activities.

    d. Small changes are made to structure over time as activities change, but the focus is mainly on making it work through better coordination mechanisms.

5 What best describes the reaction to change by those affected by it?

    a. There is a huge backlash (whether openly voiced to management or not) of cynicism, complaining, resistance, and sometimes sabotage.

    b. Efforts to communicate engage some, but many others become more resistant and cynical upon hearing the detail of proposed changes.

    c. Consultation deals with many anxieties, but some cynicism and resistance remains in pockets.

    d. Most people are involved in diagnosing the problems changes respond to, or planning change implementation, so are broadly comfortable with the changes made.

Now check your results …

For each question score: A=1, B=2, C=3, D=4

5–8: The organization shows signs of being highly solution-oriented. It is likely that any diagnostic efforts undertaken are inadequate to uncover underlying causes of problems. Initiatives to solve problems are likely to be ineffective and risk introducing new problems. The organization is probably exposed to serious risks given its inability to control performance.

9–12: The organization shows signs of being solution-oriented. It is likely that diagnostic efforts are not uncovering underlying causes of problems. Initiatives to solve problems might be ineffective and risk introducing new problems. The organization may be exposed to risks through its limited ability to control performance.

13–16: The organization shows some signs of being able to diagnose the underlying causes of problems and attain some control over organizational performance as a result. It is vital to further develop and reinforce this ability to ensure that initiatives to solve problems are effective and reduce the risks of introducing new problems.

17–20: The organization shows signs of effectively diagnosing the underlying causes of problems and attaining high levels of control over organizational performance as a result. It is important to reinforce and enhance this good practice to ensure it is sustained.

sufficiently familiar with any organization to get a rough indication of the extent such patterns exist within it.

It's important to note that this kind of subtle pattern can be reinforced by all kinds of support functions and expert providers. Interactions with functions such as HR, marketing, finance, information technology (IT), legal affairs, risk management, and so on are more than likely to lead to symptom-oriented problem solving – often inadvertently and despite working with the best of intentions. Such patterns are not limited to internal interactions. Management consultants, business advisors, IT solution-providers, outsourcing specialists, lawyers, accountants, recruiters and many others are likely to enthusiastically provide their services when requested and may not possess the information, insights, skills or incentives to contribute to proper diagnosis of perceived problems. A related external source of solution-orientation is management fads, which are worth mentioning in more detail.

Management theories

Popular management theories, techniques, and tools represent an alluring array of potential solutions for managers tackling problems that threaten implementation of their strategies. Managers may be drawn to them for many reasons – they can seem like a quick fix or a 'magic bullet', they might appear more rigorous and robust than 'home-grown' solutions and of course, they may be convincingly sold by consultants and others keen to help implement them. There are now dozens of mainstream management theories, techniques, and tools used widely in large and complex organizations around the world. The popularity of most tools varies over time and levels of satisfaction with them often lags behind their usage.[2] Many management theories, techniques, and tools do appear to be like fashion fads – they have their day and then fizzle away.[3] Recognizing this and the limitations of many of the theories is important to properly calibrate their potential value in helping implement strategy.

Because 'good' management enables organizations to be successful and therefore achieve impressive goals, there is a great deal of interest in management theories. Various groups have interests in or have benefited from the industry that has grown up around management thinking, including management consultancies, outsourcing suppliers, conference organizers, management writers and publishers, magazines and journals, business schools, professional bodies, special interest organizations, industry representative bodies, and government agencies involved in enterprise.

It is difficult to know, when presented with a management idea, how valuable it is. To be really useful, a management idea probably has to be:

- understandable by those to whom it is presented, and therefore explained clearly

- effective in producing the desired outcome when applied correctly, and therefore must be technically 'correct' and comprehensive
- relevant and appropriate to specific situations, which must therefore be identified explicitly
- realistically implementable in typical settings, so must therefore be sufficiently simple and flexible to be applied without scarce expertise or excessive resources.

Because every management idea is different and every organizational setting is unique, it is difficult to generalize about the efficacy of specific management ideas. However, many of them appear to share the following problems:

- they are too esoteric, complex or badly presented to be understood in the detail required for effective use (for example, strategic planning in its original form was probably too complex to be applied readily[4]);
- they simply don't seem to work well, raising questions about their basic validity as constructs – even some popular ideas, still commonly taught, have been debunked by empirical research;
- they have been applied successfully in some settings but not in others;
- they have proved to be difficult to implement (for example, it appears that the balanced scorecard is often implemented poorly).

It is important to recognize that a great proportion of management thinking – including some of the most popular ideas disseminated – is not the product of rigorous research. The vast majority of books, articles, conference presentations, and industry reports are often based upon little more than the ideas of one person or team. These ideas may be of great value, or they may suffer from some of the problems noted above. Even experienced 'experts' in specific sectors are prone to fall into classic traps when developing theories.

Equally, it is important to recognize that 'formal research' may or may not be rigorous. There are dozens of pitfalls that even experienced researchers fall into, and often collected data support as many conclusions as there are researchers examining it. Additionally, much academic research is of limited practical use to managers and executives in organizations.

Whatever the source of a management idea or theory, there are a number of questions worth asking to calibrate the potential value of the idea. Always bear in mind that each context in which it is being applied is unique.

- **Is the theory based on empirical observation** (i.e. real events) or simply some thinking (which may or not be logical)? Ideas that have not been empirically induced or tested may be of value, but should be treated with appropriate caution.

- **If empirical research was conducted, was it systematic?** Any observation of events is empirical. However, only a disciplined approach to data collection and analysis will produce reliable research results.
- **Did the research meet basic quality criteria?** Did it build upon or test existing theory? What kind of sampling was used? Was it representative or theoretically sound? How were the data collected? Was the collection method appropriate to the phenomenon under investigation? What role did the researcher play in collecting the data? What biases might have been introduced? How were the data analysed? Was the analysis appropriate and comprehensive? How were conclusions reached? Was it reasonable to draw the conclusions from the data? What alternative conclusions would also have been reasonable?
- **Is the 'product' of the research reliable?** Sometimes, translating research findings into an approach or technique can require an extension of logic or some important assumptions. Is this extension reasonable and explicit?
- **Is the applicability of the 'product' constrained by context?** Many theories are developed which are appropriate in one or two industries, countries, cultures and so on. This does not necessarily mean that they can be applied under different circumstances (at least without careful modification). Theorists rarely provide much guidance about how far an idea can be 'stretched' before it becomes inappropriate. It is worth noting that all of us must be aware of this problem in relation to our own experiences in organizations. What worked in one organization or job or at one point in time will not necessarily work under different circumstances.
- **Can the idea reasonably be implemented?** Management ideas can often be 'economically correct', but useless in practice. If implementation is so difficult, costly or risky as to be impractical, the idea is nothing more than an interesting observation. It is amazing how much time and money business people appear to be willing to spend hearing about concepts without learning about *how* to make them reality! This is a big frustration for those working in the area of strategy execution.

Taken together these questions set a high standard – perhaps an unassailably high one. Management theories do not have to 'tick all these boxes' to be useful – but each question is worth asking to heighten understanding of the theory and make informed decisions about how it might be used. As a general rule, the less well tested the theory, the wiser it is to proceed with caution. For example, testing out ideas using a pilot project is often useful, and even more so under such circumstances.

Common strategy execution barriers

Various researchers have explored barriers to strategy execution and some have used their analysis of these to inform the development of strategy implementation models. The key barriers identified in the research include the absence of or problems with:

- strategy execution frameworks
- task definition
- organization structure
- resource management
- information sharing
- top team functioning
- staff involvement
- budgeting systems
- conflicting priorities
- cross-functional co-ordination and conflict
- time pressure
- reporting and problem escalation
- communication
- clarity of accountability
- organizational capability
- performance measures
- management information and feedback.

Figure 4.2 summarizes these barriers.

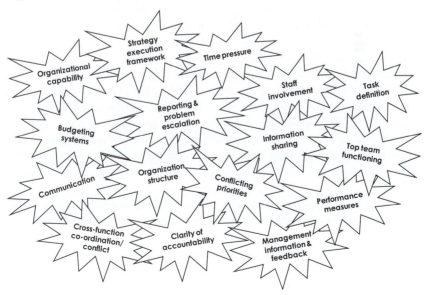

Figure 4.2 Common strategy execution barriers

Table A2 in the Appendices lists all the barriers identified in each study and categorizes them for deeper analysis. Examining the detailed findings from these studies, it appears that the identification of strategy execution barriers is to some extent based upon the level of abstraction at which they are articulated. Many barriers could be framed as subsets of more general ones – because they are likely to cause them. In other words, strategy execution barriers can be interrelated. Some of the barriers identified in studies are essentially articulations of issues at different points in chains of causal reasoning, and might be seen as somewhat arbitrary focal points within an unarticulated 'hierarchy of problems'.

Although it is useful to have a 'checklist' of strategy execution barriers to be aware of and keep alert for, such lists probably inadequately support identification of barriers in any given situation. They do not explain how barriers interrelate. In all the cases where I have examined barriers to strategy execution, there was substantial evidence of interrelationships, and it was obvious that understanding these was essential to then tackling them. Methods of exploring barriers in particular situations and accounting for interrelationships are explored below.

A diagnosis framework

Even managers who fully recognize the dangers of solution-oriented problem solving and the value of good diagnosis face a big challenge – what steps should be taken to carry out proper diagnosis?

It is tempting to gather all kinds of information that might relate to the issue at hand and trawl through it looking for clues. However, such an approach is time-consuming and laborious – a common excuse for sidestepping systematic diagnosis completely. There is rarely enough time available and elongated investigations risk 'paralysis by analysis'. This approach is also rarely productive. It is usually guided by guesses about possible causes of observed performance problems. But even intelligent guessing is inadequate because of the sheer range of factors that can constrain performance. Consider the example of the training request for salespeople outlined in Table 4.1. Underperformance of the sales team might feasibly have been caused by competitor activity, promotion mishaps, capacity management problems, resourcing failures, misaligned performance measures or a bullying manager – to name just six possibilities from dozens. Making intelligent guesses about performance problems is akin to playing darts blindfolded.

Such 'shotgun' approaches are unnecessary. A more structured approach can slice through the issues much more fruitfully. Every situation is unique, but seven suggested key steps are set out below. This framework is deliberately broad and flexible – intended to shape thinking rather than prescribe a method that is not sensitive to the particular characteristics of the situation. It is drawn from my own research and work with organizations seeking to overcome their solution-orientated problem solving. However, no claims are made that it is comprehensive or perfectly suited to all situations – the science of business problem diagnosis is in too early and fragile a state for such ambitions. The seven steps, explored below, are as follows:

- Set aside proposed solutions not founded on good diagnosis.
- Don't guess about underlying causes.
- Define the problem for the stakeholder(s).
- Determine the fundamental question.
- Use an appropriate framework to simplify the diagnosis.
- Focus on the 'hotspot'.
- Generate and test potential explanations.

Set aside proposed solutions not founded on good diagnosis

As should by now be obvious, others' assumptions about problems and solutions cannot be relied upon without decent diagnosis and need to be put to one side. However, this is easier said than done for two reasons.

First, we are all susceptible to the effects of 'framing'. When an issue is presented to us one way, it's difficult to take a step back and reframe things from first principles. Behavioural scientists have demonstrated this in simple experiments,[5] but it its perhaps most familiar to people through the example of 'leading questions'. Law enforcement interrogators often make use of such tactics, for example, by asking a suspect *why* he committed a crime even though the suspect has not admitted committing it. Such is the power of 'framing' that sometimes this tactic successfully elicits an inadvertent confession. People in organizations frame perceived problems in particular ways all the time, rarely realizing how much it constrains thinking about them.

Second, in practice, it can take considerable skill to constructively challenge solutions presented by colleagues. People can understandably be offended when their ideas are questioned or dismissed. Many managers will be reluctant to challenge the opinions of those more senior to them or those who might react badly for whatever reason. Developing the necessary soft skills to do this effectively is essential. So too is proactively influencing stakeholders to put good diagnosis before knee-jerk solutions.[6] There are many potential ways of doing this but a few examples include:

- clearly articulating the activities underway to achieve high level goals and the relationships between them (see Chapter 6);
- providing management information covering issues which are common underlying causes of performance problems;
- clearly articulating a systematic approach that includes diagnosis as part of your *modus operandi* for maximising the value you add;
- agreeing amongst a team to adopt a range of roles such as 'devil's advocate' and so on to ensure assumptions and ideas are appropriately challenged.

Don't guess about underlying causes

There are lots of 'plausible-enough-if-nobody-thinks-too-hard-about-it' answers to any apparent business problem. Many groups of managers launch immediately into an unstructured guessing game about the causes of problems when invited to undertake diagnosis. However, as explained above, the odds of hitting the right answer without diagnosis is very low, so it's as important to guard against self-induced 'framing' as that imposed by others. It can be helpful to make a note of ideas – if only to demonstrate the sheer range of possible causes of problems, thus underlining why guessing is probably futile and a more structured approach is important. Also, some initial ideas may become more useful at a later stage in the diagnostic process.

Define the problem for the stakeholder(s)

Lots of problems identified by stakeholders are disguised, whether deliberately or not. Again using the training example discussed earlier, it's useful to understand why the sales manager really picked up the phone. She said staff were "underperforming" but probably really meant, "I'll forego my bonus if they don't hit target." Understanding the genesis of problem in the eyes of different stakeholders helps to frame challenges more accurately. In particular, it's vital to understand that different stakeholders often see different problems that actually arise from a common source. In the above example, the salespeople might define the problem in a completely different way and perhaps more usefully. They might be able to point to specific problems – such as the target-setting mechanism – that help to illuminate the causes of the articulated problem. Though as noted above, every stakeholder explanation must be treated with caution – more as a possible route to the solution than the solution itself.

When stakeholders do propose solutions, it can be useful to map out the logic that seems to underlie their conclusions. Figure 4.3 outlines the likely problem logic of the sales manager in our example. It immediately expands the possible definitions of the problem from being about training and skills to include salespeople performance, sales volumes, targets, and bonuses.

Often simply articulating this logic helps stakeholders to question their own logic. Because they may have reached quickly for a solution, perhaps relying on past experiences or vague assumptions, they may immediately acknowledge weaknesses in their rationale. Even if they don't, explicit hypotheses such as the ones depicted in Figure 4.3 provide a framework for the next step.

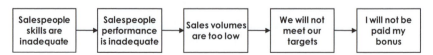

Figure 4.3 Mapping out a stakeholder's problem logic

Determine the fundamental question

One of the most important steps in the diagnosis framework is to determine the fundamental question that needs to be answered. In reality, there may be many questions that need to be answered, but the most fundamental question can be thought of as an appropriate starting point that frames diagnosis sufficiently broadly that it will uncover the underlying causes of problems, rather than just address their symptoms.

Identifying the fundamental question means starting with the triggers that caused stakeholders to identify a problem, and delving into what caused those symptoms and seeking out genuine problems for strategy execution. Again using the sales training example discussed earlier, the first question to ask is clearly not, "How can we get this training delivered?" That would be a plain example of symptom-focused problem solving, focused on the left hand side of Figure 4.3. Rather, we can determine the most fundamental question by working from the right hand side of Figure 4.3 towards the left, asking questions that test the validity of the assumptions made. If these are shaky, we may completely redefine or even dismiss the perceived problem. If the assumptions seem valid, they can be tracked back until a genuine problem for strategy execution is uncovered – and thus determine the fundamental question to ask.

An example should make this process clear. In the sales training example, our first question might be, "What criteria affect bonuses?" This will uncover whether the sales manager is right to be concerned that an anticipated failure to meet targets will preclude a bonus payment. In all likelihood, this assumption will be valid. The next questions will thus relate to the targets:

- What are the current target levels?
- How were they set?

A little diagnosis should reveal whether the target-setting process was appropriate and adhered to properly. If it wasn't that is the likely source of the problem and the diagnostic effort can concentrate on uncovering what went wrong and why. If, on the other hand, the target-setting process seems fine, attention should turn to sales volumes. Some obvious questions to ask about them would be as follows:

- What are current sales volumes?
- How have sales volumes changed and why?
- What affects sales volumes (besides salespeople performance)?

This is the point at which the fundamental question surfaces because these questions are difficult to answer without a careful diagnosis. Sales volumes will clearly be affected by numerous variables and without an understanding of how these are influencing the situation, any diagnosis will be incomplete. The fundamental question to ask in this case is probably, "Is there really a salespeople performance problem?"

The sales manager has assumed that there is a problem with the performance of the salespeople and that this is the cause of the fall in sales volumes – but these assumptions need to be checked. The sales manager *may* be right, in which case we can go on to ask questions about salespeople performance and then perhaps their skills. But doing that at this stage would be premature.

Because answering the fundamental question is usually difficult, it's essential to use an appropriate framework to simplify the diagnosis and that is the next step in the process.

Use an appropriate framework to simplify the diagnosis

Selecting the right conceptual framework – one appropriate to the fundamental question – allows 'bulk' elimination of possible causes of problems and progressive focus on a limited number of issues for deeper analysis. For example, in the sales training example, the sales process is an ideal framework, as depicted in Table 4.2.

Using a framework like the sales process enables quick filtering of possible causes by grouping them in a logical manner, in this case under the headings demand, capacity, capability and commitment. For example, if it can be determined that there has been no material change in demand – as evidenced by metrics such as volumes of queries, inbound calls, and so on – it is acceptable to rule out all external causes of poor sales performance. For example, it is unlikely that issues such as general economics, competitive activity and buyer behaviour are causing a problem. It is much more likely that the problem resides within the organization.

The next most logical issue to examine, following the sales process, is capacity. Information on activities like lead generation and call answering speedily assess capacity and determine whether sales opportunities are arising and the organization can physically handle them. Assuming there are no discernable problems with demand or capacity, it is then appropriate to examine capability and then commitment, using metrics calibrating variables such as those noted in Table 4.2.

The value of selecting an appropriate framework should be obvious. This filtering process is otherwise practically impossible and we would struggle to know what information to examine and what it told us about the fundamental question posed.

Table 4.2 Using a sales process as a framework for 'bulk' elimination of problems

Demand	Capacity	Capability	Commitment
• Unattractive products • Ineffective promotions • Suboptimal pricing • Branding or PR problems • Increased competition • Increased substitution • Telephony malfunctions	• Website malfunctions • Lack of sales people • Staff absenteeism • Excess staff turnover • Ineffective recruitment • Poor capacity management • Overwork and time pressure	• Increased administrative burden • Low morale • Poor leadership • Bullying and harassment • Flawed reward systems • Unobtainable targets • Lack of recognition	• Unsuitable working conditions • Ineffective recruitment and selection • Ineffective induction • Ineffective training • Lack of on-the-job coaching • Lack of teamwork • Poor information

Focus on the 'hotspot'

With this progressive filtering complete, the range of possible underlying causes should be narrowed-down hugely. Then a deeper analysis of specific data is appropriate. Sometimes new data need to be collected but more often, existing data simply need to be analysed through the lens of the now well-defined problem.

It is at this point that developing a basic causal model can be useful. In later chapters, we will use causal modelling for planning purposes. But it can also be used for retrospective analysis and often provides rich insights. In particular, causal modelling is helpful to ensure that the symptoms of problems are distinguished from their causes, and that causes are examined adequately deeply. This reflects the distinction between single- and double-loop learning made by Chris Argyis and Donald Schön.[7] These writers highlighted the importance of going beyond asking, "What's wrong" (single-loop learning) to asking, "Why did it go wrong in the first place" (double-loop learning). Causal analysis shows how we can take that principle further and continue asking, "Why?" when uncovering causes of problems to build a deeper understanding of why performance problems emerge.

Figure 4.4 gives an example of an actual causal analysis exploring problems in a public sector agency. This organization managed applications from eligible members of the public for a particular service. In this case, a director in the agency had requested external support to help deal with what she saw as a stubborn problem with staff shortages. For many months, staff turnover and absence had been high and difficult to reduce. The problem was perceived to be a staffing one and perhaps 'cultural' in origin.

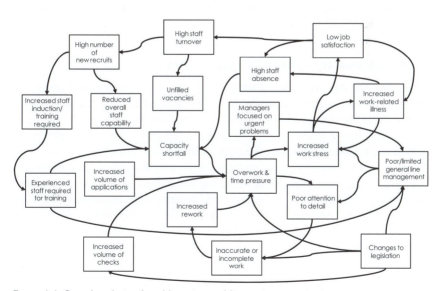

Figure 4.4 Causal analysis of problems in a public service organization

Rather than assume the director's analysis was comprehensive and valid, the external experts undertook a diagnostic exercise involving interviews with members of staff at various levels within the service. They also examined key documentation and performance metrics and developed a systematic picture of how various problems in the agency interrelated. As Figure 4.4 depicts, a large number of underlying problems were uncovered, producing a not inconsistent but much more comprehensive and detailed view of events to that presented by the director.

The 'starting points' for the story depicted in this causal analysis are two factors:

- 'changes to legislation' (that altered eligibility for the service and application process)
- 'increased volume of applications' (due in part to expansion of the eligibility criteria for the service).

These two factors, both occurring about a year before the analysis took place, triggered a 'vicious circle' of 'overwork and time pressure' causing 'poor attention to detail' causing 'inaccurate or incomplete work' causing 'increased rework' and so on. Most of the other problems in the agency occurred on the back of this 'vicious circle' of factors that sprang up quickly and proved difficult to terminate with the resources normally available in the agency.

'Vicious circles' and their much more welcome opposites 'virtuous circles' are quite common in causal analyses and often explain how a serious problem is triggered and becomes embedded. Mapping them in this way leans on the principle of systems thinking, which focuses on modelling loops of cause and effect in all kinds of systems.

Generate and test potential explanations

Examining the right rich data closely usually produces good hypotheses about problem causes. It's then essential to test theories against all the data and determine if they fit. If the data are robust and the explanation doesn't fit, it needs to be further refined or a fresh explanation explored. Typically, the right explanations fit well and point to further corroborating evidence.

In the aforementioned public sector agency example, data relating to specific issues such as rework levels, work stress and the number of new recruits all fitted the hypotheses depicted in the causal map. Perhaps more importantly, once the whole picture was presented to senior managers, it drew attention to the range of issues that were related and needed to be addressed. There was quick recognition that the diverse problems with which they'd been wrestling were in fact related. The managers realized that they were independently tackling many of the problems, without recognizing their common underlying causes and the need to develop a coordinated solution. Hence the causal analysis was an effective way of gaining control over the situation. It enabled the development of a series of action plans to tackle the problem:

- In the short term, application processing staffing levels were significantly increased though moving people from other areas and hiring temporary staff, which reduced the backlog of applications.
- In the medium term, a more efficient and effective process was introduced to manage the new application process and ensure automated quality checks of application processing.
- In the longer term, a change management process was introduced (to systematically manage foreseeable changes such as 'changes to legislation') and a capacity management system was introduced (to better manage staff levels when measurable changes in demand (e.g. due to 'increased volume of applications') was detected.

The key point to remember at this stage in the diagnostic process is that explanations must fit the data. Often people are so pleased with their theories that they don't check them against the data or ignore unexplained mismatches.

Box 4.2 provides a complete example of application of the diagnostic process.

Box 4.2 Mini case study – Staff inflexibility
Some years ago, an HR business partner joined a leading personal finance business that provided credit cards, savings products, and loans. The business relied entirely upon direct customer relationships managed primarily via the telephone and Internet.

The business was regularly applauded in the financial press for the quality of its customer service. It had developed highly efficient processes for account opening, loan sanctioning, and customer service transactions. As the majority of customer interactions were via telephone, the company sought to excel in its call centre operations. As each of the three product groups was launched, a new call centre was established to handle calls relating to that product.

Focusing on single products ensured that customer service staff were fully knowledgeable about the products they supported, could be recruited and trained fairly quickly, and were relatively inexpensive to employ. However, after rapid growth and problems in handling call volumes after promotional campaigns, the company opened a fourth call centre to handle overflows from any of the three product-based operations on busy days. This centre employed higher-skilled 'multi-tasking' customer service staff who were generally longer-serving employees and had been provided with additional training. High-performers in the overflow call centre could be paid as much as 30 per cent more than their colleagues in the single-product centres.

The HR business partner was assigned to work with the operations director who was responsible for the four call centres and ensuring they met their sales volume, service quality, and efficiency targets. The operations director encouraged the HR business partner to visit the credit card call centre, which he identified as the best-performing one. He explained that its manager ran the most efficient operation, despite also generating excellent sales figures.

Upon her first visit to the credit card call centre one morning, the HR business partner was surprised to see many workstations were vacant. Curious, she asked why so few staff were working. The call centre manager explained that it was very difficult to find staff willing to work in the early morning, but they worked around it effectively.

Over the next few weeks, the HR business partner returned to this issue, concerned about the apparent staffing inflexibility and poor utilisation of facilities. Recognizing the problem was not straightforward, she decided to adopt a systematic approach to diagnose it.

First, she set aside the explanation provided by the call centre manager, assuming that staff inflexibility might not be the underlying problem.

Second, she did not attempt to guess what the underlying problem might be – recognizing this would frame her thinking in a prematurely narrow way.

Third, she tried defining the problem in a number of ways, bearing in mind the stakeholders involved. She thought the problem ought to be defined in terms of its impact on the call centre's strategic objectives. She knew sales volumes were impressive and efficiency high, so asked more about customer service results. She was shocked to learn that the centre's call abandon rate[8] typically peaked at 20 per cent each morning – which seemed very high. She also explored the issue from the perspective of the call centre staff but could not find evidence that so few were willing to work in the early morning. Indeed, the other call centres seemed to be well staffed at this time.

Fourth, she determined the fundamental question to answer, which she decided was, "Why is the credit card call centre manager choosing not to staff adequately in the mornings?"

Fifth, she determined an appropriate framework to support her diagnosis. She realized that she needed hour-by-hour data rather than aggregated weekly or monthly performance statistics – relating to staffing, capacity management, and key performance indicators. One piece of information that caught her attention was a graph showing average call volumes and the call abandon rate throughout the day (Figure 4.5).

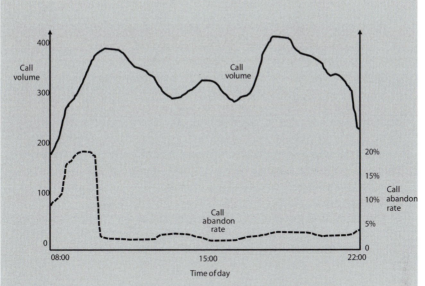

Figure 4.5 Hour-by-hour call centre performance statistics

Sixth, she focused on why the call abandon rate fell so suddenly at around 10 AM. She knew that call volumes were still rising at 10 AM and there was not a sudden influx of staff at that time. The suddenly falling call abandon rate could not be explained by the ongoing mismatch between the call volumes and number of staff available to answer them.

Seventh, a potential explanation for the data occurred to her. It was possible that the call abandon rate might suddenly be reduced because some of the calls were being transferred to the overflow call centre. The HR business partner tested her explanation by investigating how the overflow mechanism worked. She discovered that when the call abandon rate in a product call centre reached a threshold of 20 per cent, a significant proportion of the calls to that call centre were automatically re-routed to the overflow call centre for the rest of the day (to accommodate the typical patterns that followed).

Finally, the HR business partner could see what was really going on. There was no problem with staff inflexibility. The credit card call centre manager had realized that deliberately understaffing for a short time at the beginning of each day would push the call abandon rate up and trigger the transfer of a substantial proportion of calls to the overflow call centre. The business did not use an internal recharging system between profit centres, so the credit card call centre's key performance indicators – relating to sales volume, customer service, and efficiency – were all artificially enhanced by this tactic. So, too, was the credit card centre manager's bonus.

It transpired that the overflow call centre manager was fully aware of the 'scam', but pleased to play along with it as the extra business for the overflow call centre improved its apparent performance too.

In truth, the credit card call centre was not the best performing one in the business – it only appeared so because of its manager's clever misuse of the systems the organization had developed in a bid to improve performance. In reality, a huge number of customers were deliberately being poorly served each morning. Also, a substantial proportion of calls were unnecessarily being handled by the most expensive call centre staff in the business. Senior leaders had been totally unaware of the dysfunctions, seeing only aggregate weekly and monthly data, never the detailed hour-by-hour performance statistics the HR Business Partner dug out.

Organizational systems can interact in subtle and sometimes highly destructive ways, and systematic diagnosis of apparent problems is vital to uncover the true underlying causes of performance constraints.

Summary of the seven-step process

As the seven steps show, diagnosis is not easy but it need not consume vast amounts of time. With experience, the right questions can be posed early on and rapidly progress thinking in the structured fashion outlined here. Applying the seven-step process systematically, or even using it to prompt a slightly different approach to problems usually causes managers to pose different questions to those they might otherwise have asked. Box 4.3 offers a quick test of diagnosis skills using some people management support requests as examples.

As explained at the beginning of this chapter, diagnosis is a poorly understood area, but it is hugely important to successful strategy execution. After all, most

Box 4.3 Quick test – Diagnosis skill
How good are you at diagnosis-oriented problem solving? Take the quick test ...

I   The Marketing Director requests a training course on motivating staff, for all his managers. What's the most important question to ask?

   a. Do all the managers really need this training?
   b. What has triggered his request?
   c. Is a training needs analysis required first?
   d. Which supplier should be used to deliver this?

2 The Sales Director says she wants to introduce £1,000 'Golden Hellos' for new sales advisors, to speed up recruitment. What's the most important question to ask?

   a. Whose budget will this come from?
   b. Will 'Golden Hellos' attract the right kind of people?
   c. Can more than £1,000 be offered?
   d. Why is there now an anticipated gap between projected capacity and demand?

3 The Chief Executive tells you he wants to launch a world-class executive leadership development programme, delivered by a top business school. What's the most important question to ask?

   a. Will using a single business school give us access to the range of experts we need and value for money?
   b. How quickly does this need to be up and running?
   c. Should high-potential senior managers also be on the programme?
   d. Should all the organization's executives be developed in the same way?

4 The new Finance Director wants to launch a culture change programme, because the one she initiated in her last organization worked really well. What's the most important question to ask?

   a. When would she like to make the first changes?
   b. Why does she want to change the culture here?
   c. What were the objectives, context, and key elements of the programme, and how did she know it 'worked'?
   d. How long did it take, and how much did it cost?

5 The IT Director wants to increase the proportion of variable pay for some of his staff, to motivate higher performance. What's the most important question to ask?

   a. What industrial relations issues might emerge if this goes ahead?
   b. How is the current performance-related-pay system inadequate?
   c. Is pay the right lever to use for motivation of the staff?
   d. How does he assess performance and what objectives does he think might not be achieved?

Now check your results ...

Question 1:   A = 2, B = 4, C = 3, D = 1
Question 2:   A = 1, B = 3, C = 2, D = 4

Question 3:   A = 3, B = 1, C = 2, D = 4
Question 4:   A = 1, B = 4, C = 3, D = 2
Question 5:   A = 1, B = 2, C = 3, D = 4

5–8: You are a supreme tactician, but are not spotting the strategic issues and are almost certainly limiting the value you add by failing to diagnose problems appropriately.

9–12: You have a strong preference for getting on with the task at hand, but cannot be confident you are working on the right task. Developing your diagnostic skills will pay dividends.

13–16: You have the ability to spot strategic issues through diagnosis-oriented problem solving, and could usefully develop your skills further.

17–20: You are a good diagnosis-oriented problem solver and recognize the questions to ask. Provided you have the soft skills to ask them well, you can add enormous value.

managers are professionals who solve lots of problems and try to do things right. But without good diagnosis embedded in their approach, how can they be confident they are solving the right problems?

Summary of key points

- Remarkably little is known about how to diagnose business problems – it is not an area that hitherto has received dedicated focus within management science.
- Understanding how to diagnose strategy execution problems is critical to ensure both that newly developed strategies will avoid common strategy execution barriers and also to overcome barriers preventing execution of established strategies.
- Within most organizations, solution-oriented problem solving is common, whereby managers tackle the symptoms of perceived performance constraints, without seeking to uncover their underlying causes.
- Symptom-focused problem solving is reinforced by various subtle patterns of behaviour in organizations, that make it difficult to overcome, even where there is intellectual recognition of the problem.
- If diagnosis is not conducted, the probability of misdiagnosing performance problems is significant, due to the wide range of factors that can cause an apparent problem.
- When problems are misdiagnosed, underlying problems constraining business performance are not solved, investments are wasted and new problems are often introduced.

- Symptom-focused problem solving can be encouraged by external parties and the inappropriate application of management theories.
- Management theories should be carefully screened for their validity and appropriateness, as well as customized and tested before widespread application.
- There are numerous barriers to strategy execution, which form a useful checklist for managers implementing strategy.
- However, strategy execution barriers are often interrelated, so diagnosis of specific situations is essential to properly understand performance constraints.
- Systematic diagnosis can be undertaken using a seven-step process, as follows:
  - set aside proposed solutions not founded on good diagnosis
  - don't guess about underlying causes
  - define the problem for the stakeholder(s)
  - determine the fundamental question
  - use an appropriate framework to simplify the diagnosis
  - focus on the 'hotspot'
  - generate and test potential explanations.
- Causal analysis is a particularly useful method of focusing on 'hotspots' and identifying underlying causes of performance problems.

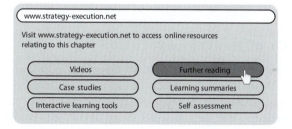

www.strategy-execution.net

Visit www.strategy-execution.net to access online resources relating to this chapter

Videos

Case studies

Interactive learning tools

Further reading

Learning summaries

Self assessment

Chapter 5

A framework for strategy execution

> The significant problems we face cannot be solved at the same level of thinking we were at when we created them.
>
> Albert Einstein

The preceding chapters have outlined what strategy execution is, why it is difficult but matters, and how to identify the barriers that can prevent successful implementation of strategy. With the context set, this chapter outlines how managers can make strategy decisions and translate these decisions into action. It introduces five crucial principles and a core framework that underpins the rest of the book.

The five Cs of strategy execution

What is the secret to good strategy execution? Of course, there is no such thing as a simple secret that can be used to unlock the challenge of implementation. Indeed, searches for 'magic bullets' in any area of management are usually fruitless. However, recognizing that the 'devil lies in the detail', it is possible to identify some essential principles. These are the five Cs of strategy execution – *causality*, *criticality*, *compatibility*, *continuity*, and *clarity*. Let's briefly examine each one.

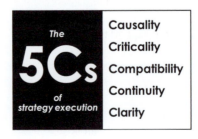

Figure 5.1 The 5Cs of strategy execution

Causality

Everyone is familiar with the basic notion of *cause and effect*. We used it in Chapter 4 to explore underlying causes of performance problems. The idea of causality allows us to understand events in the world around us. However, our familiarity with cause and effect breeds a problem – conscious and deliberate application of cause and effect thinking is rare and surprisingly difficult. In fact, it's largely limited to scientific enquiry, which systematically seeks to develop understanding of the world around us.

Nevertheless, causality is vital here because successful strategy execution relies upon undertaking activities that will plausibly cause organizations' overall objectives to be achieved. The systematic and intelligent application of cause and effect thinking can help us achieve an essential goal – linking ideas with actions. In other words, causality allows for the translation of overall objectives and strategic choices into the specific activities through which they can be achieved. Managing this translation process effectively is perhaps the most significant issue constraining the ability of organizations to execute strategy successfully.[1] However, causality on its own is not enough for good strategy execution.

Criticality

Criticality is vital alongside causality because large organizations undertake huge numbers of activities, making them highly complex systems. For those responsible for managing the performance of organizations – and therefore changing the way they operate – analysing, understanding, and manipulating all these activities is impossible. Successful strategy execution relies upon reducing this complexity to focus the resources of the organization and attention of managers and others on the limited number of *critical* activities necessary to deliver the intended strategy. Criticality is a central part of the systematic strategy execution framework introduced shortly.

Compatibility

It is not enough for managers simply to translate overall objectives and strategies into apparently critical activities. They must also ensure that the critical activities upon which they focus will pull the organization in the same direction. Activities that individually may appear to support the achievement of overall objectives may together have a different effect if they are *incompatible*.[2]

Imagine, for example, an organization that promotes and relies upon creativity and innovation but also operates a prescriptive performance management system that severely limits the scope for unplanned activities. The organization is unlikely to perform optimally unless these contradictory influences can be resolved. If compatibility is restored – perhaps by defining specific areas in which innovation is essential and adjusting the performance management system accordingly – desired outcomes are much more likely to appear.

This example illustrates a subtle but important point – organizational designs and systems heavily influence activities. Therefore, as critical activities are identified through the principles of causality and criticality, an organization's design and its systems and processes also to be need examined, to ensure they will support these activities. Chapter 7 focuses on this issue.

Continuity

Applied effectively, causality, criticality, and compatibility enable the identification of activities that will plausibly cause strategies to be realized and overall objectives to be achieved. They can help to accomplish that elusive goal of translating objectives into concrete activities. However, identifying the 'right' activities is not enough, for they must also be physically delivered.

The designs and systems of organizations may not be ideally suited to physically delivering sets of critical activities, no matter how carefully they have been identified and aligned with overall objectives. Given the nature of organizations, seemingly innocuous organizational characteristics can represent big barriers to strategy execution.

As discussed in Chapter 3, managers certainly cannot perform all the activities required to implement strategy themselves.[3] Nor, in fact, can they realistically plan executable strategies without input from those they expect to carry out activities. Ensuring this input gathers the necessary information to develop executable strategies and generates the commitment required for implementation among those consulted.

These constraints mean that the strategic decisions of an organization's senior leaders must usually be passed down through the hierarchy (which may include many levels in a large organization). As this happens, organizational units and individuals ideally must interpret strategic intentions, determine the contribution they can make, and take appropriate action. Where the *continuity* of this process breaks down, the effects of strategy makers' intentions on activities are diluted. 'Baton changes' must go smoothly if organizations are to achieve their overall objectives.

Continuity is also important over time. As organizations evolve, all activities and strategy execution efforts are threatened by short-term distractions, inertia, apathy, structural reorganizations, personnel changes, budget cuts, and so on. Many of the people involved in developing and executing a strategy can become de-motivated by such changes or cease involvement in them entirely. Transferring the necessary knowledge and goodwill to others is a challenging task. Successful strategy execution relies upon the direction and momentum generated via causality, criticality, and compatibility to be maintained despite such inevitable changes. The ability to deliver critical activities needs to be 'baked into' organizations' designs and systems.

Clarity

If the principles of causality, criticality, compatibility, and continuity are applied effectively, leaders are able to identify the critical activities required to execute strategy and make key changes to organizational designs and systems. The fifth ingredient for successful strategy execution is *clarity* – such that individuals in organizations understand overall objectives, how they are to be achieved via critical activities, how organizational designs and systems support their delivery, and their own role in making all of this happen.

Clarity of thought is vital to good strategy execution – overall objectives must be tightly defined, trade-off decisions must be logical, activities must be crispy defined, and so on. This is all easy to say, but in the pressurized reality of most organizations, it is a stretching goal. This book cites many examples of ill-disciplined or overly hasty thinking producing severe diagnostic misinterpretations and strategy execution failures.

Alongside clear thinking, excellent communication is also essential to successful strategy execution. This includes communication between executives engaged in high-level planning as much as it does communication with large numbers of individuals who will be affected by or asked to execute strategy. Imprecise definitions, ambiguous terminology, and omissions of detail all can contribute to causing severe strategy execution problems. If individuals and teams are to implement strategy effectively and take rounded decisions at the 'coalface', they need to have a clear conception of what the strategy is all about and how it is being brought to life. This essential clarity is produced by developing a shared understanding of the other four of the five Cs:

- The intended causality linking objectives to the activities that will achieve them.
- The critical activities necessary to deliver strategy.
- The necessary compatibility between activities.
- The way in which continuity will be ensured.

It also requires going one step further and showing individuals how each of these manifests itself for them *as individuals*. Employees need to know how their actions plausibly cause overall objectives to be achieved (causality) and what the most important performance drivers are to prioritize their time and effort (criticality). They must not be pulled irreconcilably in different directions (compatibility) or made unproductive and disengaged by structures and systems that do not support their most important actions (continuity). Clarity over all of these – at the individual level – increases commitment, and this in turn heightens strategy execution potential.

Role of the five 5Cs

The five Cs could be slightly differently framed, and arguments can be made for the inclusion of other principles. However, these five emerged from my own research as the most critical broad principles to help think through the challenges of strategy execution. They are threaded through the more concrete frameworks and techniques that follow in this book. In particular, they underpin the core model presented in this book as a strategy execution route map – the *inverted pyramid framework*.

The inverted pyramid framework

In many ways, the strategy execution challenge is about *alignment*. Leaders in organizations commonly use this word but rarely explain what they intend it to mean. In my work with organizations, I often introduce a metaphor to explain the nature of the strategy execution challenge and the relevance of alignment in particular.

Imagine an organization represented by an upside-down pyramid and that the tip of the pyramid is the overall objective of the organization – its ultimate purpose. The tip acts as a single foundation stone, so needs to be very strong and laid with extreme care. The rest of the pyramid represents all the resources the organization has at its disposal and all the activities it undertakes. These need to be properly *aligned* to put pressure on the overall objective – and ideally, it alone. If there is serious misalignment, the pyramid will topple, significantly reducing the pressure exerted on the tip. Similarly in organizations, misalignments can arise between the way resources are used to undertake activities and overall objectives.

When working with organizations, I often use a doctored photograph depicting an upside-down pyramid to drive home this metaphor – and with it the enormity of the strategy execution challenge. I gather a little information about budgets and headcount and use it to remind leaders of the sheer volume of tangible resources available to them and the amount of activity they are trying to align behind their

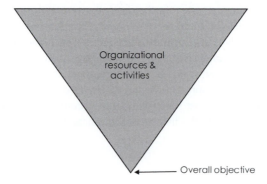

Figure 5.2 The inverted pyramid metaphor

organizations' overall objectives. Just think, for example, of the impact Walmart's employees can make if their activities are tightly aligned with the organization's overall objective – there are more than 2 million of them worldwide.

The essential message behind this metaphor is that for successful strategy execution, alignment is essential. However, the inverted pyramid framework needs more detail to enable its application in practice. Drawing upon existing strategy execution thinking and my own empirical research, Figure 5.3 outlines a series of decision areas for executing strategy successfully. These 'populate' the inverted pyramid and translate the metaphor to a practical route map for executing strategy.

The inverted pyramid framework is intended to depict a *logically sequential* series of decision areas for managers seeking to implement strategy. In other words, it offers a suggested starting point and route map to guide decision making. The starting point is, of course, the overall objective, as it should drive everything else. The large arrow in the diagram represents *alignment* – specifically the need to align all of the elements in the framework to help *cause* the overall objective to be achieved. The decision areas are split into two phases:

- *Phase 1* relates to translating objectives into activities – in other words moving from an overall objective to identifying the essential activities that will enable its achievement. This part of the framework enables managers to identify and align what is critical for successful strategy execution in their specific context.

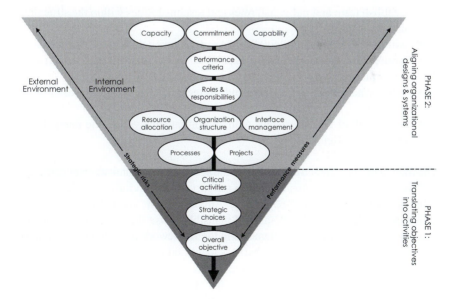

Figure 5.3 The inverted pyramid framework

- *Phase 2* relates to aligning organizational designs and systems that are generally important for successful strategy execution. Although every situation is unique, these organizational components must usually be aligned with the critical activities identified, and are presented in a logical order for decision making.

In addition, *both phases* incorporate analysis of the internal and external environment and identification of performance measures and strategic risks. The inverted pyramid framework leans on the notion of dependencies to create its logically sequential flow of decision areas. Although in practice some level of iteration is always necessary and healthy, the model implies that ideally an organization should do the following:

- determine its overall objective
- make strategic choices that will achieve the overall objective
- break strategic choices down into the activities critical to achieve them
- distinguish one-off critical activities (projects) and ongoing critical activities (processes)
- design a structure suited to ensuring that these critical projects and processes are managed effectively
- allocate resources across that structure and to the projects and processes within it
- ensure that interfaces between subunits are well-managed to counterbalance structural divisions created
- establish team and individual roles and responsibilities within the structural units
- within each team and role define the criteria that determine performance
- ensure the necessary capacity, capability, and commitment to deliver that performance
- identify performance measures and strategic risks in relation to all of these elements
- support all of these decisions with appropriate analysis of the internal and external environment.

The framework is designed to ensure that the activities the organization undertakes, and the designs and systems created to support these activities, are aligned with strategic choices and overall objectives. 'Aligned' in this context means that the activities and designs and systems will plausibly *cause* the strategic and overall objectives to be achieved. The elements in the framework deal directly with most of the common strategy execution barriers identified in Chapter 4.

It is important to note that the framework can be applied at a number of organizational levels. It could be used at the corporate, divisional, business unit, functional, or departmental levels for example. Each of these examples can have an overall objective and a strategy that it is seeking to implement. The size and complexity of the group using the framework does affect how it is used and is explored later. Suffice to say at this stage that it is important to be clear about what 'unit of analysis' (to use the technical term) defines the context for the framework's application. For simplicity, 'the organization' is used when referring to the unit of analysis.

The various elements of the framework are explained briefly next to provide an integrated overview of the framework. Each of them is then explored in detail in the remaining chapters.

Key elements of the framework

Overall objective

As discussed in Chapter 2, the overall objective is the ultimate purpose of an organization, effectively defining its reason for existence. Establishing a clear overall objective is critical for effective strategy execution. Without a well-articulated conception of what an organization is seeking to achieve, it has little chance of achieving it by adopting an appropriate strategy and consequential activities. Put another way, if you don't know where you're going, you can't decide how best to get there![4]

Strategic choices

Strategy was defined in Chapter 2 as the pattern of resource and market interactions an organization has with its environment to achieve its overall objective. The major strategic choices relate to the mix of products/markets offered, markets/segments served, and channels used.

The crafting of a strategy ought, of course, to depend on the overall objective – the strategy should plausibly cause the overall objective to be achieved. The plausibility of this causal relationship is conditioned by the external and internal environments (both elements of the inverted pyramid framework and discussed later). At its most basic level, strategy is simply a proposed method for overcoming barriers and risks and making use of enablers and opportunities in the environment to achieve the overall objective. This is not sufficient to enable strategy execution, because strategy is necessarily conceptual. It cannot, in itself, be 'done' – it can only be achieved.

Critical activities

Critical activities are the essential actions undertaken to achieve the strategy. Physical execution of strategies can only truly begin when organizations identify critical activities that will plausibly cause the achievement of their overall objectives. This is the first of the five Cs – *causality* – in action again. My own research established that achieving this is both difficult and rarely accomplished effectively; organizations undertake lots of activities, but many of them are not ones that have been systematically identified and aligned with strategy. Critical activities are explicitly aligned with organizations' overall objectives.

The inverted pyramid framework is not intended to identify every activity an organization should undertake. It should, however, isolate those essential for the delivery of the strategy, and these are the ones that need the greatest attention from managers. They are also the tasks that should be the primary drivers for later decisions about aligning organizational designs and systems.

Another important characteristic of critical activities that helps to define them relates to how abstract they are. As Chapter 4 noted, a common strategy execution barrier is that plans are not broken down sufficiently into tasks. As their name implies, critical activities need to be concrete enough to be *actionable*. Specifically, they must be detailed enough that competent individuals and teams can implement them without significant further guidance or decision making by senior decision makers. If this is not the case, further work is required by those breaking down the strategy to ensure a clear mandate can be passed to those involved in the physical execution of activities.

Critical activities should meet the 'necessary and sufficient' rule. In other words, each should be *necessary* for the achievement of the strategy, and together they must plausibly be *sufficient* to achieve the strategy.[5] This is the second of the five Cs – *criticality* – in action.

Critical activities also need to work well together and must be identified, evaluated, and aligned with this in mind. Leaders must guard against the temptation to bundle critical activities into isolated streams of work, ignoring potential conflicts and dependencies between critical activities. This is the third of the five Cs – *compatibility* – in action.

Reaching critical activities is an important milestone in applying the inverted pyramid framework. It is the point at which an organization's overall objective has been translated into activities that can plausibly enable its achievement. A conceptual idea has been broken down into a series of concrete tasks. This is perhaps the greatest strategy execution challenge. It is what distinguishes it most from change management. A more detailed explanation and examples of how it is done is provided in Chapter 6.

Projects and processes

It is, of course, vital to manage bundles of critical activities effectively. To do this, it is useful to distinguish one-off activities from those that need to be repeated many times.

Projects are coordinated sequences of activities and can be ideal packages to ensure complete delivery of these vital one-off activities. Project management, first used in domains such as construction, defence, and IT, is now an established discipline that has successfully been adapted for wide application. Many organizations run multiple projects, sometimes bundled into 'programmes' of related projects, which in turn may be parts of 'portfolios' of change-related activity overseen by organization leaders. Project management has some important limitations, chief of which is that it is not suited to determine the right projects to undertake. That is the role of an effective strategy execution model such as the inverted pyramid framework. The strength of project management lies in the systems it employs to ensure detailed planning activities of multiple related activities, their dependencies, sequencing, scheduling, resourcing, costing, and so on. These are all vital to get things done properly.

Projects that are usually best suited for unique one-off activities with a particular objective involve stakeholders and resources in ways not yet agreed and embedded in the organization. They have a natural beginning and end. Processes, conversely, are sequences of related activities that need to be repeated, often for the foreseeable future. Because they tend to be repeated many times, the design of processes is hugely important. Ineffectiveness and inefficiencies are magnified may times when embedded in a systematic routine. Well-designed and implemented processes, conversely, ensure consistent high performance. Processes play an important role in ensuring that changes introduced as part of a strategy execution effort are embedded, making new performance levels sustainable. Organizations regularly make a reasonable job of executing elements of strategy only to see the benefits ebb away as things return to normal because they were not effectively embedded.

Organization structure, resource allocation, and interface management

Organization structure is the formal arrangement of the organization into separate parts to divide labour and enable appropriate managerial spans of control and focus. Making choices about organization structures always involves trade-offs, and poor decisions can cause many problems. Identifying the essential activities for delivering strategy informs how best to make these trade-off decisions and should drive primary structural decisions. In other words, critical activities inform the core structure of the organization.

Resource allocation systems provide the separate parts of the organization structure, undertaking activities with the necessary financial, human, and other resources. It is obviously vital that resources are made available to support the critical activities needed to deliver the strategy. As with structure, any choice about resource allocation systems usually involves trade-offs, and it is those activities critical for delivering the strategy that must drive the decision.

Interface management relates to the methods and systems used to integrate the separate parts of the organization structure and ensure appropriate coordination of their approaches and activities. As mentioned earlier, making choices about organization structures always involves trade-offs. It is, therefore, essential to consider carefully how to compensate for the deficiencies of a chosen structure and seek ways of ensuring it works together properly. This subtle necessity is often under-emphasized in organizations and becomes a major cause of performance problems, which may incorrectly be attributed to poor organization structure. Major components of interface management are the information and communication systems used by an organization to inform decisions and activities of individuals. Information and communication systems can transmit a great deal of information, much of which may not be essential to strategy execution, so a systematic approach to designing these systems is necessary.

Roles and responsibilities and performance criteria

Roles and responsibilities involve the definition of individual jobs and systems used to assign particular activities to individuals within those roles. Once critical activities are established and a structure chosen, each part of that structure uses roles and the allocation of tasks to coordinate the involvement of different people. Without a systematic process for doing this, organizations run the risk that critical activities will not be undertaken or be duplicated or that the wrong people will be involved in doing them. As with structure, critical activities inform the key roles – or the key elements of them – essential for strategy execution.

Performance criteria are the standards used to establish the nature of positive performance within roles. Whenever roles are created, they can be somewhat meaningless until the performances required within them are given some definition. However, the process of defining individual performance criteria and measures is fraught with risks and is explored in detail in Chapter 8. Again, it is critical activities that should inform key performance criteria within roles.

Capacity, commitment, and capability

Capacity, commitment, and capability are closely related issues in strategy execution and can be difficult to tease apart when diagnosing and planning.

Capacity is the scope (in terms of available time and productivity) for individuals and teams to undertake activities. Leaders have the challenge of ensuring that they have sufficient capacity available to them to meet the demands placed upon the part of the structure for which they are responsible. Productivity is a complex notion, related not only to efficiency but also to the effectiveness of operations.

Commitment is the motivation of individuals and teams to undertake the activities assigned to them to a high performance standard. Highly motivated individuals and teams exhibit higher levels of productivity than those with lower commitment and are more likely to make useful contributions in relation to issues outside their roles and sets of responsibilities. However, managing commitment is a delicate art. In particular, the use of extrinsic rewards is a highly problematic area addressed in detail in Chapter 8.

Capability is the sum of practical skills and ability of individuals and teams to undertake the activities assigned to them to a high performance standard.

Capability is central to performance but often difficult to define and manage effectively.

Once again, leaders need ways to ensure that critical activities are the primary drivers behind decisions about managing capacity, commitment, and capability.

The external and internal environments

The external environment is the ever-changing situation and set of stakeholders outside of the organization but affecting its activities, the delivery of its strategy, and achievement of its overall objective. Obviously, a vast array of other parties and issues make up the external environment for an organization. However, only a limited number of these are actually vital for the organization's survival and prosperity. Identifying these is another criticality challenge – to focus attention on the issues that will most affect success or failure.

It is the initial definition of the overall objective that should narrow the scope of what should be analysed within the environment. Initially, the things that must be identified are *barriers/threats* and *enablers/opportunities* to achieving the overall objective.[6] In other words, the environment is relevant to an organization only insofar as elements of it may – now or in the future – get in the way of achieving the overall objective or somehow provide an opportunity to achieve it. Thereafter, more-specific aspects of the external environment can also inform decisions about critical activities and the organizational designs and systems. This narrowing of the focus of environmental analysis is not a common facet of conventional strategic planning but is essential to the strategy execution process.

Naturally, the unit of analysis for which the framework is being applied should drive the nature of the environmental analysis. Large corporations should, of course, bring to bear a wider and much more powerful set of tools and techniques to assess their environments than would an internal department or small business.

Many pressures in the external environment cannot be controlled by the organization or can be influenced only to a degree. However, it is essential to track these so that early responses can be initiated to changes in the environment.

The internal environment is the changing situation and set of stakeholders inside the organization, affecting its activities, the delivery of its strategy, and achievement of its overall objective. Although many organizations don't systematically analyse their internal environments, this is every bit as important as examining the external environments, as Chapter 4 demonstrated when examining how to diagnose strategy execution barriers. Organizations create their own barriers to and strengths in aiding the achievement of the overall objectives, and these can create greater threats and opportunities than the outside world. Again, awareness of the barriers, risks, enablers, and opportunities is the key and, generally speaking, there is the potential to exert greater control over internal environment.

Performance measures

As the inverted pyramid framework implies, performance measures can be identified for all the elements within it. Where historic data is available, metrics can be useful in the actual identification, evaluation, and alignment of each phase in the breakdown from overall objective to critical activities. Sometimes, the past provides reliable information about how well different strategies or initiatives work. Such data can also be used to make better-informed decisions about criticality. When considering whether critical activities are necessary and sufficient, it's important to be able to predict the impact of particular activities – and focus efforts accordingly. Of course, performance measures are also vital for tracking progress and evaluating outcomes *post hoc.* So-called leading measures relating to critical activities and the things they affect relatively directly can be used to predict less-direct outcomes, which can themselves be measured using so-called lagging measures.[7]

Performance measures can also be established for all the organizational designs and systems in phase 2 of the inverted pyramid framework. Most large organizations routinely collect many measures relating to issues such as project progress, individual performance, and commitment. Whether they are the right measures effectively interrelated and properly interpreted is another matter. We will introduce various models to help with this challenge.

Indicators relating to important factors in both the external and internal environment are also important. Some environmental factors (especially internal ones) may be affected by organizational initiatives, to an extent. However, even where environmental factors are relatively uncontrollable, tracking their movement is critical, as it may affect the plausibility of plans and necessitate re-planning.

Of course, most large or complex organizations measure lots of things. Whether they measure the right things in the right way and interpret and use metrics effectively is another matter. The process by which conceptual objectives are converted into concrete actions is important for informing, selection and design, and use of measures. Performance measurement is an extremely complex area, interacting in subtle ways with other elements in the inverted pyramid framework. As such, it is explored in greater depth in Chapters 6, 7, and 8.

Strategic risks

As with performance measures, strategic risks can be identified at every stage in the inverted pyramid framework. This is crucial. Not all strategies work, some activities are misaligned with strategic intentions, projects can fail to deliver intended outcomes, performance measures can create catastrophic unintended effects, and so on. Risk resides in every strategy, activity, system, process, and design – and in the relationships between them. What is vital is that managers know what is critical to success and can use this lens to detect risks that would otherwise go unnoticed or underestimated. It's vital to develop and execute strategy recognizing that plans are never perfect. Analysis is always limited, situations change, people don't always behave predictably, and organizational systems clash in unintended ways. Organizations constantly wrestle with some level of uncertainty in relation to everything they plan and do – which jeopardizes the achievement of their overall objectives. Some of these uncertainties don't matter – they relate to outcomes that are highly improbable or inconsequential. Others uncertainties are material because they relate to more likely or significant outcomes. The identification and management of strategic risks, within the content of strategy execution, is dealt with mainly in Chapter 7.

Important caveats for the framework

There are many elements in the inverted pyramid framework, which is in contrast with the tendency of models to be highly concise. However, it is a logical and appropriately detailed framework to guide the decisions of managers, in practice.[8] Each of the elements is explored in detail over the next few chapters, and detailed examples are provided. Before progressing to these chapters, there are some important issues to note about the inverted pyramid framework.

Comprehensiveness

No framework should ever be considered totally comprehensive. No model – and certainly none brief enough to be imparted in a single book – could detail every possible concern that leaders might address when executing strategy. This framework addresses two important areas:

- *Translating objectives into action.* Phase 1 of the framework provides a *structured process* to analyse complex situations and distill decisions through a manageable sequence, resulting in the critical activities organizations must undertake to implement their strategies. This element of the model does not prescribe what things are important for strategy execution. Rather, it gives a structure to enable leaders to identify these for themselves.
- *Aligning organizational designs and systems.* The phase 2 elements provide the 'scaffolding' to organize leaders' thinking around typically essential elements for consideration when implementing strategy. Research suggests that many of these organizational components impede strategy execution through creating or maintaining misalignments that drive activities not conducive to causing the achievement of the overall objective.

Organizations systematically addressing these areas and applying the framework intelligently should improve the probability of strategy execution success in their organizations. Success can never be guaranteed, but the value of improving the probability of success in a way that competitors do not or cannot is highly attractive.

Sequential thinking

The framework is logically sequential and, thus, represents the dominant flow of logic usually necessary for well-informed decision making. However, some iterative thinking is required, too. For example, a strategy may appear valid until the activities necessary for its achievement are identified. At that point, it may be necessary to reform the strategy, to ensure that it can be implemented. Similarly, it may ultimately be established that an organization does not possess the capabilities to undertake certain critical activities and cannot secure these capabilities. This is a strength of the framework – applied well, it tests the validity of the preceding elements.

Present reality and unique context

Many leaders dream occasionally of getting their hands on a 'greenfield' situation – an opportunity to build an organization from the ground up, without the constraints and 'baggage' that all established organizations carry. Such opportunities are of course rare and, when applying the framework outlined, it is necessary to recognize such constraints. For example, existing organizations already have structures, and though a change in planned activities may make this structure suboptimal, a decision to restructure must be made within a wider context. Often, it is simply not worth causing the upheaval associated with complete change to an 'optimal' state, given the potential benefits on offer.

No model can provide all the answers. The best way to implement strategy always depends on the specific contextual factors. This framework is designed to organize thinking so that the important issues are addressed in the right order, but intelligent thinking is still required!

Strategy versus structure

As mentioned already, the inverted pyramid framework can be applied at a number of organizational levels such as the corporate, divisional, business unit, functional, or departmental levels. It was also noted that it is extremely important to be clear about the 'unit of analysis' that defines the context for the framework's application. Some important issues related to these points now need to be addressed.

In a perfect world, every organization would apply the inverted pyramid once to the entire organization. This would have the advantages of keeping all the related thinking tightly integrated within a single sequential decision-making process. It would also make existing structural divisions easy to ignore – with decisions about structures being left until their designated stage in the decision-making sequence.

For small- to medium-sized organizations or relatively simple ones (e.g. those with one dominant product line), doing this is feasible and attractive.

However, very large and complex organizations are more likely to confront a dilemma. Should they try to apply the inverted pyramid framework to the entire organization or apply it to subunits or some combination of these options? Selecting subunits has the advantage of making application more manageable because of the smaller and less complex nature of business units/functions. However, this decision reinforces existing structural arrangements and the thinking paradigms associated with them. There is a risk of the 'structure tail wagging the strategy dog'.

The right choice always depends on the context. In a decentralized corporation, in which strategic business units operate relatively independently, it is perfectly feasible to apply the inverted pyramid to these subunits. Conversely, if a complex organization incorporates many centralized processes and needs to avoid assumptions based on existing structural divisions, it is best to start with an entire organization application of the framework. Doing so may reveal unmanageable complexity, which in itself is an important challenge to leaders, as it may imply that strategy is not executable in such an unmanageable context. Alternatively, it is possible to use both an overarching corporate application of the framework and more detailed applications to subunits, 'nested' within that, once the ideal corporate-level structure is established.

Deterministic versus emergent strategy

Another dilemma that senior leaders must consider are the relative merits of 'deterministic' strategy and 'emergent' strategy. This is a well-established distinction in the strategy field. Debates have raged about whether it is right or realistic for senior leaders to try to impose strategic decisions on organizations that behave 'organically' or whether it is better to allow organizations to evolve in a less coordinated fashion to respond fluidly to environmental changes. The inverted pyramid framework looks, on the face of it, like a relatively deterministic model – starting with overall objectives, determining activities, and ideally being initiated by those in senior roles. However, it is less prescriptive than that.

Though the model is *logically sequential*, it is also recognized that iteration and feedback are essential parts of the ongoing refinement that must occur to keep an organization in alignment with its objectives, within its changing environment. Rather than debate whether deterministic or emergent strategy is better, it is perhaps more useful to suggest that the nature of the environment, and in particular levels of uncertainty within it, should determine the nature of strategy and how it is executed. For example, in a fast-moving and unpredictable environment, strategy might rightly be focused purposefully on fast innovation and developing organizational flexibility and change capability. Achieving these things is not easy and, ironically, might require a *determined* programme of change. Conversely, in relatively stable environments, strategy and its execution might naturally focus more on long-term positioning, more domain-specific capabilities, and longer-term process-based effectiveness and efficiency. In other words, both deterministic and emergent strategies perhaps have their places in both dynamic and static contexts; rather, it is the content, nature, and focus of the strategy itself that should adapt to the context.

It is also worth noting an insight drawn from my own field research – that much apparently 'emergent' strategy is much less emergent than it appears. In several settings, I detected changes that looked bottom-up or emergent and were subsequently adopted much more widely. However, having been in the field conducting longitudinal case studies for some time, I was able to track these activities back to deliberate decisions by senior leaders made at some time in the past. These leaders recognized that imposing their planned changes on wide swathes of an organization's population was time-consuming, difficult, and unreliable. So, rather than attempting this, they quietly chose high-potential areas to start executing elements of strategy, refining implementation as they went. Then they sat back and watched as other divisions and departments jumped on the bandwagon and started systematically copying (and in some cases bettering) the performance of the 'guinea pigs'. You might call this 'deterministic emergent' strategy!

Summary of key points

- The are five broad principles useful for thinking through the strategy execution challenge – the five Cs of strategy execution – *causality*, *criticality*, *compatibility*, *continuity*, and *clarity*.
- Causality relates to identifying activities that will plausibly cause achievement of an organization's overall objective (and later ensuring alignment of organizational designs and processes).
- Criticality relates to focusing attention on those activities most essential to realize the strategy.
- Compatibility relates to ensuring that critical activities will pull an organization in the same direction and do not conflict with one another.
- Continuity relates to aligning organizational designs and systems with objectives and critical activities to ensure sustained physical delivery of activities and responsibility for outcomes.
- Clarity relates to ensuring clarity of thought in the strategy execution process and that individuals have clear understanding of strategy, how it is being executed, and their related roles and responsibilities.
- The inverted pyramid framework is a logically sequential decision-making framework to guide leaders through the strategy execution process.
- Phase 1 of the inverted pyramid framework relates to translating objectives into action and includes the following:
  - Overall objective

- Strategic choices
- Critical activities.
- Phase 2 of the inverted pyramid framework relates to aligning organizational designs and systems and includes the following:
    - Projects and processes
    - Organization structure, resources allocation, and interface management
    - Roles and responsibilities
    - Performance criteria
    - Capacity, capability, and commitment.
- Both phases of the inverted pyramid framework require the following:
    - Identification of strategic performance measures
    - Identification of strategic risks
    - Analysis of the internal and external environment.
- The inverted pyramid framework should not be seen as a prescriptive or perfectly comprehensive model – every situation is unique, so intelligent and flexible application is always necessary.
- Although the inverted pyramid framework informs how organizational designs and systems should be aligned to deliver critical activities, the benefits of any change must always be weighed against the costs and disruption it causes.
- The inverted pyramid framework can be applied to entire organizations and subunits, but leaders should bear in mind the risks of reinforcing assumptions and paradigms based on existing structural arrangements.
- Application of the inverted pyramid framework should incorporate iterative decision making and feedback to ensure that it is responsive to fast-moving and localized environmental pressures.
- The nature of strategies developed should be conditioned by the relevant environment and correspondingly content- and domain-focused or process- and change-focused.

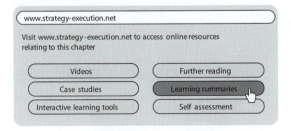

Chapter 6

Translating strategy into action

However beautiful the strategy, you should occasionally look at the results.

Sir Winston Churchill

The challenge of moving from plan to action

In Chapter 1, distinctions were made between strategy execution and strategic change (changes in the content of strategy) and managing change (operational improvements, not necessarily designed and prioritized to achieve strategic objectives). This distinction was important because it explains why some organizations have great-sounding strategies and slick operations but no obvious relationships between the two. It is often difficult to see how everyday activities,

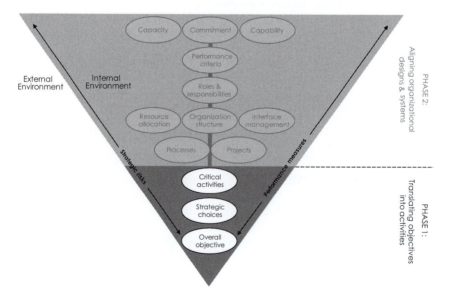

Figure 6.1 Translating objectives into activities highlighted in the inverted pyramid framework

projects, and initiatives might plausibly deliver strategic objectives. Bridging the gap between strategy and operations is the core strategy execution challenge, represented by phase 1 of the inverted pyramid framework – translating objectives into activities – highlighted in Figure 6.1.

Phase 1 incorporates the overall objective, strategic choices, and critical activities – and along with phase 2 necessitates consideration of the internal and external environments and identification of performance measures and strategic risks. All these elements were briefly described in Chapter 5. This chapter and the next tackle this challenge via two complementary perspectives. This chapter explores translating overall objectives into action (top down), and Chapter 7 explains how to align activities with strategic objectives (bottom-up). As already discussed, both these perspectives are useful in different situations and partly reflect the simultaneously 'deterministic' and 'emergent' nature of strategy and strategizing.

As discussed earlier, a great deal more is known about strategic planning than strategy execution, and this is reflected both in organizations' usage of strategic planning techniques and in their satisfaction with them.[1] Assessing the quality of strategic planning efforts or their ultimate effects on performance is more complex, but there is limited evidence that the practice is statistically associated with superior financial performance of corporations.[2] However, reported strategy execution failure rates do suggest that relatively few strategies result in the performance outcomes they aim to achieve. The research into strategy execution barriers summarized in Chapter 4 provides some indication of problems specific to strategic planning, and these include the following:

- strategy having insufficient market or technical validity
- strategy not being broken down far enough
- there being no strategy execution framework
- strategy not being understood by those responsible for implementing it.

Some corroboration and more concrete clues were provided in my own case study research, and this is explored in greater detail later in this chapter. All these findings reinforce the common complaint that strategies are often developed by senior teams and written up but not properly used to drive actions. Various explanations are provided for this common tendency:

- Formal strategies are required to justify budgets and are otherwise seen as being of little use by executives.
- Executives are not interested in the detail of implementation, this being a job for lower-level managers.
- The process of planning is seen as more important than the plan it creates.
- Breaking strategy down is too difficult and, perhaps, executives are embarrassed by their inability to do this or lack of knowledge about operations.

Each of these explanations is probably true in some circumstances, but none of them excuse leaving strategies in conceptual form, existing only on paper and as vague memories. If execution is to succeed, strategic objectives must be broken down into concrete activities that will plausibly achieve them. Alone it cannot guarantee desired performance–identified actions must also be performed effectively – but it is the first step and a necessary one.

Models to translate strategy into action

One might think that such a seemingly obvious challenge would have been thoroughly addressed by practitioners, consultants, and researchers. Though confidential techniques may exist in some organizations, a review of academic research and other publications reveals that there is no widely accepted method for breaking strategy into activities. Of course, this partly reflects the fact that the amount of research and guidance on strategy execution is very small.

Within the field, a number of the early contributors proposed integrated 'content' models to help guide strategy execution.[3] These models defined *what* issues managers should consider when implementing strategy and were reasonably consistent at a high level. The elements of the main models are summarized in Table A3 in the appendices. Although largely unsupported by empirical research, these models were in part based on theory from other management disciplines and certainly helped define the strategy execution challenge. However, a change of direction followed. A second stream of authors proposed 'process' models.[4] Rather than prescribe what issues managers should consider to implement strategy, they outlined how they might determine the most appropriate issues to address in their particular situations. Again, not all these models are strongly supported by empirical research but usefully draw upon theory from other established disciplines.[5] More recently, ideas developed in other areas may prove useful clues about how strategy might be translated into actions.[6] The best known of these is the notion of strategy mapping, which has been used to depict strategic logic within the managerial and organizational cognition field for some time and more recently within the performance measurement arena. Once again, these ideas are built upon shaky empirical underpinnings and were not developed with strategy execution in mind, but they nevertheless provide useful clues for the challenge of translating strategy into action.

Having cantered through the development of thinking in this area, the question arises of what approach to adopt to tackle the critical challenge of translating strategy into activities 'top down'. My research provides empirical support for an approach that, along with the other elements of the inverted pyramid framework, draws together and extends all these ideas.

The core process

The inverted pyramid model depicted the primary strategy execution challenge as translating overall objectives into critical activities, employing the principles of causality, criticality, and compatibility along the way. The first step in the process must be clearly identifying the 'unit of analysis' to which the translation process relates. As described in Chapter 5, this can vary from an entire organization to a department.

Overall objective

Establishing the overall objective is the critical next step. As the inverted pyramid framework implies through resting only on its tip, everything depends on the overall objective. It is the foundation stone that should shape strategic choices, critical activities, and all organizational designs and systems.

Overall objectives are often poorly framed. Organizations may develop and publish missions and visions and other grand-sounding statements, but often these lack clarity and meaning. They frequently don't describe the real intent of the organization's senior leaders but rather are 'sales pitches' aimed at influencing stakeholder groups such as investors, customers, staff, regulators, and the media. Because they are often public, they must avoid the problem of sending conflicting messages to these different groups and therefore are 'watered down'.

A quick look at a typical corporate website illustrates this phenomenon. The 'mission' published on Starbucks's website is, "To inspire and nurture the human spirit – one person, one cup, and one neighbourhood at a time".[7] Immediately following this, several 'principles' deal with the interests of coffee growers, partners (employees), customers, communities, and shareholders. However, the company's annual report has a slightly different focus:

> The Company's objective is to establish Starbucks as one of the most recognized and respected brands in the world. To achieve this goal, the Company plans to continue disciplined expansion of its retail operations, to grow its specialty operations and to selectively pursue other opportunities by introducing new products and developing new channels of distribution.[8]

This focus is reflected in the company's 2009 Fiscal Business Update (an investor presentation) that presents key financial results, earnings per share, geography and channel reach, margin improvement, cash flow, store growth, store sales, and so on. The cynical observation is that there isn't much reported to investors on progress inspiring and nurturing the human spirit. However, Starbucks is not unusual or acting oddly in its presentation of objectives. Like all complex organizations, it has a tricky job reconciling the expectations of different stakeholder groups, all of which can affect the achievement of its overall objective through their actions.

Managing this dilemma creates a common problem – it's not entirely clear what many organizations' overall objectives are. Even in internal strategy development sessions attended only by senior executives, attempts to define overall objectives can be thwarted by concerns about stakeholder perceptions. Executives know that as strategy is cascaded to more junior employees, winning their hearts and minds will be important for successful execution. Consequently, they state objectives that sound motivating. Executives also know that information leaks become more likely as strategies are put into practice, so they hedge their bets by making statements palatable for outsiders. The result is the watered-down statements with which we are all so familiar and have been the butt of so many jokes in the business world.

However, staff motivation is not the only strategy execution consideration. My own research repeatedly found that unclear overall objectives couldn't effectively be broken down into critical activities that will plausibly achieve them. Moreover, employees find it difficult to align the activities they oversee with unclear overall objectives. If this 'line of sight' between actions and overall objectives is weak, effort is likely to be wasted on initiatives that will not plausibly cause desirable outcomes. Using the metaphor of the inverted pyramid, the considerable might of the organization is not aligned to exert pressure on the pyramid's tip – the overall objective. Unclear 'line of sight' is also, ironically, de-motivating for employees.[9]

The lesson here is that organizations must distinguish stakeholder communications from setting objectives. They must clearly define why they exist and what they seek to achieve, in such a way that the critical activities they thus need to undertake can thereafter be determined. How best to communicate with and influence different stakeholders is a consideration for much later on in the strategy execution process. Indeed, before setting a clear overall objective, it is tricky to know who the important stakeholders are for the organization.

This lesson is easy to present and understand, but managers can find it incredibly difficult to do. On many occasions when helping senior teams define the overall objectives of the organizations they run, I have outlined this argument and secured explicit agreement that it is correct but later heard someone voice concerns about how a particular word or phrase will 'play' with a stakeholder group.

Setting aside stakeholder concerns makes setting overall objectives much simpler. However, there are still challenges to overcome. The right balance between simplicity and complexity is important for ensuring clarity. Simple overall objectives look clear and neat, but complex objectives leave less room for ambiguity. There is no single formula for getting this balance right, but one approach that can be helpful is to agree on a simple overall objective and then separately define the key terms in it to remove any doubt about their intended meanings. Usually, this extra effort amounts to little more than capturing the conclusions of the debate that inevitably arise when defining what an organization's overall objective should be. A good example is provided by a stockbroking business, the overall objective of which is as follows:

Our Mission is to maximize long-term profit through the provision of execution-only stockbroking services to UK-based customers.

This short statement of the business's overall objective is fairly clear and avoids the problems associated with statements oriented toward influencing multiple stakeholders. However, even this statement can benefit from some definitions to reduce any ambiguity. For example, what does "long-term" actually mean? What exactly does "execution-only" mean? Why did the business elect only to serve United Kingdom-based customers? These questions and others are answered by defining (as shown in Table 6.1) the key phrases used in the statement, emphasized here:

Our Mission is to maximize *long-term profit* through the provision of *execution-only stockbroking services* to *UK-based customers*.

A fair question can be raised about how narrowly the overall objective should constrain factors such as the product range or geographical market. After all, these issues might be dealt with via strategic choices, and the organization might feasibly decide one day to maximize profit via other means (e.g. providing advice or overseas expansion). There is no one right answer to this question but, if for the foreseeable future this represents the specific overall objective of the business, it is useful to constrain it clearly in this fashion. It keeps people focused on achieving a tangible result within defined parameters and makes the challenge of translating strategy into action a little easier. In the long-term, the objective can be changed if need be but, in the meantime, it is better that people are not diversifying the organization's activities in ways that are not explicitly agreed. On more than one occasion, I have come across businesses where the CEO was unaware of the true extent of market development (e.g. into unpalatably risky countries) or product extension (into areas where the business had alarmingly limited expertise).

Table 6.1 Example of overall objective defined for stockbroking business

"maximize long-term profit"	"execution-only stockbroking services"	"UK-based customers"
• Long-term means as far as the environment in which we operate is reasonably predictable in terms of its key characteristics, which we recognize varies. Generally, we will seek to maximize profit over a 10 year horizon	• Execution-only means trading by customers on their own account without the active provision of advice relating to specific transactions • Execution-only does not preclude the passive provision of market data, economic data, publicly available analysts' forecasts and explanations of how stock markets operate and trades can be placed. • Wherever possible, customer assets may be held in government tax-free 'wrappers'	• UK-based customers means customers domiciled in the United Kingdom of Great Britain and Northern Ireland • These customers and interactions with them are subject to the laws of the United Kingdom and, as appropriate, Scotland, Northern Ireland and England and Wales • Offers made to, and interactions with, these customers are subject to regulation by the UK's Financial Services Authority (FSA)

Getting the balance right is usually the result of asking good questions. When working with businesses to pin down what they are really trying to achieve, I often ask how much they might change their activities to make a profit. Would they enter new industries? Would they expand into any country around the globe? How much long-term profit would they forsake in favour of achieving espoused ethical aims? The answers help to define the *real* overall objective.

Environmental analysis

Defining key phrases in the overall objective has an immediate payoff. Early on (and throughout) in the strategy execution process, it is vital to examine the internal and external environments in which an organization operates. Many organizations systematically consider the external environment, seeing it as important for strategic planning. However, they can underestimate the importance of the internal environment, which is also crucial because it so heavily affects strategy execution. It is in the internal environment that many of the barriers to and strengths supporting strategy execution reside. It needs to be systematically examined, too, if the conceptual strategy developed is to be executable and strategy execution itself is going to succeed.

Many organizations undertake broad-brush environmental analysis. Any MBA graduate will recall using models such as PEST to frame examination of key political, economic, social, and technical environmental factors – or SWOT analysis to examine strengths, weaknesses, opportunities, and threats. There is nothing inherently wrong with these models, but they are weakened when applied without a clear objective in mind. This is the main reason that when using SWOT, strengths are often also identified as weaknesses and opportunities as threats – all adding to the confusion and diminishing the usefulness of the analysis. Defining the overall objective is hugely helpful because it provides a specific frame of reference for environmental analysis. Analysts are not simply identifying apparent 'opportunities' but specific opportunities to achieve the well-specified overall objective. This narrows the focus of environmental analysis significantly and gives it much more traction.

This book is about strategy execution, so is not the place to provide an extended guide to what is a task undertaken at the strategic planning stage. Suffice to say that strategy execution is helped enormously by a multi-lens but focused environmental analysis. Large or complex organizations can usefully use models such as PEST, SWOT, industry structural analysis, competitor analysis, market analysis, and scenario planning when examining the external environment. Internally, a much wider range of tools can be employed, depending on the shape and nature of the organization. Needless so say, financial analysis is critical but so, too, is analysis of activities (be they projects or processes) and their impact on intermediate (non-financial) objectives. Issues such as staff engagement, process efficiency, customer service, technical effectiveness, system responsiveness, and so on might all be important. Generalities are made difficult because each organization is unique. Google Inc. might place a high focus on technological innovation, for example, whereas the Red Cross might see its global logistics as being critical to its success.

What really matters is that organizations develop a clear understanding of what does or might help achieve their overall objectives and what does or might threaten achievement of overall objectives. In other words, the implications of the environmental analysis can be positive or negative in terms of achieving the overall objective. They can also be already present or only possibilities that may arise in the future. Figure 6.2 identifies these four alternatives as barriers, enablers, opportunities, and risks.

These barriers, enablers, opportunities, and risks may be referred to in other ways. For example, an internal enabler could also be called a *strength*. Sometimes, a barrier is called an *issue*. The labels don't really matter as long as the analysis is conducted systematically and understood properly by those interpreting it.

There are also other refinements to these distinctions that can be made. For example, as implied earlier, most aspects of the environment can be categorized as external or internal, though some relate more accurately to interactions between the two. It is also worth assessing the controllability of environmental factors. Some may be easily manipulated (e.g. pricing of directly sold products), whereas others are entirely uncontrollable (e.g. inflation within the general economy). Broadly speaking, internal factors tend to be more controllable than external factors, but this is not always the case, and there are wide variations within each category. Clearly, for a strategy to be executable, it must focus on changing or influencing environmental factors that can realistically be altered.

Suggesting that the implications of an environmental factor are simply positive or negative is artificially polemic. Rather, this is more of a dimension and can be constructed as such for assessing and recording the significance of the factors identified. Table 6.2 gives the example of a systematic analysis of several environmental factors affecting the stockbroking business described earlier. It

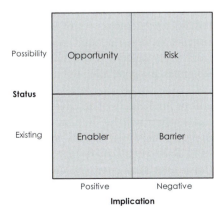

Figure 6.2 Environmental factors: Barriers, enablers, opportunities and risks

Table 6.2 Example of environmental analysis for stockbroking business

Related overall objective element(s)	Environmental factor	Location (internal-interaction-external) score (-10 to +10)	Positive/ negative score (-10 to +10)	Controllability score (-10 to +10)	Occurrence probability score (0 to 1.0)
Execution-only stockbroking services	Only 39% of trades are conducted within nominee accounts, creating high trading costs	+3	−3	+3	1.0
	Only 32% of trades are conducted online, increasing trading costs	+2	−5	+5	1.0
UK-based customers	25% of the UK population own stocks, a figure that is increasing steadily	+9	+3	−9	1.0
	Stock trading activity is expected to grow by 3–6% per annum over the next 5 years	+9	+4	−9	0.7

uses quantitative scales to 'dimensionalize' the location, positivity, controllability, and occurrence probability of several environmental factors related to two elements of the overall objective. These quantifications are not strictly necessary but make it easier to calibrate the scale of the opportunity or challenge facing the organization. They also enable simple sorting, to prioritize the most important and controllable factors, deserving of the greatest attention in terms of strategic options and choices.

Some caution has to be exercised. It is easy to get carried away with such quantifications and build elaborate models that over-extend the analysis and create an illusion of control. Staying close to reliable raw data wherever possible is wise.

At this point, it is worth noting that environmental analysis has to be an ongoing activity. The environment can, of course, change quickly, and few organizations can afford to leave their monitoring of the environment until annual strategy reviews (or even less often). Developing a set of environmental indicators – at least for the most significant factors – is vital.[10] Some environmental indicators are relatively reliable and finely quantified. Obvious examples include national statistics such as inflation rates and population numbers, which may be used with relative confidence.

Sometimes, the status or implication of an environmental factor is unknown or unforeseeable. Many readers will be familiar with the notion of 'known knowns', 'known unknowns', 'unknown knowns' and 'unknown unknowns' – if only because of former U. S. Secretary of Defense Donald Rumsfeld's amusing attempt to explain it in a television interview during the Iraq War. The key point is that it's important to recognize that no environmental analysis is ever comprehensive or perfect, and maintaining a close watch on the environment is crucial.

We have discussed analysis of the environment in some detail, especially given that this book is about strategy execution, not strategic planning. However, this is deliberate. Strategy execution often fails because the strategy that has been developed is simply not plausible. It may look good on paper and at first glance but does not incorporate sufficient analysis of the external and (in particular) internal environments upon which success always relies.

The final consideration in relation to the environmental analysis is to consider how it should actually be used. The reason the environment is so important is that it *conditions* the relationships between activities and their outcomes (including, ultimately, organizations' overall objectives). The environment determines whether the cause-and-effect assumptions underlying particular courses of action will hold true. Will the new pay deal really motivate staff to be more productive? Will the new process design reduce waste? Will new customers be attracted by the new advertising campaign? Will costs come down if IT is outsourced? Will complex combinations of actions such as these all roll up into increased sustainable profitability (or whatever the overall objective happens to be)? The environment will determine all this, so understanding it matters.

In many strategic planning models and even some strategy execution ones, environmental analysis follows mission/vision setting and precedes the examination of strategic options, it obviously being possible after the former and necessary for the latter. This logic is sound; however, it is inadequate to limit environmental analysis to this stage in the strategy development and implementation process. At this stage, the analysis is inevitably high-level and often conceptual. It is too broad to incorporate all the detail that might be useful as strategies get broken down toward activities. The environment conditions relationships at all levels of detail. For this reason, it is essential to see environmental analysis as something that must be 'wrapped round' all the stages of both strategic planning and strategy execution. As more detailed options, initiatives, programmes, projects and, ultimately, concrete actions are defined, more specific 'mini' environmental analyses are needed to uncover those factors that will help or hinder strategy execution. With this final caveat in place, we can turn attention to the question of how to start breaking the overall objective down in a manner that will facilitate successful strategy execution.

Strategy execution maps

A great deal has been written about identifying, evaluating, and making strategic choices, and it is not the job of a book on strategy execution to repeat it. However, the way in which strategy itself is articulated, interpreted and, of course, broken down matters greatly for strategy execution. Strategy cannot be planned in isolation and 'tossed over the wall' for execution. It must be planned with execution in mind, and that means describing it in a format that can be picked up and used for breaking down strategy toward activities.

As discussed earlier, causality is a vitally important notion for strategy execution. It is at the heart of one of the simplest questions that can be put to managers – how will the organization's overall objective be achieved? Logically, any answer must articulate something that will plausibly *cause* the achievement of the overall objective. However, it is fairly rare that the answer – such as a description of an organization's strategy – convincingly describes this hypothesized (or implicitly assumed) causal relationship. This is perhaps unsurprising. Strategies are necessarily conceptual – relating to patterns of interactions, as described in Chapter 2. Strategies are difficult to pin down and articulate. Activities, conversely, are much more concrete, but they are much more numerous and do not cause overall objectives to be achieved *directly*. Describing how they do this is also tricky.

My research over the last decade suggests that an effective solution is to base breakdowns of strategy around causal diagrams that depict causal relationships. Causal mapping is far from a new idea and has been used to describe systems and even strategic logic. However, it has a great deal to offer here, because we can think of breaking down overall objectives and then strategy as moving from outcomes (or ends) to identifying their causes (or means).[11] This particular application of causal thinking necessitates some special treatment, as my research has also identified a series of common pitfalls into which managers often fall when employing this method. These are dealt with once the basic approach is outlined.

At a high level, depicting causal hypotheses is relatively simple, as there are often fairly few variables at work. Let's start with the simple example of an electrical goods retailer. Figure 6.3 shows how a typical overall objective (simplified for the purposes of mapping) of 'increased profit' might be broken down into two plausible direct causes. Put another way, asking, "What could cause increased profit?" leads to two obvious answers – increased revenue or reduced costs. This is a simple accounting equation. Although things tend to get much more complicated, it is essentially this logical approach that can be continued until critical activities are identified.

Before breaking this example down further, an important observation is immediately worthwhile. It may well be that this retailer could or would not wish to reduce costs. Of course, because it ultimately seeks to maximize profit, increased revenue or decreased costs, or both would deliver this. In the early stages of developing a strategy execution map, it is best to identify and explore

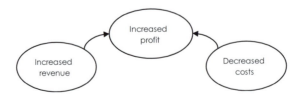

Figure 6.3 Basic high level casual relationships

Figure 6.4 Beginnings of a strategy execution map

options before moving toward decisions about choices. As that happens, a more polished map of choices can be developed.

Before moving to an example of such a map, we can continue breaking down the preceding map. Taking just the revenue side for the moment, we can ask, "What could cause increased revenue?" Two direct causes of this outcome are obvious – increasing volume of sales or increasing price. Again, either or both would cause increased revenue.

Once again, these are options being identified rather than choices being made. As the breakdown continues, short chains of causal logic appear. For example, increasing volume of sales would plausibly cause increased revenue, which would plausibly cause an increase in profit – all other things being equal.

This last point is important. The causal hypotheses developed in an early strategy execution map are made in relative isolation of one another. Difficult trade-off decisions are apparent and will need to be resolved as choices between options are made. For example, increasing prices may decrease volume of sales, depending upon price elasticity of demand (as every student of microeconomics knows). What is the optimum price the business should adopt? Systematically breaking objectives down into possible causes in this way structures these trade-off decisions (and more subtle ones) clearly – but they do still need to be resolved through decisions.

Before breaking this example down further, another important observation is worthwhile. As discussed, maps can be simplified and polished into depicting choices rather than a larger number of options. They can also be usefully simplified as they are developed by employing another of the five Cs – criticality. As objectives break down into more detail, strategy execution maps would become extremely complex if every sub-objective and activity necessary in an organization were mapped. Rather, to isolate *critical* activities, some prioritization must occur. It is important to isolate the most influential and most plausible causes of desired effects. This allows decision makers to focus their attention on critical decisions and for the challenging process of translating strategy into activities to focus on defining performance that is truly required for success. Often, the most important sub-objectives are immediately clear to knowledgeable decision makers. At other times, they are hotly debated, or dedicated research is necessary to inform decisions. Such choices are always made with some uncertainty, and judgment is always necessary. Along with the move from options to choices, the move from many causes to the critical ones makes strategy execution maps progressively more manageable, simpler, and more useful to depict the organization's strategy and means of its execution. Figure 6.5 summarizes the progressive development of evolving strategy execution maps, moving both from options to choices and from a wide to a critical focus.

Figure 6.6 shows the next iteration of the evolving strategy execution map for the electrical goods retailer. To keep this example simple, only one cause is shown broken down each time. The evolving map suggests that increasing the number of customers and/or volume of sales per customer would increase volume of sales. The next layer down shows that decision makers recognized that customer numbers could be increased by increasing customer acquisition and/or retention. Finally, the map depicts three potential causes of increased customer acquisition – acquiring other businesses, increasing promotion impact, or increasing sales impact.

At this point, it is worth noting a key strength of this kind of systematically developed causal map. Although the potential causes of the effects shown in Figure 6.6 look obvious when laid out on the page, in practice they tend not to flow out of discussion easily and clearly. This is especially true if a systematic approach such as the one being outlined here is not used. More often, strategy-related assumptions are made in free-flowing or facilitated debates or even by individuals preparing documents and presentations. Under such circumstances, it is all too easy for managers to ignore important possibilities. For example, an organization that has conventionally focused on fast growth may hotly debate methods by which more customers can be acquired but may ignore customer retention. Such tendencies are exacerbated when organization designs and systems, such as structures, performance measures, targets, rewards, capabilities,

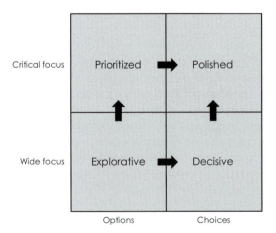

Figure 6.5 Progressive development of strategy execution maps

and so on orient attention toward particular modes of operation. Systematically developed strategy execution maps can help guard against these tendencies.

It should be obvious from Figure 6.6 that asking what could cause an objective to be achieved and repeating this process many times translates high-level conceptual goals (such as an organization's overall objective) into progressively more concrete means by which these conceptual goals may be achieved – through a chain of cause and effect relationships. However, Figure 6.6 does not go far enough. Though a performance variable such as 'increased sales impact' is much more tangible and specific than 'increased profit', it is not an activity. It would be risky for senior decision makers to ask even competent teams or individuals to go and achieve that without considerable further debate or guidance. This is an important point. Existing applications of strategy mapping – although a really

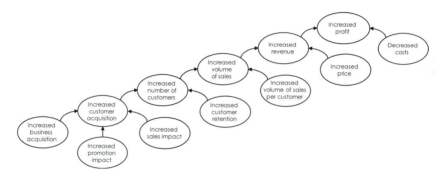

Figure 6.6 Early stage strategy execution map

Box 6.1 Retail banking confusion
A large retail bank that was developing its strategy execution map stumbled across a worrying problem. For many years, it had focused on attracting new customers, and many systems had been tuned to achieving this. As the executive team debated the evolution of the map, a discussion revealed that although both customer acquisition and retention rates were tracked, the bank had no idea of the relative value of these different ways of increasing the size of its customer base. No one had ever calculated the average revenue derived or costs generated from these alternative causes of (what everyone agreed was) a critical effect. The executives reflected that the way they had designed performance measures, targets, and reward systems would have reinforced the impression that retention was not critical. Later analysis revealed that retention was far less costly than acquisition and was likely to generate as much, if not more revenue.

useful development – typically have several serious limitations from a strategy execution perspective, and this is one of them. For successful strategy execution, maps cannot suddenly stop at a conceptual level. They must identify concrete actions. Strategy execution maps link critical actions with overall objectives.

Figure 6.7 shows a further evolution of the retailer's strategy execution map. It shows that the managers recognized that increasing sales capacity and/or sales effectiveness would increase sales impact. They knew that they could increase the amount of sales activity and/or seek to make sales efforts more successful (meaning a greater proportion of customers to whom a sales attempt was directed proceed to make a purchase). Four plausible causes of increased sales capacity were identified – increased intermediary sales, increased online sales, increased sales staff numbers, and increased sales staff capacity.

This last option was an attractive one for the retailer. It was thought that increasing the capacity of existing staff might create a big impact at relatively low cost. Initial insights suggested two ways of achieving this – reducing sales team absence (which was higher than average for the sector) and reducing the time taken by sales staff to process customers' orders. The map shows two activities deemed critical to achieving the latter – improving the ordering system and improving order-processing training.

Figure 6.7 is significant. It is the first example of an overall objective (increased profit) being explicitly linked to critical activities (improved order-processing system and improved order-processing training). This is an example of how the core strategy execution challenge – translating conceptual objectives into concrete activities – can be overcome. Taking one example, improved order-processing

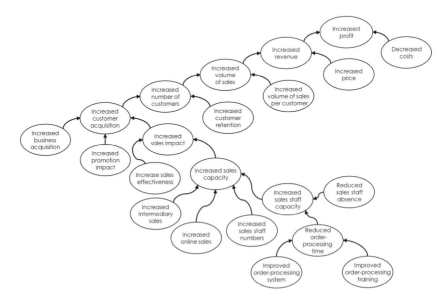

Figure 6.7 Evolving strategy execution map including two critical activities

training can be considered a critical activity as it is specific enough that learning specialists could reasonably be expected to develop a small project aimed at producing this as the project's 'product'. They would still need to break it down into individual tasks, sequence and schedule them, ensure adequate resource management, and so on. However, these are well-established project management methods. They are not inherently strategic and would require little if any oversight from senior decision makers.

It is useful to examine the chains of cause and effect logic contained within this evolving strategy execution map. Anyone seeking to understand how strategy is to be implemented can start at the top with the desired effects and trace down the map to see plausible causes. Equally, anyone seeking to understand why particular critical activities have been identified can start at the bottom of the map with causes and trace upward to see the effects they might plausibly produce. This contributes to increased clarity – one of the five Cs described in the last chapter.

Of course, Figure 6.7 is not a complete strategy execution map. For simplicity in this example, a limited number of effects have been broken down to identify their plausible causes. Also as Figure 6.5 summarizes, the map requires progressive development from options to choices and from a wide to critical focus. At this stage, it is important to reflect that some of the initial options identified may not even be plausible. As information and insights are gathered and the early stage map reviewed, it is often the case that some less convincing causes of the desired effects can be discarded.

However, even at this stage, consideration can be given to compatibility between critical activities – another of the five Cs. The map suggests that conducting order-processing training would be beneficial. However, a compatibility check alerts us that it would almost certainly be worth conducting as part of the rollout of the improved order-processing system. After all, there is little point in training sales staff in using a system that will shortly change, and it is likely that training would be required to introduce the new system in any case. The evolving map has confirmed compatibility between these critical activities – subject to this sequencing and integration of these activities.

Polished maps representing critical choices are discussed and presented later in this chapter. However, before exploring these, it is important to discuss the challenges getting from an early stage map such as the one in Figure 6.7 to such a polished specimen.

General pitfalls in working with causality

Strategy execution mapping, when done well, produces maps that look clear, logical, and simple. However, producing them is typically far from easy. There are numerous pitfalls that teams can fall into when they apply this technique – as there are with all such techniques. Some pitfalls relate to working with causality in general and are fairly well documented already. Others relate specifically to translating strategy into activities and have more recently been identified via my own research. These are outlined shortly.

The concept of causality is fundamental to our lives and learned from an early age. Newborn babies instinctively cry when they are hungry or uncomfortable and quickly learn that their parents give them attention in response. They begin to use this mechanism to secure attention, even when they are not hungry or uncomfortable, as every parent soon discovers. As humans develop, they recognize a great many cause-and-effect relationships: smile at people and they usually smile back at you; drop something and it will fall; and so on. As we grow older, continued mental development is largely about recognizing more subtle and sophisticated cause-and-effect relationships in operation and recognizing these more quickly. In organizations, every activity or event forms part of a complex series of cause and effect relationships.

Of course, few of us live our lives thinking actively about these relationships. As we learn of them, we tend to embed them in our thinking so that we don't have to rely on conscious thinking to perform simple tasks. This is just as well, or simple actions such as opening a door or brushing your teeth would become time-consuming cognitive challenges requiring us to identify our desired outcomes, establish what would cause them to occur, and sequencing our actions to perform the task at hand. Thankfully, because our ability to learn is highly sophisticated from an early age, we normally are not aware we're doing it. We can detect and understand apparent cause-and-effect relationships with little conscious thought and embed this learning into our everyday thinking. Psychologists call this learning *conditioning*, and famous experiments, such as those conducted by Pavlov, exemplify the power of this type of learning. Pavlov demonstrated that dogs quickly responded to a stimulus (a bell ringing) by salivating, because he had previously rung the bell before feeding the animals. The dogs had detected an association between the stimulus and being fed and thus started responding (by salivating) to the stimulus (the bell) even if no food were produced. In management, Chris Argyris and his colleagues have conducted a great deal of research into the links between learning and management in organizations.[12] He has also applied some of this thinking to the specific issue of strategy implementation.[13]

Most sciences are oriented toward understanding cause-and-effect relationships. Almost all scientific enquiries aim to explain *why* and *how* things happen; to do this means to understand cause and effect relationships. Consider the following questions that scientists have posed and how these aim to explore cause and effect:

- Does smoking increase the chances of suffering from lung cancer?
- Why is there more crime in areas affected by poverty?
- Do children who start school early perform better academically?

Interestingly, many scientists see *prediction* as being the ultimate goal of science. Though it may be useful to recognize patterns and even explain them, being able to use that understanding to predict what will happen in the future is extremely valuable because it can enable us to alter our current actions in anticipation of causing a preferred future outcome. All managers in organizations have a real interest in prediction and, through it, management control.

Unfortunately, because learning is so easy and largely unconscious, there are numerous related problems with human cognition. This affects managers' capacity to handle complex problems such as strategy execution. Relevant problems include the following:

- the basic cognitive limitations of individuals for processing large amounts of complex information[14]
- relying too heavily on limited data in reaching conclusions[15]
- placing undue emphasis on easily or already available information[16]
- placing undue emphasis on vivid and memorable information[17]
- placing undue emphasis on consistent information[18]
- placing undue emphasis on information recently obtained[19]
- ignoring important statistical constraints or implications[20]
- tending not to seek disconfirming data[21]
- discarding or neglecting disconfirming evidence[22]
- distorting reality[23]
- assuming causality (or its direction) from association of variables[24]
- placing undue emphasis on data obtained from senior people ('elite bias')[25]
- maintaining hindsight biases in assessment of past events[26]
- reacting differently to events based on the language used to describe them[27.]

Evidently, there are many fundamental human information-processing limitations that affect most judgments, and all of these can affect strategy execution decisions. Several are particularly relevant to the use of the cause-and-effect thinking described in this chapter and the next, so they are discussed in more detail next.

Construction

As noted in the discussion about environmental analysis, we can process only the data we have and often fail to recognize when we are short of information. This can in itself lead us to make incorrect inferences. As the psychiatrist R. D. Laing put it:

If I don't know what I don't know,
I think I know.
If I don't know what I know,
I think I don't know.

Most magic tricks rely upon lack of full information. An audience may gasp at levitation but only because they don't know that a mirror is being used to create an illusion. With full information there would be no magic. Managers make similar mistakes all the time. Many profitable companies, for instance, service large numbers of unprofitable customers. However, relatively few firms acknowledge this possibility and undertake the analysis required to identify these customers. Because of this lack of information, managers are unable to find ways of making these customers more profitable or deciding to stop servicing them. The development of customer relationship management is partly a response to this problem, as it aims to track and analyse the behaviour of individual customers to support better management decision making. Most people working in organizations come across even simpler situations in which somebody is putting significant effort into doing things in a certain way in blissful ignorance that it is not necessary or could be done more effectively.

Humans are good at 'filling in' information where it doesn't exist to 'complete' apparent patterns. Numerous psychological experiments demonstrate that we unconsciously apply both logic and previously developed thinking frameworks to explain gaps in data, often thereby 'inventing' information that may or may not reflect reality.[28] It has been known for 'witnesses' of car accidents to explain in detailed visual terms events which they did not actually see. Typically, they heard a car skid and an impact but turned only in time to see the aftermath. However, the scene together with the audio stimuli is enough to cause the brain to recreate the event as if it had actually been seen in full, and this is the way it is remembered. These witnesses are not liars but simply unaware that their brains have filled in missing information for them.

In management, construction occurs all the time. Managers often leave meetings assuming that their colleagues agreed with a course of action, recalling it that way later when they become confused about the lack of commitment from the team. The angry scenes that often follow may not be justified by the actual

Box 6.2 Processing failure at an airline

The freight division of an airline hired a consultant to advise on how efficiency might be improved in its administrative operations. Among the operations he reviewed was a large office with staff responsible for the processing and systematic filing of paper copies of completed orders. Curious about why such effort was being expended on a process that might normally be computerized, he asked what happened to the files. It transpired that they were collected weekly and taken to be stored at one of the airline's warehouses.

The consultant tracked the deliveries to the warehouse and asked the manager there what happened to all the files. The manager explained that every month a contractor's lorry arrives and uplifts all the files. "What do they do with them?" the consultant asked. The manager nonchalantly explained, "They incinerate them!"

events, but it is *recalled* events that drive the emotions of those who feel let down by their colleagues.

Assuming causality

It is extremely common to assume that, because a second event closely follows a first, that the first event caused the second one. If an electrician does some rewiring work in your house and the next day a circuit fuse blows, it is tempting to assume that there must be some problem with the work and call the electrician back to check that everything's been done properly. However, a fuse blowing is a fairly common occurrence, and the laws of probability, therefore, suggest that it is equally likely to happen on any given day.

It is common to assume that because patterns of occurrences seem to vary with one another, one is causing the other. This is a significant problem even in advanced scientific research. A great deal of research is based on hypotheses about causal relationships between two or more variables (e.g. whether smokers die earlier than non-smokers). Researchers seeking to examine this kind of hypothesis typically collect quantitative data relating the relevant variables and test the data for correlations (a correlation is a measure of the extent to which sets of data relating to variables tested vary predictably with one another). They also go to great lengths to ensure representative samples by selecting large numbers of subjects at random to survey. If it is found that the two variables appear to vary with one another, it is frequently assumed that one factor causes the other (e.g. smoking causes increased likelihood of early death). In management research, this kind of scientific approach has long been employed and, among practitioners, it is increasingly popular as the basis for management decisions.

However, there are huge potential problems with this kind of study. Unfortunately, correlation analysis can only establish *association* between variables, not *causation*. The fact that two variables are associated does not mean that there is any causal relationship between them. The reason is that any number of *co-variables* may exist. A co-variable is another factor that has a causal relationship with the variables under investigation. In other words, two variables being tested in a research study may vary with one another but only because of a third factor that influences both of them.

For instance, it might be true that people who don't own cars eat in restaurants less frequently than car owners. It's tempting to assume that this might be because they cannot travel to restaurants easily, and this might partially explain the association. However, there can be little doubt that those with low incomes are less likely to own a car *or* eat in restaurants frequently, because both are costly to do. In this case, car ownership and frequency of restaurant dining are both affected by the co-variable, level of income.

The problem with most quantitative research is that though measures can be taken to try to eliminate some co-variables (by controlled experimentation and careful sampling), it is never possible to eliminate all co-variables because we can never know what they might be. There is an infinite number of potential co-variables in any study, and it is usually only practical to isolate and eliminate a few. This means that there is also an infinite number of potential hypotheses that could be developed to explain any patterns of association that emerge from the data.

What this means is that it is usually insufficient to rely upon quantitative data and the kind of analysis techniques described earlier. To examine causality normally requires qualitative data analysis that examines actual events, sequences, and the detailed nature of the relationships between wide-ranging factors. This is even more important when investigating social and organizational phenomena, which include most management and strategy issues. This issue is a significant problem in organizations. All management decisions are based on assumptions about cause and effect, and it seems that even systematic testing of these assumptions can provide unreliable conclusions.

Loops of cause and effect

Where causality does exist, it is worth remembering that it may be in one direction (e.g. working long hours causes managers to have successful careers), the other (e.g. career success causes managers to work long hours), or both (e.g. working long hours causes managers to have successful careers and vice-versa). This last possibility is an example of bi-directional causality, which is far more common than one might expect and is often undetected. It can be very important as it is the basis of 'virtuous' and 'vicious' circles, which can cause unparalleled success or speedy failure in organizations, as we saw in Chapter 4. It is all too easy to ignore the possibility of loops of cause and effect.

Ignoring time lag

It is useful to remember that there may be a significant time lag between cause and effect. In organizations, this can cause severe problems. Most leaders (especially those in quoted companies) are under significant pressure to deliver results over short timescales. Some choose to use management techniques to improve performance but decide after a short time that the techniques they have implemented are not working and move on to another method. Though many management techniques are flawed, it is sometimes the case that they would have worked well if there was sufficient patience to embed them properly and give the positive results enough time to appear.

Bounded rationality

Organizational strategies and plans for executing them are based on *hypotheses* about cause and effect and in many respects are no different from other attempts to predict and thereby manipulate future outcomes. However, as we have seen, so severe are the problems with human information processing that a difficulty is created when we come to use cause-and-effect thinking in organizational planning. Because we don't think consciously about such relationships in everyday working life, we often find it difficult to map out cause-and-effect relationships in a rigorous fashion. Bounded rationality is a principle that acknowledges that humans can never properly take into account all the relevant factors that could go into making any given decision.[29] No matter how apparently simple a decision, if we were to start considering all the factors that should perhaps influence our thinking, we would quickly be overcome with information, ideas, and options. We are forced to ignore lots of issues that might be relevant because, if we don't, we would be unable to operate effectively in the world around us. Most of the time, we don't worry about ignoring much of the detail because our decisions have limited potential consequences, but when we are faced with important decisions, bounded rationality becomes a problem.

Leaders' ability to acknowledge bounded rationality and 'cut through' information to reach a decision is important. Those who find it difficult may suffer from analysis paralysis and fail to make a decision and fail to exploit short-lived opportunities. Most of us know people who are highly intelligent and, well-educated and also poor at making hard decisions and getting things done because they tend to 'get lost' in the detail. Leaders who fall into this trap are usually destined to fail because, ultimately, clear decisions must be made for organizations to follow.

Most strategic decisions, by definition, deal with high-level decisions that theoretically take into account a huge number of variables from both outside and inside organizations. No matter how sophisticated the planning, it cannot take proper account of all of these. A framework is required to help leaders identify and think through the *most important* issues. The very process of having to make choices about what seems most important, based on the best evidence you can reasonably gather and take into account, is what enables choices to be made. This is applying intended rationality to make progress in the world around us. Applying *causality* factors problems into smaller parts, and the principle of *criticality* necessarily narrows the scope of decisions for managers, thus making successful strategy execution achievable.

Overcoming these thinking challenges

Strategy execution maps are well suited to strike the right balance between rigour and practicality in decision making. Applying them involves the following:

- clear identification of a specific unit of analysis for which a strategy execution map can feasibly be produced;
- identification and articulation of the overall objective, focusing attention on limited, specific desired outcomes (by implication ruling out alternative objectives);

- analysis of the external and internal environment using the framework of the overall objective to identify the specific factors that help or hinder its achievement;
- the development of explicitly articulated causal logic that depicts strategic thinking and enables debate and research to validate or falsify hypotheses;
- the progressive development of options and then choices to uncover assumptions, broaden thinking, and then make explicit trade-off decisions;
- the application of criticality to simplify strategy and the framework used for its implementation, focusing attention where it matters most.

Specific pitfalls in translating strategy into activities

Other writers have noted that for managers, thinking about strategy implementation is particularly difficult.[30] Some of my own case study research provides empirical support for this view. It focused on how organizations identify what activities to undertake to achieve strategic objectives and uncovered a series of pitfalls into which managers fall when attempting this. In order of frequency observed, the problems observed were as follows:

- lack of strategic logic and clarity
- inadequate breakdown of strategy
- leaps of causal logic (between means and ends)
- the use of vague and/or ambiguous terminology
- strategy that deals only with changes
- strategy oriented to influence multiple stakeholders.

Each of these is explained further.

Lack of clear strategic logic

Many problems in translating strategy into activities are caused by strategies that do not incorporate clear strategic logic. In some of the organizations in which I conducted research, there was no documented strategy, meaning that individuals, teams, departments, and functions saw what was often described as a 'strategic vacuum', making development of their own strategies, operating models, and programmes of action difficult. In other cases, strategies were not described with sufficient detail or logical clarity to make their intent understandable by those charged with execution. Lack of strategic logic and clarity makes the already difficult challenge of identifying and planning activities even more so. In particular, my research also suggested that managers were confused about how to manage trade-off decisions (e.g. between revenue, costs, and risk) when strategy was unclear. Strategy execution maps, as described here, can help by ensuring that strategy hypotheses are both plausible and clear. They necessarily demand that arguments or assumptions about cause and effect are explicitly defined. Graphic representation of causal relationships also helps people interpret them. It also has the distinct benefit of being able to show the interrelationships between multiple effects and causes – hence, strategy execution maps often include variables with more than one arrow 'going in' or 'coming out' of them. These interrelationships are difficult to convey via strategies explained in words.

With this all said, strategy execution maps are not a panacea. They must be constructed with care, debated properly, and evolved effectively to move from a wide range of options to ultimately represent critical choices. They also have a limitation that needs to be recognized – sometimes simplification of the variables contained within them is necessary. For example, Figure 6.7 portrays the overall objective of the retailer as being 'increased profit'. This is a simplification of a more fully developed overall objective statement that included more context and caveats – specially relating to long-term, sustainable profit through operating within a particular retail sector. Of course, it is perfectly possible, as the retailer did, to include some of this more specific detail elsewhere. (In many cases, 'hyperlinks' are used in electronic versions of strategy execution maps to link to more detailed explanations of variables and associated measures, etc.). The key point is that managers should recognize the need for sufficient detail around the causal logic incorporated in their strategies.

Inadequate breakdown of strategy

In every case studied in my research, strategy was not broken down adequately to enable the identification and subsequent planning of activities that might plausibly achieve strategic objectives. In many instances, the least abstract elements (of plans that had been broken down to inform implementation) were highly abstract and could not have been executed without considerable additional planning. This is a problem that other writers have recognized.[31] When strategies are articulated only at high levels of abstraction, numerous questions remain unanswered about *how* they should be implemented. In many cases, strategies are broken down into broad 'programmes' but no further. It is difficult to generalize about precisely why strategies are rarely broken down to the activity level, but it seems that, in many cases, managers do not attempt to do this because they:

- do not assume that strategic planning should be connected to operational activity (perhaps based on the assumption that strategic planning is a low-value formality, is of value in terms of a process more than its outputs, or is intended only to generate highly generic outputs for communication to colleagues – rather than actual implementation);
- assume that those responsible for implementing elements of the strategy will break strategies down into activities (and, presumably, that this will be adequately performed in this less integrated fashion);

- consider the level of detail to which strategies were broken down to be adequate to drive activity; and
- prefer not to formally articulate how a strategy would be implemented, to 'leave their options open' or camouflage their own uncertainties about how to implement the strategies.

This last explanation is sadly often the case. Some managers see precise definition of future activities, outputs, performance measures, and targets as unwise because this information might be used by superiors or peers in the future to challenge or damage credibility or for other political purposes. My research found this was particularly prevalent in organizations with high levels of managerial political activity.

Obviously, the core purpose behind using strategy execution mapping is to overcome this translation challenge and link overall objectives all the way to concrete activities. However, it is all too easy to start developing a strategy execution map and, when the going inevitably gets tough, stop – pretending that there is enough detail there. If the lowest-level variables in a map are not ones that competent individuals and teams could execute without significant additional guidance and input, they are not critical activities and need to be broken down further.

Leaps of causal logic

Often, when developing strategies and breaking them down, managers make (unarticulated) assumptions that amount to leaps of causal logic. These leaps of logic mean that highly indirect causal relationships are implied within strategies. Managers are prone to identify highly specific means to achieve conceptual objectives without articulating intermediate means and ends. Highly indirect relationships are much harder to articulate, explore, evaluate, and measure. This has two serious consequences. First, visibility of different means of objective achievement is severely reduced because alternatives for each intermediate means have not be identified. Second, if the selected means are chosen for execution, they will be further planned and performed without reference to a rich context explaining more precisely what they were intended to achieve, why they were chosen as a means, and how they relate to other means.

Figure 6.8 Leap of causal logic

A simple example makes these problems clearer. A team of managers with whom I was working were exploring how profitability could be increased. Someone quickly suggested the business should seek to increase its advertising activity to boost profits (as depicted in Figure 6.8). This was not an outrageous suggestion – it was plausible that (all other things being equal) increased advertising would have caused increased profitability as long as it was effective advertising.

However, as those who have examined Figure 6.7 closely will foresee, this causal argument is too simplistic and indirect to be useful. A more comprehensive and explicit articulation of the manager's hypothesis is that (all other things being equal) increased promotional activity would cause increased promotional impact, which would cause increased customer acquisition, which would cause increased number of customers, which would cause increased volume of sales and thus increased revenue and profit.[32] This revised causal chain is depicted in Figure 6.9, which shows there are six causal links between seven variables rather than simply one causal link between two variables.

So, though the manager's suggestion was not necessarily wrong, the way in which the question of how to increase profitability was approached led to a suboptimal exploration of potential answers. In particular, because intermediate means to increasing profit were not identified, obvious alternatives means were ignored. For instance, advertising – depending on how it is conducted – might cause increased sales volumes per customer or increased customer retention. And, of course, there is no reason to limit the thinking to advertising. Perhaps an increase in price would plausibly cause increased profit. Figure 6.10 shows these

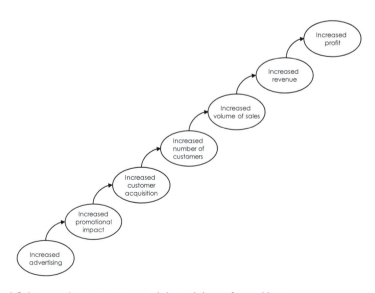

Figure 6.9 Intermediate means ignored through leap of causal logic

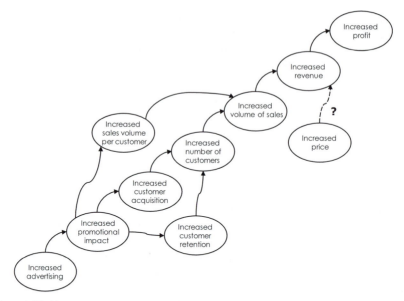

Figure 6.10 Alternative means ignored through leap of causal logic

alternative means that are ignored through the leap of causal logic. Of course, there are many others – the point is that such leaps cause thinking and debates to become 'stuck in the weeds' very quickly. A more systematic step-by-step approach avoids these problems and helps create a strategy execution map that provides a more comprehensive framework for future planning.

Another important point arises from our discussion about leaps of causal logic. Because attraction of customers and increased customer base were not specified as means, it was not entirely clear what the *immediate* objective of the increased advertising would be, even though this would likely affect its detailed planning and implementation. Advertising might, for example, be oriented to attract non-users of a product, retain existing customers, or increase current users' usage. The effectiveness of promotional activity would likely be increased were such specific objectives made clear by a strategy breakdown. This problem has enormous implications. Failure to articulate reasonably detailed chains of causality and explore an appropriate range of alternative means of objective achievement causes the following:

- suboptimal strategic choices
- misallocation of resources
- ineffective strategy execution.

Managers need to keep an eye out for leaps of causal logic. They are rarely laid out as explicitly as they are when developing strategy execution maps. Such leaps not only occur in manager's thinking and discussions but are contained within various management tools and ideas. For example, the service-profit chain is a well-known tool focused on the links between employee satisfaction, customer satisfaction, and profitability.[33] Although it builds on the notion of causality, it incorporates a number of leaps of causal logic, of the sort outlined earlier – for example, linking customer loyalty directly to revenue and profitability. This relationship may hold true in some circumstances, but it is difficult to tell without identifying intermediate causal relationships particular to each context.

The use of vague and/or ambiguous terminology

As fans of Scott Adams and his cartoon creation Dilbert know, ambiguous language regularly creates lack of clarity about the intended meaning of overall objectives and strategies. What is less well recognized are the difficulties this in turn creates for the identification of activities that might plausibly cause overall objectives to be achieved. In some cases, strategic objectives seem to 'overlap', often because they were defined at different levels of abstraction and were causally related (a problem that typically goes unrecognized). In others, managers have even had to try to 'break down' strategies represented pictorially. Although pictures might create useful metaphors to explore strategy, they are probably impossible to break down. In many cases, words with ambiguous meanings are used to describe strategy. For example, managers frequently use the single word 'sales'. However, it is often unclear whether it is intended to mean revenue or sales volume. Even the scholarly management literature is replete with ambiguous terminology of this sort.[34]

Strategy execution maps are not immune from ambiguous language, and those developing must guard against the tendency to use meaningless or confusing terms. It can be tempting to use ambiguous terms when precision requires time and dedicated thinking. However, such ambiguity can create problems with both the development and interpretation of strategy execution maps – and have a significant knock-on effect on strategy implementation.

Strategy that deals only with changes

My own research has revealed an intriguing problem with strategies that has significant implications for their translation into activities. A high proportion of espoused strategies deal only with *changes* to strategic direction, rather than also articulating organizations' existing strategies or business models. Many written or presented strategies apparently ignore all other aspects of the organization, including many that are central to existing performance. As Chapter 2 outlines, strategy relates to products, markets, channels, resources, and so on, not simply *new* products, markets, channels, and so on. This problem prevents managers from making well-informed decisions about integrating new initiatives with existing activities and ensuring compatibility between them. It also makes trade-off decisions difficult, when managers have to decide where to focus limited resources and attention.[35]

The real problems arise when managers seek to translate these incomplete strategy articulations into activities, because the interdependencies between what is required to bring about the changes specified and what is required to maintain existing operations become more relevant as the level of planning detail develops. Leaders typically demonstrate limited awareness of this problem, but they need to recognize that effective execution relies on explicit integration of the new with the old.

Strategy oriented to influence multiple stakeholders

Earlier, the problems with worrying about stakeholders when defining an organization's overall objective were discussed. A similar problem can occur when strategies are articulated, which causes problems for translating them into activities. My research has found widespread evidence of strategy plans and presentations being developed to influence stakeholders, at the expense of seeking absolute clarity for those involved in developing and implementing the strategy. Many strategic plans read like 'sales documents', using grand but imprecise language about ambitions, highlighting past successes, seeking support, and avoiding 'negative' issues such as important strategic risks. This problem contributes to creating a lack of strategic clarity and logic along with the use of vague and ambiguous language, both described already. Once again, strategy execution maps are not immune to this problem, and managers must be alert to it, whatever method they select to translate strategy into action.

Polished maps and competitive advantage

With the various pitfalls to developing strategy execution maps explored in some depth, we can turn attention to how more-polished strategy execution maps look and can be used. Well-developed strategy execution maps are selective, no longer showing every plausible option for achieving overall objectives. Rather, they depict only critical choices made by organizations. I deliberately avoid the use of the word *final* when describing well-developed strategy execution maps because, of course, they can always be refined and refreshed. They should be 'living documents' that evolve along with the organization and its environment.

Strategy execution maps also provide a useful lens through which to examine firms' competitive advantage and the role of strategy execution in securing and sustaining it. This is also examined through two polished strategy execution maps that use some well-known companies as examples – IKEA and Apple.

IKEA strategy execution map

IKEA is a well-known high-performing organization and, as such, makes a good example for a polished strategy execution map. The company, founded in 1943 in Sweden by Ingvar Kamprad, has grown to be a 123,000-employee business generating sales of €21.5 billion from operations in around 40 countries. It sells a wide range of home and office furnishings items from around 300 large stores.

Its strategy is well documented, having been examined by many writers. Notably, Michael Porter mapped IKEA's 'activity-system' by identifying strategic themes and linked activities.[36] Porter's depiction of IKEA's strategy was very useful, but using a strategy execution map to examine IKEA's business model offers another dimension useful from an implementation perspective. It allows articulation of the organization's overall objective (assumed to be high profit) and depiction of the means by which this is achieved at multiple levels of abstraction, via interlinked causal relationships.

Figure 6.11 depicts the polished strategy execution map for IKEA. As with the previous strategy execution maps, the direction of causality is upwards, with concrete activities at the bottom of the map and the more conceptual objectives towards the top. It is useful to think of the map as containing performance variables, which are causally related and therefore exist at varying levels of abstraction.

The way in which IKEA has translated its overall objective into critical activities is pretty obvious from Figure 6.11 – that clarity (one of the five Cs) is one of the advantages of strategy execution maps. However, a few observations are worthwhile.

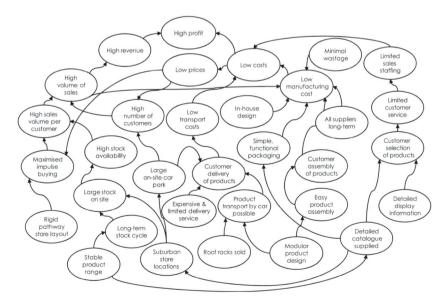

Figure 6.11 A strategy execution map for IKEA

IKEA's strategic position requires it to sell high volumes of products at low cost. It therefore relies on attracting high numbers of customers through its doors every day and for them to spend significantly when in store. It relies heavily on advertising and word of mouth to bring customers to its suburban stores. However, even more important is the IKEA catalogue, which is delivered to homes within a wide reach of its stores. Every year, IKEA prints around 200 million copies of its catalogue – which is also now available on its website.

Most IKEA stores are in suburban locations in very large units, which can carry a great deal of stock. On site, large car parks and spacious layouts ensure that huge numbers of customers can browse in the store. Each store is laid out according to a rigid plan that incorporates a one-way pathway from which it is difficult to divert. The pathway passes every product on offer, laid out in attractive settings reflecting their intended use. IKEA relies on this layout (and the enormous bags they provide customers for small items) to induce impulse purchasing, which it usually does. In addition to the catalogue, detailed product display information is available, encouraging customers to make their own product selections both mentally and then physically in the warehouse area that they ultimately reach.

Very few employees are present, considering the numbers of customers. Although limited and expensive delivery options exist, customers are generally expected to transport their own products home by car. The modular design of large items such as furniture makes this easier, as does the availability of roof racks in stores. It also makes assembly relatively easy – at least compared with similar self-assembly products. Most IKEA assembly instructions are multi-lingual, as they include only pictures.

The effort to maintain low costs (and thus prices) continues behind the scenes. In-house design and long-term manufacturing and supplier arrangements keep costs to a minimum, as does the functional packaging (promotional packaging is not necessary, given the catalogue, displays, and display information). Wastage and costs are minimized further by challenging designers to design products from off-cuts produced from the manufacturing of other items in IKEA's range.

The result of this strategy's execution has been IKEA's steady and solid growth over many decades. Financial information for the firm is not widely available, as it remains privately owned. IKEA's Netherlands-based parent company, Ingka Holding B.V., filed accounts in 2004, reportedly revealing post-tax profits of €1.4 billion on sales of €12.8 billion (a healthy margin of 11 per cent); its value has thus been estimated at €28 billion.[37] As another broad indicator of the success of the business, Ingvar Kamprad and his family are estimated to hold a $22 billion fortune, making him the fifth richest person in the world.[38]

Polished strategy execution maps play an important role in picking up the last two of the five Cs – continuity and clarity. In the case of IKEA, such a clear strategy and execution model makes managing continuity relatively easy. Critical activities have been identified clearly, which obviously helps when trying to determine how different individuals and subunits within the organization should be involved in their execution. This topic is explored in greater depth in Chapter 8.

The IKEA strategy execution map immediately demonstrates a useful method of increasing clarity about strategy and how it can be executed. Imagine that you joined IKEA as an employee and sat down with your new line manager over lunch in IKEA's restaurant to learn about your role and how it fits in to the business. It would take little time to get to grips with the fundamentals of the business if your line manager had the map in Figure 6.11 to hand. This kind of tool can be used to increase line of sight, which as already discussed is vital to motivate employees and align their behaviour with strategy.

Apple strategy execution map[39]

Another example of a polished strategy execution map is useful to illustrate the shape of what organizations might aim for as they move from exploring wide options to isolating critical choices. Apple Inc. provides a good example of how a well-executed strategy can deliver superior business performance. In recent years (many would say since Steve Jobs returned as CEO), Apple has overcome serious troubles to once again compete as a serious force in several related (and converging) industries. In the eighties, it transformed the computer industry with its easy-to-use desktop computers. More recently, it has played a leading role in transforming the music and mobile phone industries through its iPod and iPhone, respectively.

Those who dismiss Apple as a small player in the PC industry miss an important point. Although fewer than 10 per cent of personal computers sold in the United States are Apple Macs, 91 per cent of the revenue generated from sales of computers costing more than $1,000 is from Mac sales.[40] Similarly, although it entered the mobile phone industry only in June 2007 by launching its iPhone, Apple became the world's most profitable manufacturer just more than two years later despite only having a market share of around two per cent.[41] Apple enjoys a premium position in all these markets, offering relatively expensive products that a substantial minority of buyers are willing to purchase. More than one Apple executive is quoted as saying that the company's goal is not to build the most computers but to build the best. This neatly sums up the company's intended strategic positioning, but the strategy execution map in Figure 6.12 helps to explore how this strategy is executed.

Once again, the strategy execution map makes the business model and its means of implementation pretty clear, but a few observations and deeper explanations are useful. Because Apple seeks a high-value and premium-price strategic position, its focus is squarely on creating high perceived product value. This ensures that the relatively small proportion of buyers who purchase Apple products buy more products and are prepared to pay a premium for them. Apple does not ignore costs, which are constrained by high levels of outsourcing and assembly in relatively low-cost countries such as China. Nor does Apple ignore the need to acquire new customers but approaches them with long-term loyalty in mind. Its heavy focus on the educational sector ensures that thousands of young people experience Apple

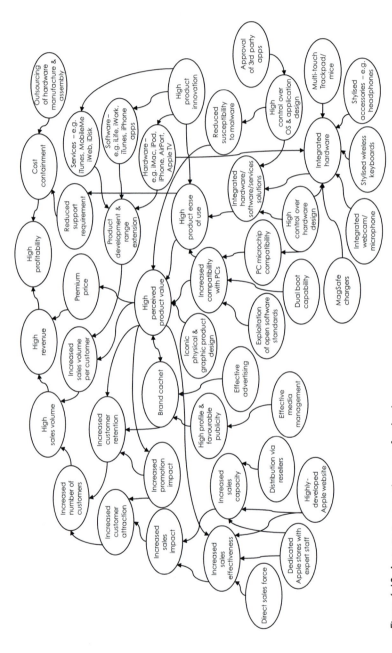

Figure 6.12 A strategy execution map for Apple

technology long before they become prospective customers themselves. And when they do, Apple offers discounts to customers still in education.

Apple's use of channels closely reflects its premium positioning. It has rolled out its own iconic stores in premium locations (and buildings) around the world, staffed by knowledgeable experts. In these stores, customers can 'touch and play' with all Apple's products. This is a deliberate tactic – everyone knows what it's like to use a PC, but not everyone has actually used a Mac or an iPhone. So easy to use are Apple's products that many users develop a strong loyalty to the brand once they start using them.

Apple plays on the strength of its brand and fanatical consumer loyalty with polished media management. Secrecy is well maintained before product launches, which are dramatic enough to create a stir. Apple receives a great deal of media attention – much of which is positive and centres on its product features or customers' obsession with the brand.

A huge amount of effort is put into aesthetic design in Apple products. Careful attention is paid to colour, shape, material, and size. The result is that many consumers consider Apple's products to be not only the easiest to use but the most beautiful, too. The incredibly thin and light MacBook Air is a great example.

Historically, hardware and software incompatibilities between Apple Macs and PCs running Microsoft operating systems (i.e. the vast majority of personal computers) deterred some potential customers from purchasing Macs – especially business users. However, Apple switched to using Intel chips in 2006, meaning that Macs can now run Microsoft operating systems natively (i.e. without additional emulation software). Apple also exploited new standards enabling its business productivity suite to exchange files with Microsoft's equivalent package much more easily.

Apple does not licence its hardware designs to other manufacturers or allow them to install the Apple operating system on their machines. It designs all the core software used on Macs and retains high levels of control over the design and distribution of third-party software, particularly iPhone applications (downloadable through its 'App Store', only once approved). This helps Apple to ensure that its hardware and software work well together (and reduces susceptibility of the platform to malware, a major headache for PC users). For example, various software applications make use of the Web camera and microphone built into the screens of all new Macs. Apple also offers expensive but high-quality wireless keyboards and the world's first 'multi-touch' mouse that can be used like a trackpad and mirrors the touch-screen of an iPhone. These nifty gadgets work automatically with Macs without the need to install new software drivers and so on. Apple aims for things to work 'out of the box' and knows that this, along with attractive aesthetic design and clever branding, make people love its products. That is why the design and introduction of these peripheral products are critical activities.

Apple has gone a step further than simply ensuring compatibility between its products. It now builds upon this interoperability to create new value-adding features. For example, an iPhone can control a multi-media presentation (via a downloadable 'App') and music streamed to a room via a wireless network from a Mac situated elsewhere.

In addition to this hardware and software integration is Apple's development of value-add services, such as the iTunes store (offering music, TV, video, audio books, and software) and MobileMe service (providing e-mail/contact/calendar synchronization and data backup). Access to these services is made easy through the software distributed on every Mac. The potential for cross-selling is obvious.

Apple's focus on proprietary software and tight hardware, software, and services integration does also have the effect of 'entangling' consumers. Apple gets some negative press about this, and it must be the case that some consumers choose to stay with Apple because migrating away from the integrated bundle of products the company offers is difficult. However, most Apple customers seem happy to accept this constraint to use technology that works well together.

Apple's product developments reflect an extraordinary product innovation capability. The company spent $1.3 billion on research and development in 2009.[42] Apple remains one of the most attractive places for talented people in the industry to work, and benefits from a seemingly exceptional focus on customer-centric product design.

Does Apple's financial performance reflect what might be expected from this apparently well-devised and executed strategy? Of course, lots of factors affect financial results but, on the face of it, Apple has delivered impressive results. Its gross margins are extremely healthy at around 35 per cent. It has no debt and has huge reserves. Over the 5- and 10-year periods to date, its share price has grown by far more than all its major competitors – enough to have pushed its market capitalization beyond Google's and into the top five companies in the United States. No business is immune from unforeseen problems but, for the time being, it seems the strategy is largely working.

Apple's strategy execution convincingly demonstrates causality, criticality, and compatibility in action. The causality between the company's activities and strategic objectives is clear and plausible. There is an explicit focus on trade-offs and critical activities. The integrated nature of the business model reflects the inherent compatibility between these critical activities. The strategy execution map also helps inform how continuity and clarity can be managed. With critical activities and the relationships between them clearly defined, it is feasible to make coherent decisions about organizational designs and systems around these. The clarity of the strategy execution model is also obvious – anyone from a new board director to a new start in an Apple store could readily comprehend the essential elements with a model such as that shown in Figure 6.12.

Strategy execution and competitive advantage

The lack of serious attention that strategy execution has thus far received belies an important point. Effective strategy execution is a critical source of sustainable competitive advantage. Firms do not operate in a vacuum. They need to compete effectively with industry rivals to survive and prosper. Competitive advantage is thus a key concern for commercial organizations and is created through the interlinked processes of strategy development and implementation. Organizations that are able to implement strategy more effectively than their competitors to undertake unique activities can create sustainable competitive advantage. Strategy execution ability is, therefore, a key route to obtaining superior returns.

Though the notion of competitive advantage has greatest resonance for profit-making businesses, its principles can also be applied to understand the pressures and choices facing public sector and not-for-profit organizations – most of which compete with other organizations for the right to use limited resources to provide their products and services.

Competitive advantage is the ability to outperform organizations operating in the same industry.[43] Michael Porter is the best-known thinker on the topic of competitive advantage.[44] He outlines three essential sources of competitive advantage:

- industry structure
- strategic positioning
- the 'fit' of value-creating activities.

These three areas are explored briefly here because though they relate primarily to strategic planning, they help to illuminate why strategy execution is a logical and important addition to this list of sources of competitive advantage. Important aspects of strategy execution thinking can usefully be meshed with Porter's models, producing a more comprehensive and integrated view of all these issues.

Porter points out that out that profitability in different industries varies hugely over extended periods, owing to their structure. He proposes his '5-forces' model to analyse industry structure, essentially examining supply and demand and the 'share of wallet' that firms can command in the chain of supply to end-consumers. This encourages strategists to think widely about future sources of competition (e.g. from substitutes and new entrants) and become sensitive to the dynamics shaping their industries. Occasionally, such analysis leads to decisions to diversify into other industries, but this is generally highly risky. Most firms must use their understanding of the dynamics of their industries to try to secure sustainable competitive advantage relative to rivals.

Hence, Porter further argues that firms should adopt deliberate strategic positions that distinguish them from competitors. He essentially suggests that strategic positions emerge from choices about products, markets, and channels (closely reflecting the descriptions of strategy explored in Chapter 2). In particular, Porter focuses heavily on how firms' offerings differ in relation to perceived pricing, differentiation (i.e. the value to buyers), and breadth of market appeal.

His three generic strategies, based on combinations of these positions, are now well-established frameworks within the strategy field:

- cost leadership – based on offering lower-value cheaper products with mass-market appeal, through a low-cost base and economies of scale;
- differentiation strategies – based on offering high-value offerings but at a correspondingly high price, thus securing high margins;
- focus strategies – based on either cost leadership or differentiation but aimed at a narrow market segment.

Porter argues that firms can outperform others in the same industry through superior positioning; however, his theory illuminates three key mistakes, each of which is relevant to strategy execution:

- competing head-on with rivals – which favours consumers and diminishes returns for industry players;
- adopting a strategic position 'in the middle' – with 'medium' perceived pricing and value, thus at risk of developing neither sufficient economies of scale or high margins to compete effectively;
- seeking to implement a mix of generic strategies simultaneously by adopting a broad range of positions across a product range – thus risking out-performance by rivals with more narrowly focused offerings or market appeal.

This last mistake relates to 'trade-off' decisions, which Porter argues are central to strategy. Making trade-offs means making clear decisions about what activities to undertake – and conversely, those not to undertake. Porter mentions strategy execution in this context, saying, "Effectively implementing any of these generic strategies usually requires total commitment and supporting organizational arrangements that are diluted if there is more than one primary target".[45] He also uses maps of 'activity systems' to explore fit between activities produced by trade-off decisions, which is cited as a third source of competitive advantage.

We can usefully build on Porter's models to locate the role of strategy execution in securing and sustaining competitive advantage and highlight a further role of strategy execution maps. There are two areas to consider (only the first of which Porter mentions); both of these are discussed further:

- choosing an executable strategy
- developing superior strategy execution capability.

As discussed earlier, Porter generally advises against competing head-on with rivals, and this advice seems sound advice for choosing an executable strategy, from a strategy execution perspective. So difficult is strategy execution that organizations with experience of implementing a particular strategy are likely to be at an inherent advantage and, as Porter says, direct competition will likely reduce returns for all industry players.

Porter's concern about organizations getting 'stuck in the middle', in terms of strategic positioning, deserves more challenge. Although he acknowledges that there are situations (such as oligopolistic markets) in which firms can 'get away with it', Porter claims that companies stuck in the middle generally cannot compete with cost leaders and those with high-value offerings. He notes these firms cannot exploit economies of scale and/or reap the benefits of customer loyalty and high margins that differentiators enjoy.

Porter has been criticized by various theorists who disagree that firms are generally not successful if positioned 'in the middle'.[46] These criticisms have some weight. It is worth remembering that economies of scale, for instance, are not a binary characteristic. Firms don't have economies or lack economies. Rather, they secure economies of scale to varying extents. The same is true of high margins generated by premium pricing. Given this rather obvious clarification, there seems no reason why a 'middle positioning' would not be as feasible as any other. Table 6.3 summarizes this configuration.

Table 6.3 Key characteristics of generic strategies and the possible 'in the middle' strategy

Variables	Cost leadership	Differentiation	'In the middle'
Economies of scale Priority to cost minimization and low price	High	Low	Medium
Price premium Priority to value maximization	Low	High	Medium

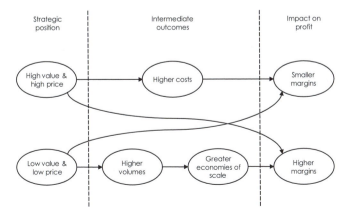

Figure 6.13 Variables affected by generic strategic positions

Figure 6.13 suggests that adopting either of the two main generic strategies has both cost and revenue impacts, by representing how these cause-and-effect relationships tend to operate. What firms must determine is how, by manipulating these dynamics, they can secure margin increases that are greater than the margin reductions concurrently created.

It is certainly more likely that being 'in the middle' is a legitimate option in:

- developing markets in which the objective is fast growth rather than competition for scarce customers;
- fast-changing markets in which a more extreme position may quickly become unprofitable as the industry restructures or customer behaviour alters without sufficient warning; and
- industries in which a structural analysis reveals the pressures upon existing firms to be low and in limited danger of increasing in the foreseeable future.

Ultimately, decision makers must decide for themselves – giving consideration to the structure of their industries and situations of the firms – whether to follow Porter's guidance or take a stance 'in the middle', if it is appropriate. However, though being positioned in the middle may be a sensible option in some cases, there are other reasons why the third caution – having a *mixture* of strategic positions – might create serious problems for organizations. (Interestingly, Porter does not appear to make this distinction and groups middle-positioned and mixed-position firms together.) These potential problems relate not only to strategic positioning but to the implications it has for the 'fit' of value-creating activities and how firms implement strategy.

Porter's activity maps go some way to explaining fit and supporting this argument for clear trade-offs, but strategy execution maps make this logic easier to follow and analyse more forensically. At a basic level, we can use the notion of line of sight and consider how employees would make everyday trade-off decisions, using strategy execution maps. If you were a shop assistant in IKEA looking for something useful to do, should you (a) look for customers to assist or (b) check that products have their display information showing properly? The answer is certainly (b) – this helps to execute IKEA's strategy and will reinforce performance, according to the strategy execution map.

Strategy execution maps also explicitly show the outcomes arising from undertaking specific activities and allow us to see how altering these activities would affect the business model. For example, several years ago, IKEA announced that it would launch 10 stores in city centre locations in the United Kingdom.[47] This contradicts the business model captured in the strategy execution map in Figure 6.12. In fact, IKEA has made this decision reluctantly, stating that its strong preference is to build stores on the edges of cities. However, planning restrictions in the United Kingdom have constrained further growth in this way, and the business has calculated that this limited alteration to the business model is worth making.

Implementing this change brings with it risks, and Figure 6.12 makes it easy to see the implications of this reversal of relevant trade-offs. Higher building costs may ultimately push up prices (a point made by IKEA publicly), and this could of course affect impulse buying and volume of sales and so on. It will also be difficult for IKEA to carry the same stock in city centre stores (or, at least, at anything like the costs it can in existing stores). Where smaller stores are built, this may affect stock availability and, therefore, sales volume per customer. The layout of stores is also problematic, with city centre locations typically offering a smaller footprint. This necessitates many floor levels in a store, affecting layout, stock movement, and the all-important one-way pathway. Traffic access in city centres is also more problematic, potentially affecting customer numbers. Similarly, the strategy execution map suggests that smaller car parks will affect the number of customers IKEA can serve and limit scope for customers to transport some products home. In fact, in Coventry, where the first in-town store was located, IKEA initially charged for parking (perhaps in part to deter non-customers from using its parking facilities) and offered a relatively cheap home delivery service for high-spending customers. More recently, it has made its parking free to IKEA customers and offered temporary price cuts on its delivery service. In Southampton, where IKEA has built another town store, it promotes an on-site van rental partner to help customers transport bulky items home. All these tactics have cost implications for IKEA, and the hope must be that they will be outweighed by associated revenue increases.

Similarly, Apple's strategy execution map provides a useful lens through which to explore the basis of its competitive advantage, and in particular Apple's trade-off decisions and critical activity compatibility. The map shows how activities, some of which may seem almost trivial at first glance, may be critical for Apple. The development of its multi-touch wireless mouse might seem a tiny sideshow set against Apple's leading products, but it further cements the software/hardware integration and consistency across products that the company seeks to deliver. Any of the millions of iPhone fans (even those owning no other Apple products) using one of these mice will immediately be able to use its advanced features, because they reflect the functions of the iPhone's touch screen.

We can again use a topical example to test the clarity and logic of Apple's trade-off decisions. Some commentators are arguing that Apple should launch a 'netbook' (a cheap small and simple laptop with a cut-down operating system, intended mainly for Web access and e-mail). Apple's executives have not showed great enthusiasm thus far, indicating that unless they see a way to offer a far superior equivalent offering in a way that complements Apple's other products, it is unlikely to happen. Apple sees risks in cutting out features and/or product quality available in its other products to compete with other computer manufacturers on their terms. Removing features would potentially mean not exploiting Apple's existing integrated hardware designs. It would potentially limit the scope for using Apple's software and services, reducing the scope for cross-sales. All of this means that were Apple to introduce a small laptop, it would almost certainly not be as cheap or simple as existing netbooks are.

As these examples demonstrate, strategy execution maps offer the scope to explore trade-offs systematically and predict the implications of changes to business models. They enable analysis of the knock-on implications from altering particular variables, tracking their effects all the way through to overall objectives. As Chapter 7 shows, it is possible to use explicit causal models of this sort for sophisticated risk analysis, performance measurement, and even cost-benefit modelling – much enhancing decision making in relation to strategy execution.

There is a final consideration worthy of mention before concluding this section on choosing executable strategy. Over the last couple of decades, there has been a re-emergence in the strategy field of the so-called resource-based view.[48] This stream of thinking complements market-based strategic planning, which is externally focused and responds to customer requirements and competitive forces. The resource-based view encourages deeper consideration of internal strengths – and in particular strengths that are unique in an industry – to help shape strategy. Some of the related rhetoric suggests that, as markets move faster and competition intensifies, seeking optimal strategic positioning becomes a less feasible option. Instead, flexibility and responsiveness can be developed to enable organizations to be first to take advantage of opportunities thrown up in the unpredictable environment.

From a strategy execution perspective, the resource-based view seems a sensible balance to purely market-driven strategy. It seems wholly logical to be aware of what distinctive resources or capabilities a firm possesses, as these can *potentially* be used to outplay competitors through unique positioning (this is a long-established idea[49]). It also seems that being flexible enough to exploit opportunities – or at least keep up with the changing environment – is a fair objective. Perhaps most important of all, given the subject of discussion, firms need to develop strategies that they actually have the capability to execute. Doing this clearly requires a deep understanding of what the resources of the organization are capable of in terms of activities.

Having said all this, it is vital to recognize that – as with so much management writing – the debate about market- and resource-based strategy is unnecessarily polemic. Firms must take into account both their external *and* internal environments. Barriers/risks and enablers/opportunities to the achievement of high-level goals exist both inside and outside an organization. If strategy is not developed to address both these areas, it is unlikely to result in the achievement of primary objectives.

Besides choosing an executable strategy, organizations also need to consider how they develop strategy execution capability. Although Porter does not explore this issue, some firms are better than others at executing strategy. It seems an obvious extension of Porter's logic to say that both selecting an executable strategy *and* the capability to implement strategy are important sources of competitive advantage. Put another way, if two firms in the same industry seek the same strategic position and activity configuration, it is logical to expect that (other things being equal) the firm that chooses a more executable strategy and has a superior strategy execution capability will perform best – through achieving intended performance faster and at lower cost.[50]

Managing the strategy translation process

Thus far, this chapter has explored a framework via which overall objectives can be translated into critical activities and integrated it with the notion of competitive advantage. However, managers need to know more than the technical details of how this kind of model can be applied. They also need to manage the actual process within their organizations, ideally integrating this translation process with existing strategic and operational planning. Every situation is unique, and some level of customization is always required. This section offers some ideas and evidence to support this process.

One of the most obvious questions to ask about strategy execution maps is who should develop them? Although there is no one simple answer, a key principle should be applied in most situations. That is that those executing the strategy should have as much input to the process as possible. Even if they do not take the final decisions about what critical activities to pursue, their involvement is usually critical. Research shows that managerial edicts and attempts at persuasion tend to produce a mixture of resistance and apathy – yet these tactics are among the most popular employed by managers making strategic decisions, being used in two out of every three decisions studied.[51] The use of participation, conversely, is consistently more effective in creating superior decisions and higher commitment.[52] Wise senior teams dare not manage the translation of strategy into action alone.

Involving lots of people in breaking down strategies can be problematic from a logistical perspective. However, there are ways around this. For example, it is usually neither practical nor preferable to break an overall objective down to critical activities in one workshop. Though this might be the right kind of gathering to get things started, lots of other forms of collaboration can be used to develop and refine strategy execution maps and move them from representing broad options to critical choices. Multiple mini workshops with key stakeholder groups to break down particular aspects of a strategy execution map may be useful. Similar sessions can be used to provide feedback and constructive challenge of maps created by a lead team. One-to-one meetings can be useful for deeper exploration of important issues with technical experts. Even remote collaboration is possible – perhaps inviting feedback using e-mail or other more advanced Web-based tools such as discussion boards or online conferencing.

Another common question relates to facilitation and whether this is useful or essential in developing strategy execution maps. Again, there is no simple answer. In organizations with positive experience of such tools and highly collaborative teams that are comfortable challenging one another constructively, facilitation is less crucial. Without this backdrop, however, the expertise and impartiality of a facilitator are a worthwhile investment. However, it is ideal if an independent facilitator helps to build a facilitation capability within the organization, so that a wider range of participants can be involved in the strategy translation process and a sustainable ongoing process evolves over time. As mentioned earlier, strategy execution maps should be living documents, subject to regular analysis, ongoing development, and continual refinement.

As more and more stakeholders become involved in developing and using strategy execution maps in different ways, it becomes more important that there is a clear 'owner' of the maps and the processes by which they are created, recorded, distributed, applied to support operations, reviewed, evaluated, updated, and so on. This can be problematic, because strategy execution is rarely well managed within organizations. Few organizations have a well-developed strategy execution process that incorporates the data collection, analysis, options development, decision-making structures, and detailed planning necessary to translate ideas into action effectively. Rarely is the strategy execution process owned and driven by a senior executive with a dedicated professional team. Accountability for strategy execution sometimes cannot be located at all. Sometimes, the same is true of strategy generally, which may be a process buried deep in the finance function in which it is a process adjunct to the budgetary planning cycle. A related problem is that the strategy process is often narrowly focused, being limited to strategic planning only. It should by now be obvious that complex organizations also need an explicit framework to guide the execution of strategy (not to mention organization change, project management, performance measurement, and risk management). In summary, if developing useful strategy execution maps and applying them effectively is a serious ambition, it needs commensurate commitment.

Summary of key points

- Research into strategy execution barriers suggests that strategic plans are often not broken down into action, perhaps because of leaders' beliefs about the purpose of strategic planning and assumptions about how their plans will used by others.
- There is no widely available guidance on how to translate strategy into action, and most existing strategy execution theory incorrectly assumes managers are able to this effectively.
- Phase 1 of the inverted pyramid framework deals with translating overall objectives into critical activities.
- It is crucial that organizational leaders do not develop overall objective statements intended to influence stakeholder groups – this undermines their accuracy and clarity, which are essential.
- It is useful to define the key terms used in statements of overall objectives, to reduce ambiguity.
- Environmental analysis is critical because the environment conditions cause-and-effect relationships, including those hypothesized in strategies and implementation plans.

- It is essential to examine the internal and external environment – many strategy execution barriers are internal to organizations.
- Many tools can be used for environmental analysis, but it is critical to establish barriers/risks and enablers/opportunities relating to the specific elements of the strategy execution map.
- Barriers and enablers already exist and will foreseeably affect outcomes, whereas risks and opportunities are possibilities that may become relevant in the future.
- Strategy execution maps use the principles of causality, criticality, and compatibility to help translate overall objectives into critical activities.
- Strategy execution maps can initially depict a wide range of options and progressively be simplified to depict only critical choices in polished maps.
- Strategy execution maps are a useful method for depicting beliefs and plans, supporting constructive debate and communication.
- In particular, strategy execution maps are useful to help those planning strategy and its execution to consider a wide range of options for achieving objectives.
- Strategy execution maps must be broken down until they include concrete activities that competent individual individuals and teams can implement without substantial additional input or guidance.
- There are many general human information-processing limitations that affect how we think about cause and effect – in particular, we are prone to draw erroneous conclusions when information is missing, assume causality from association, miss loops of cause and effect, and ignore time lags.
- Research specifically examining the translation of objectives into activities established that the following problems damage this process:
  - Lack of strategic logic and clarity
  - Inadequate breakdown of strategy
  - Leaps of causal logic (between means and ends)
  - The use of vague and/or ambiguous terminology
  - Strategy that deals only with changes
  - Strategy oriented to influence multiple stakeholders.
- Polished strategy execution maps depict organizations' critical choices – they are living documents that can be readily used to communicate an organization's strategy and strategy execution model (see the IKEA and Apple strategy execution maps in Figure 6.11 and Figure 6.12, respectively).
- Strategy execution maps provide a useful way to examine fit between activities, associated trade-offs, and how proposed changes to activities are likely to affects these.
- Competitive advantage can be secured through selecting an executable strategy and developing superior strategy execution ability.
- To develop strategy execution maps effectively, leaders should ensure involvement of those who will implement strategy and use a facilitator if appropriate.

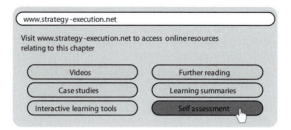

Chapter 7

Aligning action with strategy

Never mistake motion for action.

Ernest Hemingway

The strategy execution maps outlined in Chapter 6 are powerful tools for translating strategy into action. However, starting with overall objectives and translating them into activities represents only one way of creating alignment to execute strategy. Top-down planning can be a relatively deterministic process, usually relying upon initiation by senior managers. Desired outcomes (effects) are determined first and then used ultimately to establish critical activities (causes) that – it is hoped – will indirectly cause these outcomes. In this chapter, we turn to look at how alignment and causality can be applied bottom-up. This is useful for two reasons:

- to focus on particular critical activities and test more precisely whether they will plausibly cause the achievement of overall objectives and inform *how* they should be carried out to do this;
- to handle more emergent opportunities and ideas and ensure that they are aligned with overall objectives.

Aligning actions with strategy bottom-up relies much less on senior leaders producing formal statements of overall objectives and high-level strategic decisions. In fact, though these are certainly useful, this bottom-up approach can be used even when no clear strategy exists. It empowers more-junior managers to ensure that their intended activities will plausibly cause desirable outcomes.

Value of bottom-up planning

The deterministic approach to planning is favoured by many firms and advocated by many theorists.[1] It assumes that leaders have the ability to influence the future through manipulating current activities and that long-term plans to mange these manipulations are worthwhile. There is another school of thought that eschews deterministic planning in favour of what advocates see as a more realistic approach to strategy. Some theorists hold that strategy tends to evolve largely bottom-up.[2] They say that a legitimate pattern of activities emerges in organizations and that excessive top-down planning and control is not only unrealistic (essentially because of the problems of bounded rationality, explored later) but can crush the natural development of strategy emanating from responsive activities at the sharp end. This approach has been called *emergent strategy*, *evolutionary strategy*, *logical incrementalism*, and *muddling through*. It has been informed by fields of study such as cybernetics and can be a useful way of approaching strategy – especially in fast-moving, unpredictable early-stage industries. Many leading theorists remain highly skeptical of what sometimes they see as 'throwing planning to the wind' and instead being swept along by the environment in the hope that it will lead the organization in the right direction.

Emergent strategy doubtless has some important lessons for all strategists (particularly in relation to developing management information systems and control systems). However, research into the value of strategic planning does suggest an association between its use and higher financial performance.[3] (There is also some work that fails to find such a relationship.)[4] Moreover, my own research suggests that *some forms* of strategic planning coupled with systematic strategy execution efforts are effective in helping to close the gap between desired and actual outcomes in complex businesses (e.g. where methods such as strategy execution maps are used to move beyond planning conceptual strategy to detailed execution).

As mentioned already, the heated debate between the two views of strategy is probably unnecessarily divisive. Organizations need to make clear decisions about how to position themselves if they are to have good chances of creating sustainable competitive advantage. However, it is also vital to recognize that top-down planning cannot be 'perfect' and is never comprehensive and that organizations will not always implement plans with ideal rigour. Imperfection in planning results from bounded rationality, imperfect information, and changing internal/external environments – meaning hypotheses about cause and effect will sometimes be wrong. Also, opportunities and ideas definitely do emerge from day-to-day activities – that may be quite legitimate and consistent with strategic direction.

As a result, there are inevitably multiple occasions when there is a requirement to deal with some issue or undertake activities not addressed in top-down planning. From the perspective of a manager in an organization, such occasions may include the following:

- an *edict* from a senior executive to launch some initiative (without practical scope for challenge)
- an unanticipated *problem* that appears and requires a coordinated response
- an unanticipated *opportunity* worthy of consideration and possible action.

In each case, it is sensible to make an attempt to tie the resulting work back into the overall objectives of the organization. Solutions to problems should be oriented toward goal achievement (not just problem solving for its own sake), and any issue is relevant only to the extent that it constitutes a barrier or risk to achievement of overall objectives (or perhaps a failure to exploit enablers/opportunities).

To those dealing with specific management issues day to day, edicts from senior executives often feel as if they bear little relationship to overall objectives (or they can seem imbalanced, perhaps too heavily focused on cost reduction or upon some relatively unimportant issue). On occasion, such orders are based on unappreciated wisdom, but they often are the dysfunctional results of imperfect information, frustration, or organizational politics.

Even in circumstances in which an initiative is misaligned with objectives or is a sub optimal method of achieving them, causal chains can be useful to work out ways of *extracting* value from mandatory activities (perhaps through adding some small additional steps to ensure objective achievement) that might otherwise achieve little.

Introducing bottom-up causal chains

Choosing the right activities

There are typically many proposed activities (or clusters of related activities) that arise and are worthy of explicit alignment with strategy and overall objectives.

Box 7.1 Bottom-up integration planning

A multinational business once became involved in a large and complex merger. The human resources executives were dismayed when, as integration began, the dominant CEO insisted that employee terms and conditions should be harmonized. Although this would have been necessary at some point, the HR teams were under severe pressure to deal with much more urgent and fundamental issues, such as selection, de-selection, redundancies, re-structuring, and so on. Nobody could see any immediate benefits of integrating terms and conditions.

However, deciding that challenging the CEO's decision was not a practical option, they used causal mapping to explore the potential linkages between this initiative and the business's overall objective. They established that they *could* extract significant value from integrating employee terms and conditions *if* they offered the highly competitive flexible benefits package used by one of the merging companies to the employees of the other. This benefits package was a strong differentiator, having had a proven impact on attraction, motivation, and retention of high-quality staff. Furthermore, it was realized that the lure of the flexible benefits package could be used to drive up the acceptance rate of the new terms and conditions. This is what was done, and the project was a success.

These might be called projects, initiatives, or change programmes or, if they are ongoing, might be labelled as processes. For simplicity, we'll refer simply to projects, as they are perhaps the most common 'container' used to plan, manage, and deliver important new activities.

My research suggests that it is common for projects and other initiatives to be defined as ends in themselves. When possible projects arise emergently, perhaps owing to a perceived problem or opportunity, they can quickly gather momentum and start to feel like something that must be delivered. Excitement can grow and, before long, what emerged only as an idea starts being called a *project* or *initiative*. A team may be pulled together to start fleshing out how it may be delivered and begin to engage stakeholders more widely. Often an experienced and well-qualified project manager leads such efforts. Projects may be delivered within a strong governance process that necessitates explicit sign-off, tracking, reporting, and evaluation. Usually, this means that the products of projects (i.e. the concrete changes it will produce – such as a newly installed IT system) are extremely clear, as are the timescales, costs, and resources required to deliver it.

However, in spite of all this expertise and systematization, explicit alignment between the product of a project and the strategy or overall objectives of the organization is often absent. As we have seen, making such alignment explicit is not trivial, so this is perhaps unsurprising. However, often little, if any, effort is made to make this clear. Many managers – and project managers are typically no exception – are action-oriented and like to focus on delivery of a defined output. After all, typically it is this delivery that is taken as success – formally and informally. A project manager who repeatedly delivers on time to budget and to specification is valued highly. As soon as delivery is complete, most project teams are disbanded. Its members are often keen to get back to the 'day job' or on with the next project. Of course, none of this expertise, governance, systematization, reporting, or apparent performance actually means that the project has had any material impact on execution of the organization's strategy or achievement of overall objectives. The project could have been delivered perfectly but have been the wrong project in the first place or have become misaligned with strategy owing to changes in the strategy or (more commonly) environment. A conventional approach to project management typically ensures that projects are 'done right' – but rarely ensures that the right projects are being done. This is unacceptable. Projects and other change activities consume huge amounts of cost and managerial time – not to mention attention, effort, and motivation. It is imperative that explicit efforts are made to ensure that projects are the right ones and that they are shaped in such a way as to maximize their impact on organizational objectives. That is where bottom-up causal chains can be of great help.

It is tempting to assume that such explicit alignment is ideal but perhaps not strictly required – surely, one might think, most of the projects that organizations undertake add value. My research suggests otherwise. In many of the cases examined, not only were the plausible strategic outcomes from projects not clearly defined but when causal analysis was performed to test for alignment, material impact on strategic outcomes did not appear likely. It appears that managers are often overoptimistic about the impact their activities are likely to have on strategy and overall objectives.[5] With the importance of bottom-up alignment underlined, we can now turn to how it can be ensured.

An example from an airline

An example helps to convey the logic and value of bottom-up causal chains. Several years ago, an airline became interested in the use of automated check-in machines, after a close competitor became one of the first airlines in the world to install some (of course, they are now commonplace). This was not a critical activity defined through the airline's strategy, which was determined top down. The opportunity arose by virtue of changes in the environment and led to serious consideration of what would be an important change to the airline's customer-facing operations and a significant investment. A bottom-up causal chain was developed, which mapped both potential cost and revenue implications. Figure 7.1 depicts the causal chain developed (slightly simplified for ease of understanding).

As with strategy execution maps, good causal chains are fairly easy to interpret. Figure 7.1 shows on the far left the proposed change, or 'product', of the project that would be launched. On the far right is the organization's overall objective – increased profit. The causal chain shows the two primary mechanisms by which it was thought the project's product might (indirectly) positively affect the overall objective. Put another way, the causal chain shows a series of performance variables plausibly causally linking the output of the project with increased profit.

Dealing with the cost implications first, a fairly obvious opportunity to reduce the number of check-in staff and associated costs was predicted, as a result of customer use of the automatic check-in terminals. On the revenue side, a less certain logic was developed, anticipating that reducing queuing time would increase service quality and thus customer satisfaction, and so on.

The development of causal chains like this is typically a useful step. It depicts the logic of implementing a proposed project with greater clarity than conventional reports or presentations. It can cause and inform constructive debate across a range of stakeholders with an interest in the project. This is one of the most immediate benefits of causal chains. Often, stakeholders suggest other possible project outcomes not previously considered. Others may challenge the logic of what was presented. Some might be able to point to existing management information or research data that provide empirical support for or against some of the causal hypotheses incorporated in the chain. In the airline example, data relating to the relationship between customer satisfaction and retention were particularly important and re-examined with this project in mind. All this helps to enrich and refine project plans. At the same time, it engages important stakeholders intellectually and emotionally.

It should be noted that Figure 7.2 depicts a positive scenario – a set of intended outcomes (as most plans do). At this early stage of exploring the logic of the

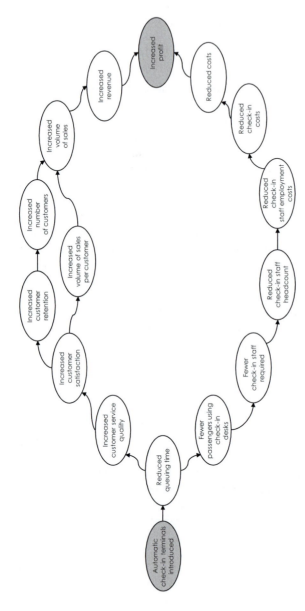

Figure 7.1 Bottom-up causal chain: Airline automated check-in

project, the focus is naturally on the possible upside of undertaking the activity in question. We will deal with the possibility of negative outcomes shortly. Similarly, Figure 7.1 shows no quantifications to these positive outcomes – it does not specify how *big* an impact the project might make. Again, this is dealt with later.

It is also worth saying that, in some respects, Figure 7.1 looks obvious. Partly this reflects the choice of a simple first example, but this is also a fairly common feature of good causal chains. Logically considered, well-articulated causal chains *do* look obvious. In fact, ideally they *should* look rather obvious – *once they are complete*. Developing them against a typical backdrop of overoptimistic expectations about outcomes, vague ideas, and shaky strategies is usually much more difficult than Figure 7.1 might lead one to think.

This point is important to mention for two reasons. First, managers can become frustrated when they work at developing causal chains, thinking it should be easy. Actually, to do a good job, they must overcome hidden assumptions and rules of thumb they use when deciding what to do, how, and why. This is genuinely difficult, and recognizing this makes it less emotionally draining. Second, most managers need a fair bit of help to become skilful at developing causal chains. This might come in the form of written guidance, training, facilitation, coaching, or some combination of these – what is important is that it is available. There are various pitfalls into which most people fall when developing causal chains, and these are explored later.

Another example of a completed causal chain is depicted in Figure 7.2. This relates to a stockbroking business that was looking at allowing customers to trade stocks using Smartphones. Offering this service necessitated some substantial changes to the Web technologies employed by the business, but it was thought that it might reap considerable rewards, especially given the explosive growth in this segment of the mobile phone industry. The causal chain was developed to explore and articulate this option.

Once again, the product of the proposed project (Smartphone access introduced) on the far left is connected via a series of cause-and-effect hypotheses with the organization's overall objective (increased profit). Once again, there are both revenue and cost implications from this project depicted. This causal chain is a little more complex than the one in Figure 7.1 in that it includes many inter-linkages and different paths by which, it was anticipated, a positive impact on the overall objective might be made. This is quite common and broadly speaking is a good sign – as there are many ways in which the project may bring positive results.

Figure 7.2 makes a subtle but important point. Attentive readers will have noticed that many of the more conceptual elements of strategy execution maps and causal chains are common across different examples. This is unsurprising – performance variables such as sales volume and number of customers are important to many businesses. However, as Figure 7.2 shows, assumptions along these lines are dangerous. Such are the dynamics of stockbroking that a different language makes more sense in places (trades, not volumes, for example), and

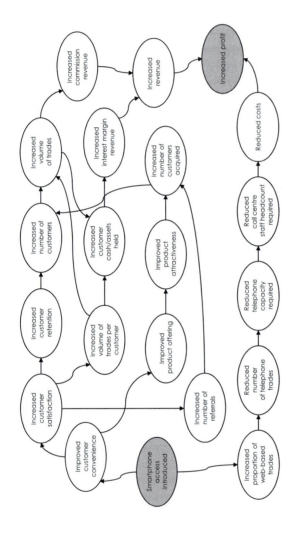

Figure 7.2 Bottom-up causal chain: Stockbroking business Smartphone web access

unique distinctions (such as between commission revenue and interest margin revenue) are important. Those who favour a 'copy-and-paste' approach to their work beware – for causal chains, often a clear mind and blank page are the best starting points.

One of the many challenges facing support functions is that their activities typically lie furthest back from overall objectives, in terms of their causal impact. That is not to say they are not important – on the contrary, they are often critical to the long-term success of any organization. It is tempting to think that explicitly aligning support function activities with overall objectives is not essential, as the investment made in support functions is a 'leap of faith', or that doing so would simply be too difficult to justify trying. However, this causal complexity makes such alignment even more important – it means that assumptions and optimistic expectations are even more dangerous. Causal chains appear to work well for this purpose. The explicit causal arguments they demand push managers to articulate logic that often goes unexplored. Figure 7.3 provides an example of a causal chain developed by the HR function of a large retail chain. This organization recognized a need to improve the performance of its sales staff and, after some diagnostic investigations, determined that focusing on the sales managers held perhaps the greatest potential to trigger a leap in performance. It was proposed that all sales managers across the group should be given sophisticated training specifically designed for sales managers, to help them lead and manage their teams more effectively on the ground.

The causal chain in Figure 7.3 shows the logic developed by the HR team. They had to think carefully about the direct outcomes of the training and determined that they were seeking to improve sales managers' skills in relation to sales staff management (specifically). This, they intended, would improve the management of sales staff and, thus, sales staff performance. The two direct outcomes from this, they anticipated, were increased sales effectiveness and increased sales capacity. The outcomes beyond this will by now be familiar.

This clarity of outcomes led to a rather different approach than that conventionally followed by the business in relation to training. Historically, once managers had attained a certain level of seniority, they were provided with generic management and leadership training unspecific to their functional specialty. There was a tacit assumption that managers would have been promoted from these functional areas and understand them deeply. However, it became recognized that specialist sales staff management training offered sales managers skills they did not generally develop through their career paths. The causal chain also oriented the intended outcomes of the training clearly – something that had been a long-standing problem. Training has conventionally been seen as a rather 'woolly' activity that is difficult to link to the achievement of business objectives. However, using causality to articulate the intended outcomes of training interventions challenges this view.

It is important to note that causal chains are also viable and useful in non-commercial settings. Figure 7.4 shows a causal chain developed by a government

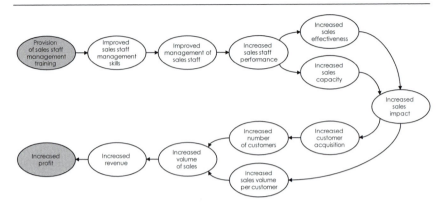

Figure 7.3 Retailer casual chain: Sales manager training

authority responsible for a city in which there was a problem with road accidents – specifically pedestrians being knocked down by vehicles. Several solutions were being considered, one of which was the installation of more controlled crossings. The authority's overall objective was essentially to improve the quality of life for citizens in and visitors to the geographic area for which it was responsible. The causal chain developed clearly mapped the plausible causal relationships between introducing more controlled crossings and this overall objective.

As with some earlier causal chains, Figure 7.4 looks rather obvious when laid out neatly in this fashion. However, the authority recognized the value of exploring this option in a structured fashion. Experience told managers that easy assumptions about what would impact quality of life did not always hold true. Sometimes, hypotheses were simply invalid. At other times, unanticipated factors derailed their causal logic. Further, of course, the authority had numerous competing initiatives, all theoretically contributing to improving quality of life, too. The following sections explore how further developments using these basic causal chains can help address these challenges.

Applications of causal chains

Some of the potential uses of developing causal chains are immediately obvious. However, others are more subtle. Causal chains allow managers to explore the outcomes they might plausibly expect to result from activities. (This is the converse to top-down strategy execution maps that allow managers to identify possible means of achieving objectives.) Importantly, it allows the construction of a compete chain of cause and effect hypotheses, linking activities with conceptual objectives such as organizations' overall objectives. The creation of such chains makes the possible causal relationships between activities and objectives explicit – something that is rarely achieved. This makes it easier for managers to think

Figure 7.4 Government authority casual chain: Controlled crossings

Box 7.2 Try it – Causal chains
As discussed earlier, causal chains sometimes look simple once they are developed but can be remarkably difficult to develop properly. The best way to become skilled at developing and using them effectively is, of course, practice. It is worth trying to develop a causal chain for a project or initiative with which you are familiar.

about these relationships, communicate them to stakeholders, and debate them in groups. This enables more effective discussions between those involved in developing and executing strategy – an important process to ensure strategy is executable, and there is sufficient engagement among those expected to deliver it. Stakeholders are helpful to assess whether hypothesized cause and effect relationships are reasonable and question the assumptions underlying them.

It is possible to develop different causal chains, representing different means to achieve the same ends. This helps to consider the relative merits between mutually exclusive options. It also allows for easier consideration of the compatibility (or dependencies) between related activities. These efforts help organizations to make better investment decisions.

Because causal chains articulate intended strategy execution means clearly, they are potential mechanisms for creating a clear 'line of sight' between objectives and activities for those responsible for managing an organization's primary objectives (usually senior executives) and those charged with implementation of projects or activities (usually more-junior staff). This clarity helps to put activities in context and supports day-to-day decision making, which may involve making minor *ad-hoc* trade-off decisions informed by an understanding of objectives. Causal chains should also help to orient project managers toward ensuring that their projects have positive impact on strategic outcomes rather than simply successful delivery (i.e. on time, within budget, with satisfactory quality).

Finally, building upon many of the uses outlined earlier, causal chains are useful for risk identification, performance measurement, and cost-benefit analysis, all of which are explored shortly.

Pitfalls in using causal chains

As with strategy execution maps, there are various pitfalls into which managers can fall when trying to develop causal chains. My own research explored this in some depth. Many of the common problems reflect those encountered when translating strategy into action top down. Of the pitfalls explored in Chapter 6, the following are also common problems with bottom-up causal chains:

- lack of strategic logic and clarity
- leaps of causal logic (between means and ends)
- the use of vague and/or ambiguous terminology.

In addition, a problem specific to bottom-up causal chains is confusion between causality and task dependency. Each of these four issues is discussed briefly next.

Lack of strategic logic and clarity

Although causal chains help to explore and ensure alignment in a bottom-up fashion and thus do not depend on perfectly formed strategies, there is no doubt that lack of strategic logic and clarity does not help this effort. In fact, causal chains often make problems with poorly formed or articulated strategies highly apparent. Managers can find it difficult to see how seemingly logical activities 'hook in' to the strategy articulated by senior executives. Sometimes, this is because the activity is genuinely misaligned but, more commonly, the strategy does not provide sufficient clarity to evaluate alignment or lack of it.

Leaps of causal logic

When exploring strategy execution maps, the problem of making big leaps of causal logic was explored. The same pitfall awaits those developing causal chains bottom-up. It is common for managers to make overambitious 'leaps of faith' when articulating the intended outcomes of proposed activities. This is a serious problem because it makes the true plausibility of these hypotheses difficult to estimate. For example, consider the stockbroking business project described earlier. If a manager proposed introducing Smartphone access to increase trade volumes, this may at first have sounded reasonable. However, Figure 7.2 shows how limited this logic is and how many intermediate performance variables would have to be successfully affected for the project to make a positive impact on trade volumes. In particular, it is difficult to make even a broad estimation of how much the project might affect trade volumes without articulating these intermediate effects. It is also tricky to consider alternative methods of driving up trade volumes and making initial comparisons of these alternative approaches. My research suggested that leaps in causal logic (whether or not portrayed in a causal chain) led to superior investment opportunities being ignored in favour of obvious or conventional tactics. As with strategy execution maps, occasional small leaps of causal logic probably don't matter too much, but developing a disciplined approach to developing more precise causal chains pays dividends.

The use of vague and/or ambiguous terminology

Earlier, the danger of using vague or ambiguous terminology was discussed in relation to strategy execution maps. The same risk exists with bottom-up causal chains. Once again, minor ambiguities such as referring to 'sales' rather than 'sales volume' or 'turnover' rather than 'staff turnover' can cause confusion. More common, however, is the use of 'woolly' words when precise thinking about the outcomes of activities is absent. Even when attempting a precise articulation of outcomes via a causal chain, managers can be tempted to refer to outcomes such as 'world class performance' or 'a best-practice approach'. Terms such as these, unless defined clearly elsewhere, are meaningless and have no place in any strategy execution work. Even more convincing terms such as *high performance* or *preferred choice* are meaningless out of context and best avoided in most cases. Some organizations deliberately introduce a 'ban on bull***t', and this is a good idea for successful strategy execution. Ultimately, if the plausible outcomes of an activity or project cannot be articulated in precise language, it is highly questionable whether desirable outcomes will plausibly result from it. There are several questions useful to test the rigour of a causal chain:

- What do the variables used really mean, and how can they be defined unambiguously?
- Are the causal links between the variables realistic?
- How could each of these variables be measured?

The answer to this last question is telling. If the variables in a causal chain can feasibly be measured, it is probably made up from unambiguous, specific elements. Measurement is explored later in this chapter.

Confusion between causality and task dependency

A common pitfall specific to developing causal chains bottom-up is to inadvertently establish chains depicting task dependency instead. Project managers are typically schooled in critical path analysis, a method of establishing the optimal order in which activities should be undertaken, given dependencies between them, to minimize the time required to deliver a project. This is a great methodology – it's important to schedule tasks in the right order to deliver projects quickly. However, mapping task dependencies is not the same as mapping the chain of cause-and-effect relationships impacted by a project. Task dependency and causality are completely different things – the former informs *how* to do a project; the latter informs *why* it should (perhaps) be done in the first place.

Various contextual issues contribute to making this mistake a common one. Excessive action orientation, unclear business objectives, and a disconnection between operations and strategy can all contribute to a rather introspective approach by those undertaking projects or activities in organizations. The planning of many support activities falls into this category. Departments that don't deal directly with end-customers but instead support the organization itself often find it hard to link their activities to overall objectives. They run the risk of undertaking activities for their own sakes. This is common in finance, IT, human resources, and so on. However, let us take an example from marketing. Figure 7.5 shows a simplified critical path analysis for promotional activities carried out by a marketing team. In this example, it is clear that the marketing team needs to 'select promotional channels' before it 'commissions promotions' and so on.

However, Figure 7.5 is not a causal chain because 'evaluate promotion success' is not an overall objective. Rather, every element of the chain is an *activity* that the marketing team would carry out. No causality is evident. For example, selecting promotional channels would not *cause* the promotions to be commissioned. That would require further intervention after the promotional channels were selected. In the example in Figure 7.5, it is conceivable that none of these activities would contribute to the achievement of any legitimate strategic objectives. We cannot tell because no linkages are made with objectives. There isn't even any evidence that the strategic objectives are known or understood by the marketing team.

In summary, there are important pitfalls to avoid when using causality to help translate strategy into action or align activities with strategic objectives bottom-up. The most common ones are explored here because developing high-quality causal chains is essential – not just for the reasons discussed so far but because they can usefully be built upon, as is discussed next.

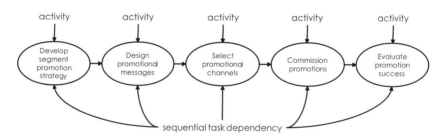

Figure 7.5 Sequential task dependency in a marketing project

Strategic risk management

Overview

The notion of risk management is well established in management and particularly advanced in specific areas such as finance, investment, credit, health and safety, and so on. Numerous models to identify, analyse, and manage risk exist for particular purposes, and some of these are embedded in wider frameworks such as project management. However, it is relatively recently that strategic risk management has emerged as a distinct concern. Recognition that isolated risk management in specific areas is inadequate and that many risks are 'strategic' in their nature and impact has led to the emergence of the field and terms such as *enterprise-wide risk management*. Given the early stage of these developments, it is perhaps little surprise that strategy execution risk management is far from well developed. Of course, a fair bit of research has been conducted into strategy execution barriers, but this does not address how organizations should manage the uncertainty that underlies the notion of risk.

A definition of risk is needed here, and we can think of risks as events, occurrences, or situations that limit or prevent the achievement of objectives. Risk is thus contextual, and if we see successful strategy execution as the objective for the purpose of this discussion, we can define strategy execution risks as events, occurrences, or situations that limit or prevent successful strategy execution.

Being based on the same fundamental concepts, both strategy execution maps and causal chains are useful tools for strategic risk management. Here we will look at the latter.

> *Box 7.3* Risk definitions
> Risks are *events*, *occurrences*, or *situations* that limit or prevent the achievement of objectives.
>   Strategy execution risks are *events*, *occurrences*, or *situations* that limit or prevent successful strategy execution.

Implementation risks

Project management frameworks and processes have for a considerable time incorporated the notion of risk. Indeed, most advanced project management systems include initial risk assessments, risk management plans, risk tracking (often captured in risk logs), and so on. Project managers, naturally concerned with project delivery, know that there are many factors that may (or may not) make delivery difficult, or even prevent it. Project managers conventionally think in terms of managing time (schedule), cost (budget), and quality (specifications). They know that when problems arise in one area, trade-offs must often be made in another. For example, if a project starts to slip behind schedule, it can perhaps be brought back on schedule by allocating additional resource, albeit at a cost. Contingency plans, often manifested in unallocated budget contingency or a deliberately extended forecast delivery date, are designed to accommodate common risks.

Project managers with deep experience of the domains in which they are working typically know what kind of risks to expect. They know that project teams can become stretched, especially if depleted. They know that software development often takes longer than expected. They know that some stakeholders will not release resources to the project in time. They foresee that certain costs might rise and so on. Usually, good project managers know how to mange such risks if they can identify them. Project managers typically assess risk in terms of probability of their occurrence and extent of impact. Clearly, risks with a high probability and high impact attract a great deal of attention when it comes to managing them.

In summary, implementation risks threaten the *delivery* of projects or activities. Managing them is an operational matter, and important though that is, it isn't a direct concern of strategy execution. However, *post-implementation risks* are firmly in the domain of strategy execution.

Post-implementation risks

There are two types of post-implementation risk, both of which can arise even after a project is 'successfully' delivered on time and to budget and specification:

- failures of intended outcomes
- negative unintended effects.

Failures of intended outcomes occur when the objectives a project or activity was intended to cause fail to materialize. The only rational reason to plan and implement any sort of project is to cause its intended outcomes – no activity is worth undertaking for its own sake. However, any project, no matter how perfectly delivered, is at some risk of this occurrence. An activity or project can fail to achieve its intended outcomes if:

- the cause-and-effect hypotheses developed to link activities with achievement of objectives are incorrect or substantially weaker than expected; or
- factors present in the internal or external environment 'neutralize' the effect of an activity (perhaps because of poorly calibrated dynamics or unforeseen changes).

This type of risk does not seem to have received attention within the strategy execution field or related areas – perhaps because explicit causal reasoning has not been widely applied as a method in the field. With conventional strategy development or project management methods, it is difficult to see how such risks might effectively be identified. However, causal chains support identification of the risks of failures of intended outcomes. This kind of risk can be identified by examining each link in a well-developed causal chain and asking, "What might prevent this cause and effect relationship operating as intended?' A knowledge of the technical issues relevant to the change activity or project is, of course, helpful, but this approach appears to produce a systematic analysis of failure risks.[6] Very importantly, examining *each* link in a causal chain makes it easier to see how even apparently small risks might have a significant impact on the ultimate success of a change effort or project. It is clear using this analysis that every weak link compounds the weakness of all the links that follow it. Unlike their physical equivalent, these chains are typically *much weaker* than their weakest link.

Projects or other initiatives may be delivered brilliantly but completely fail to make their intended impact or even create a negative impact if these risks are ignored. An example of this analysis helps. Figure 7.6 shows potential failures of intended outcomes for the airline automated check-in project, using the causal chain first shown in Figure 7.1. Failures of intended outcomes are shown with arrows pointing toward the links in the causal chain (i.e. affecting cause-and-effect links in the chain).

As with causal chains, Figure 7.6 should be fairly clear upon first reading. To take two examples, the managers were concerned that the introduction of the automatic check-in terminals might not lead to reduced queuing time to the extent hoped if they suffered from malfunctions. If they were out of commission or their reliability was not trusted by regular passengers, the check-in desks would be busier than expected. Similarly, there was recognition that some customers would elect not to use the facility, and this would moderate the causal relationship between the reduced queuing time offered by the machines and increases in customer service hoped for as a result. Both these examples are of risks of failures of intended outcomes. They acknowledge that the original causal chain in Figure 7.1 was a statement of potential benefits. The risk identification takes things to the next level, acknowledging that there are factors that threaten realization of these potential benefits.

Of course, these risks identified can be assessed like any other in terms of their probability and impact. Equally, they can be managed. In this case, careful testing of the machines was essential, as was access to a speedy repair service in case malfunctions did occur. Similarly, conducting customer research by including a pilot scheme more accurately predicted the likely usage of the machines. Plans were also developed for how staff would assist customers initially to manage the transition and 'educate' them in using the new facility. A key point, however, is that the management of these risks added to the complexity, timescales, and costs of the project. Once they were recognized and management options considered, the project plan and business case were altered. For some projects, identification of risks can and should ultimately mean that they are cancelled – if the case for undertaking them over others is not adequately made.

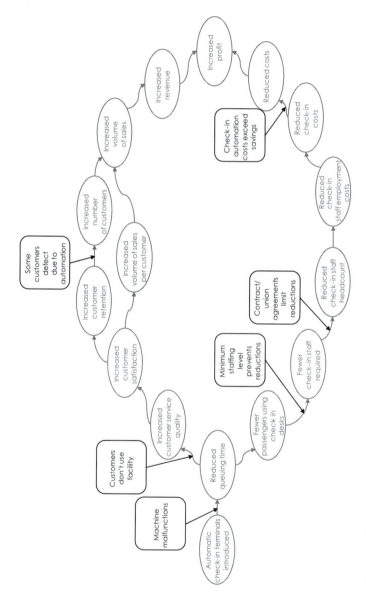

Figure 7.6 Risk identification (failures of intended outcomes): Airline automated check-in

The second type of post-implementation risk is negative unintended effects. This phenomenon is more widely understood and discussed in the management field – most managers recognize that sometimes their efforts 'backfire'. Any activity or project can have negative unintended effects. Often, these are not anticipated (partly because few managers consider the possibility of their occurrence or look for them after change has been implemented). Again, however, systematic analysis of a causal chain makes their identification easier and more effective. In this case, we can ask for each variable in the causal chain, "What negative outcome might also appear if we achieve this"? Often, these negative unintended effects may cause problems if they are not avoided or managed.

Figure 7.7 gives examples of negative unintended effects for the airline's automated check-in project. Again, this builds on the casual chain shown in Figure 7.1. Negative unintended effects are shown at the end of arrows pointing away from the causal chain (i.e. being caused by the elements in the chain).

It was realized that if customers used the check-in machines (a desired outcome), they would interact with staff less and, as a result, less oversized hand baggage would be spotted and more sharp objects would be left in hand luggage (both undesirable outcomes). There were similar concerns that the reduced customer interactions might damage the customer experience for some passengers who valued the 'personal touch'. Another potential negative unintended effect recognized was the disastrous scenario where the automated check-in system might fail, making all the machines inoperable and placing huge stress on the depleted check-in staff teams. These and other unintended effects were assessed and managed as part of this project, the scope of which again changed substantially as a result of this form of risk identification.

Figure 7.8 shows some of the post-implementation risks (of both types) identified by the stockbroking business in relation to the project to introduce Smartphone access. This builds upon the causal chain depicted in Figure 7.2 and is self-explanatory.

It should be obvious that effective post-implementation risk identification relies heavily upon the development of high-quality causal chains. It is difficult to see how these risks could be identified systematically without a structured tool such as graphic causal chains.

Thus far, we have examined risks using causal chains rather than using strategy execution maps. This is perhaps the most manageable way to approach this task and helps to focus the examination of risk on activities that are seriously being

Box 7.4 Try it – Identifying post-implementation risks
If earlier you developed a causal chain for a project or initiative with which you are familiar, try identifying post-implementation risks relating to it. Try to identify both possible failures of intended outcomes and negative unintended effects.

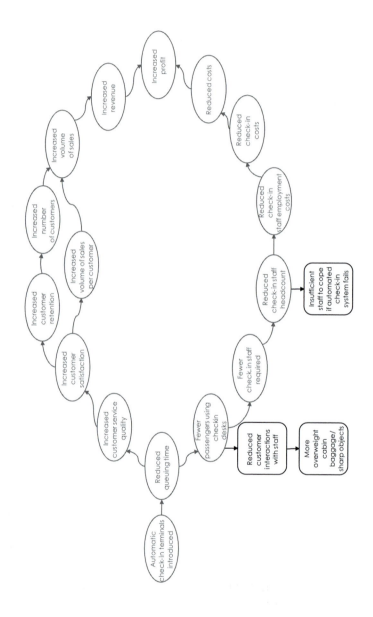

Figure 7.7 Risk identification (negative unintended effects): Airline automated check-in

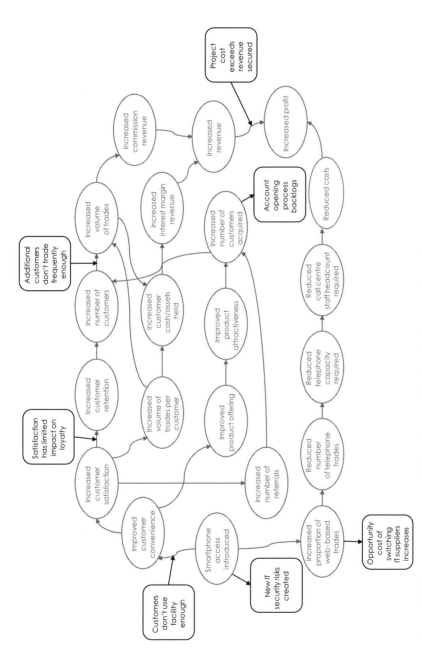

Figure 7.8 Post-implementation risk identification: Stockbroking business Smartphone web access

considered (whether these were identified deterministically or more emergently). However, risks can systematically be identified using strategy execution maps. Exactly the same process can be applied using a strategy execution map. It is useful to do so as such maps develop, often relatively informally at first and then in a concentrated fashion as more definitive critical activities emerge.

Both causal chains and this risk identification are important stages in the development of alignment between activities and overall objectives. Each of them supports the next two developments – performance measurement and cost-benefit analysis.

Strategic performance measurement

Overview

Performance measurement is a hugely important but difficult area for organizations of all kinds. Accurately calibrating performance of activities and their outcomes has many advantages – and some risks. Performance measurement is, therefore, central to successful strategy execution.

Measures always perform two roles in organizations – 'feedback' and 'feedforward'. Feedback tells us about past performance and can be used to inform decisions about the future – relating both to strategy development and strategy execution. Feedforward, conversely, is the effect that selecting measures has on people's behaviour. As Peter Drucker and many others since have said, "What gets measured gets managed". This means that the way measures are chosen, designed, and used has an enormous impact on strategy execution success.

So potent are performance measures that a great deal can be inferred from them about how managers in any organization approach the strategy execution challenge. Performance measurement data themselves may offer limited insights. They can fluctuate for many reasons, are of limited significance without baselines or benchmarks, and might be inaccurate or irrelevant. What really matters is how organizations approach measurement. How are measures selected and designed? How is information collected and analysed? To whom is it reported and how is it really used? What happens when measures tell an important story, be it good or bad? Performance measurement is hugely revealing about how organizations create and try to implement their strategies.

In this chapter, we examine the strategic role of performance measurement – and in particular how measures can be identified using some of the frameworks already introduced. In Chapter 8, we look at motivational issues related to measures and in particular the effects of 'feedforward'.

Leading and lagging measures

The principles about using measures for feedback are well established. It is accepted that organizations should complement 'lagging' measures reflecting performance in terms of ultimate objectives (such as financial outcomes in a business) with 'leading' measures reflecting performance of indirect drivers of these objectives. This provides a more balanced, sustainable, forward-looking view of overall performance that acknowledges the need to secure the resources that create value indirectly. Conventionally, many organizations have focused heavily on using lagging indicators, but this approach has been likened to driving a car looking only in the rear-view mirror.

Numerous strategic performance measurement systems have evolved, seeking to operationalize these principles, including the balanced scorecard and European Foundation for Quality Management (EFQM) excellence model, for example. These frameworks prescribe that attention should be paid to particular categories of measures that reflect this notion of leading and lagging indicators. However, such tools bring with them risks. Prescriptive lenses shape the way managers see their organizations and, with such a potent force as measurement, it is crucial that these lenses are focused appropriately.

Performance measurement frameworks

There are several key points to consider to avoid the risks and forge a more customized and useful approach to strategic performance measurement. First, the measurement tail should not wag the strategy dog. It is essential to establish strategic objectives and determine how they might best be achieved without being constrained by a prescriptive framework for performance measures. Using a measurement framework that is not built around a solid strategy designed for the overall objective and unique situation of an organization is fraught with danger. It is impossible to be sure that the right measures are being used or that the emphasis naturally placed on them is driving the organization in the right direction. My own action research examining the application of strategy execution maps suggests that this non-prescriptive tool rarely produces a business model reflecting the layout of the popular measurement frameworks. This is not surprising. There is no reason why any organization's strategy should reflect the balanced scorecard's four categories, EFQM's nine criteria, or any other prefabricated model. It is dangerous to design strategy around these, and of limited value to categorize existing measures in such an arbitrary manner as suggested by the design of the balanced scorecard and EFQM models.

One of the attractions of most management tools is that they find neat ways around fundamental dilemmas. However, this is also one of the greatest threats they pose. Use the balanced scorecard and you may feel you don't have to detail how activities will achieve strategic objectives, because the model implies that people-related initiatives positively impact internal processes, in turn driving customer behaviour and financial outcomes. These assumptions are so conceptual and broad as to be meaningless. My research suggests there is no substitute for clearly breaking down strategic objectives into specific, concrete activities that will plausibly deliver them.

Using strategy execution maps to identify performance measures

Given the limitations and risks of prescriptive measurement frameworks, it is useful to point to alternatives. My own research suggests that strategy execution maps can be used for this purpose. As Chapter 6 showed, well-developed strategy execution maps systematically articulate how critical activities might plausibly cause the achievement of overall objectives. They map causally related performance variables at varying levels of abstraction – from conceptual down to concrete. If these performance variables are well articulated, it is feasible to attach performance measures to them. In doing so, a strategic performance measurement framework emerges that is naturally customized around the unique strategy and business model of the organization.

Figure 7.9 shows an example set of performance measures relating to (for simplicity) a chain of seven related performance variables included in the IKEA strategy execution map in Figure 6.11. It demonstrates how it is possible to establish measures for variables at all levels of abstraction from the organization's overall objective right through to critical activities. This naturally produces a progressive mix of measures from ones that can be considered lagging to ones that are leading.

It is worth noting that the performance variables in Figure 6.11 and the measures in Figure 7.9 do not fall naturally into the measurement categories proposed in prescriptive tools such as the balanced scorecard and EFQM model.

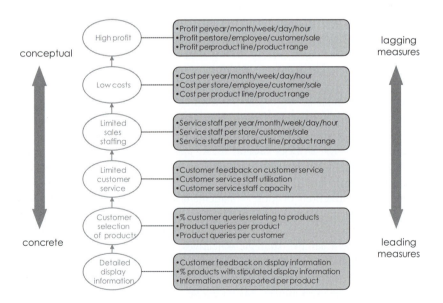

Figure 7.9 Example measures developed for variables in IKEA strategy execution map

This is because the IKEA strategy execution map was developed around the unique business model of that business – not force-fitted into what might be seen as an arbitrary series of measurement categories.

Using causal chains to identify performance measures

Causal chains relating to specific critical activities are also useful for identifying performance measures. This is particularly useful for change programmes or projects to enable planning, evaluation, and tracking.

Estimating and tracking project outcomes has conventionally been difficult, especially for projects led by support functions such as human resources and marketing. Managers find it difficult to identify what they should measure and how to do it. One of the biggest problems is clearly articulating the means by which desired outcomes will be achieved – a challenge reflected in the drive toward using leading measures as well as lagging ones.

As with strategy execution maps, causal chains identify the activities and outcomes resulting from them around which leading measures can be developed. Because of time lags, leading measures can provide early warnings of likely problems in achieving overall objectives. Using a mix of leading and lagging measures enables easier identification of *why* problems in outcomes occur, enabling action to be taken to remedy such problems.

Figure 7.10 builds on the sales management training causal chain shown in Figure 7.3 to demonstrate how measures can readily be added to each element of a causal chain. These may be quantitative or qualitative – what is important is that each measure helps to calibrate the variables included in the causal chain and, over time, movement in these variables. In practice, usually more measures than would be necessary to collect, can be identified. Figure 7.10 gives examples of measures that might be used in this kind of situation.

Detailed design of performance measures

An issue generally overlooked by performance measurement thinkers is how to design actual performance measures. Happy to focus on broad frameworks intended to help select indicators, they often ignore the importance of critical measures being accurate and balanced. This advice gap is perhaps matched by managers' reluctance to get into too much detail, believing complexity to be the enemy of progress. 'Keep It Simple, Stupid' (KISS) is often heard in discussions about measurement. It's sometimes appropriate but subject to the importance of the performance variables being measured. It's baffling that KISS should blindly be applied to critical strategic measures. Organizations are inherently complex systems – they need to be to survive and prosper in their complex environments. The Apollo Program, which put a man on the moon, involved 400,000 people and 20,000 organizations in the design, manufacture, assembly, and lift-off of more than five-and-a-half million parts, all working together. The Apollo team probably

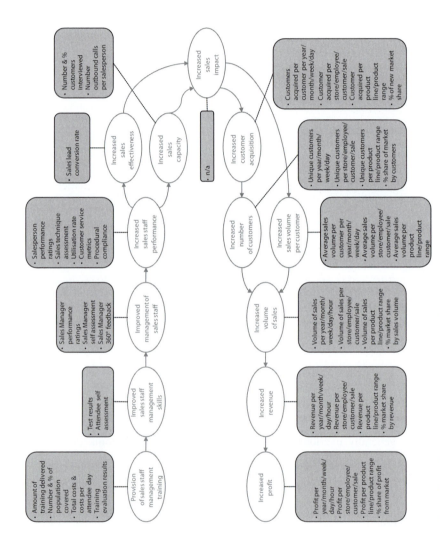

Figure 7.10 Example measures developed for the retailer management training project

Box 7.5 Try it – Identifying performance measures
If you earlier developed a causal chain for a project with which you are familiar, try identifying measures relating to each of the variables in the chain. Try to use measures that would accurately show how these variables changed over time.

applied KISS often – but at the right moments and in the right way. Inherent complexity was managed rather than avoided.

It should be obvious that measures need to be accurate, yet often their design means they are unnecessarily blunt. Two key issues to consider are triangulation and timing.

Careful examination of Figure 7.10 reveals that one variable cannot be measured directly – 'sales impact'. This is because it is an entirely conceptual notion, really intended to enable a distinction between sales effectiveness and sales capacity. Occasionally a variable such as this cannot be measured directly but is measured by 'encircling', by measuring variables either side of it in a causal chain. This technique is known as *triangulation* and is a particularly useful principle when measuring intangible performance variables. Consider, for example, customer service quality. Quality is difficult to define and notoriously so in relation to customers. However, using a cluster of related measures provides a good calibration of customer service quality. Factors typically measured include customer feedback (often using surveys), complaint levels, referrals, and context-specific factors such as call abandon rate. Figure 7.11 shows an example of triangulation to measure customer service in a retail financial services organization. Typically, results from multiple sources such as these are weighted and pulled together into a customer service index. An index of this sort is effectively a manufactured value giving a strong indication of how good customer service is at a given point in time.

The point to note here is that all of the variables shown in Figure 7.11 are either causes or effects of customer service quality. Improving the queuing time or call abandon rate would plausibly improve customer service quality. Conversely, improved customer service would plausibly increase customer satisfaction and referrals, improve mystery-shopping results, and reduce complaints. Indices of this sort rely on causality for their construction, and causal chains thus help to inform their design.

Timing of measurements ought to be led by common sense but, remarkably, often it is ill judged. Annual employee surveys conducted just after Christmas bonuses have been paid are likely to produce warped results (perhaps this common practice is a deliberate tactic!). Training evaluations conducted immediately after training events are never going to provide accurate feedback on actual application of new skills in practice.

Figure 7.11 A cluster of measures to calibrate an intangible performance variable

Similarly, many errors are made with the time horizons over which measures are collected. Using the example of employee opinion surveys again, it is mystifying as to why many organizations should conduct one huge survey every 12 months. Rolling surveys of samples of employees will produce more representative and continually up-to-date data. Similarly, some leaders request updates on sales volumes every few hours. In most circumstances, such short periods can offer absolutely no representative samples of performance data because of uncontrollable pattern variations. Unless these leaders really can act in some way to improve performance in such short timeframes, they are more likely to do harm than good with their perpetual enquiries.

More accurate measures can enhance feedback hugely – making important decisions much better informed ones. They also help with feedforward. Imbalanced measures focus attention and performance assessment too narrowly and encourage self-interested trade-off decisions. If, for example, time to recruit is measured but the quality of candidates is not, it's natural for recruiters to focus on speed at the expense of quality. Targets and rewards, based on such measures, add rocket fuel to the mix and encourage even more ruthless focus on measured variables at all costs. This issue is explored in more detail in Chapter 8.

Developing cost-benefit models

As discussed in Chapter 5, performance measurement is an essential component of the inverted pyramid framework. It provides leaders with *feedback* about an organization's progress toward delivering critical activities, executing strategy, and achieving overall objectives. Indicators of the external environment also enable tracking of barriers/risks and enablers/opportunities. Feedback is crucial to ensure that leaders can:

- monitor the delivery of planned activities;
- evaluate the validity of the causal assumptions used and thus learn more about the organizational systems they are manipulating; and
- initiate corrective action where necessary to improve the probability of strategy execution success

Taking corrective action relies upon being able to predict that an overall objective will not be achieved because performance measures show that intermediate objectives are not being achieved as intended. This reflects the distinction between leading and lagging indicators.

Thus far, we have examined measures in a fairly static fashion. We have examined each performance variable depicted in a chain of cause-and-effect relationships and determined what measures could be used to calibrate each one. Over time, of course, these measures might produce different readings from which we may draw conclusions. However, we can go much further. With a good causal chain developed and set of measures identified for each performance variable within it, it is possible to start exploring the relationships between the measures to create a sophisticated cost-benefit model. Cost-benefit modelling allows both prediction of the impact an activity or project might make and the tracking and evaluation of this impact after implementation.

In terms of predictive modelling, developing a cost-benefit analysis that compares the anticipated benefits of implementation with the costs of implementation is useful to accomplish the following:

- determine whether a project or initiative is worth undertaking at all (Obviously, the benefits of a project or initiative should outweigh the costs of planning and implementing it.);
- prioritize projects or initiatives that compete for scarce resources (optimising resource allocation);
- highlight which activities are the most critical ones required to achieve an objective and so should be favoured in trade-off decisions.

The direct costs of a project or activity are relatively easy to estimate. The potential benefits are more challenging to quantify. A cost-benefit analysis cannot (and should not) attempt to predict *exactly* what the financial impact of a project or initiative will be. This is impossible for several reasons:

- The numerous cause-and-effect hypotheses used in planning may be wrong.
- Measures will always be imperfect.
- Unforeseen risks may materialize, or foreseen ones may be more serious than anticipated.

Despite these challenges, it is almost always possible to place a *reasonably anticipated* quantified value on a project or initiative contingent upon the following:

- explicit assumptions about cause and effect (which can be evidentially based)
- identified measures that can be highly sophisticated, if required
- identified risks
- the notion of 'all other things being equal'.

In other words, in most cases, it should be possible to make a reasonable assessment of the potential impact of a project or initiative based on a model using measured variables and the cause-and-effect relationships between them. This approach puts decision makers in a position to make informed choices based upon a clear understanding of what could happen under particular circumstances. Decision makers can then decide for themselves whether they think the underlying assumptions of the model (and the evidence supporting them) are or are not fair – and even change them to see the impact of their own expectations on the potential outcome of a project.

Moreover, it is possible, once a project or initiative has been implemented and made its impact, to test the assumptions used and determine whether they were accurate.

A causal chain explains *how* an activity might contribute to the achievement of an objective. A cost-benefit analysis can be thought of as using some of the measures identified alongside it to anticipate *how much* an activity might contribute to an objective being achieved. Figure 7.12 shows a simplified example of how a causal chain informs the application of cost-benefit analysis, using key measures from the sales management training example in Figure 7.10.[7]

Table 7.1 shows the calculations summarized in Figure 7.12 in more detail.

Figure 7.12 makes the assumptions underlying the model explicit. If, for example, decision makers do not accept that the improvement of sales staff performance would be as significant, they can make their own assumptions and test how the outcome would be affected.

Using this example, it is extremely unlikely that the next reported profit will be exactly £53,960,000 but, *if* the assumptions are correct and no unforeseen exogenous factors neutralize the impact of the training, we can be reasonably confident that the profit will be around £14m or 35 per cent higher than it would have been had the training not been conducted.

Of course, in many cases there will be evidence to support some of the assumptions. For example, if historical data show that, on average, sales staff who are achieving a 2.75 rating for their behavioural performance (i.e. relating to application of sales techniques, etc. but not reflecting actual sales outputs) do indeed generate three per cent more sales opportunities than average salespeople and convert an extra one per cent of their sales opportunities into sales, it is entirely

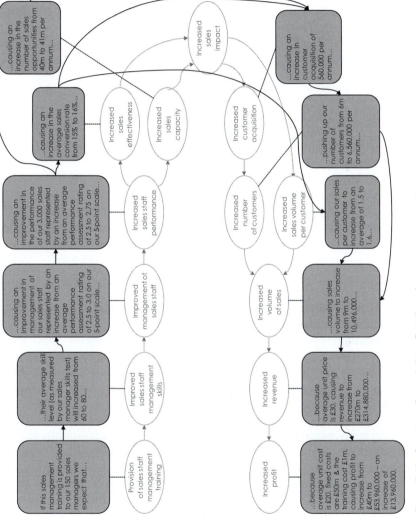

Figure 7.12 Cost-benefit modelling: Retailer sales management training

Table 7.1 Detailed cost-benefit projection: Retailer sales management training

Performance variable	Baseline	Projection	Change	% change
Sales manager skill test average score	60	80	+20	+33%
Sales manager average performance rating	2.50	3.00	+0.50	+20%
Sales staff average performance rating	2.50	2.75	+0.25	+10%
Number of sales opportunities	40,000,000	41,000,000	+1,000,000	+3%
Prospect to customer conversion rate	15.0%	16.0%	+1.0%	+7%
Customers acquired	6,000,000	6,560,000	+ 560,000	+9%
Average sales volume per customer	1.50	1.60	+0.10	+7%
Sales volume	9,000,000	10,496,000	+1,496,000	+17%
Revenue	£270,000,000	£314,880,000	+£44,880,000	+17%
Variable costs	£180,000,000	£209,920,000	+£29,920,000	+17%
Fixed costs	£50,000,000	£50,000,000	–	+0%
Additional sales management training cost	£0	£1,000,000	+£1,000,000	–
Total costs	£230,000,000	£260,920,000	+£30,920,000	+13%
Profit	£40,000,000	£53,960,000	+£13,960,000	+35%

reasonable to expect the anticipated sales volume increases – if salespeople performance increases as expected.

Interestingly, when *planning* an activity, assumptions toward the 'effect' end of the causal chain tend to be associated with high levels of confidence. For instance, we can be quite sure that – all other things being equal (in this case 'other things' being costs) – a specific increase in revenue would lead to a specific increase in profit. Conversely, at the other end of the chain, it is clearly harder to predict the exact nature of the relationship between training provision and skills increases.

Conversely, when *reviewing* the impact of an activity, we can typically be rather confident about the cause-and-effect relationships at the 'cause' end of the chain. Because so few other things affect skills increases, if they measurably go up soon after training is delivered, it's fair to argue that the training was the cause of this effect. However, how confident could we be that it was an increase in sales staff performance that led to higher sales volumes? This clearly can be influenced by many other factors such as demand levels, competition, and so on. Our confidence about the extent of this causal relationship, when analysed *retrospectively*, is low.[8]

See Figure 7.13 for a representation of this contradiction, using a simplified version of the causal chain for the airline's automated check-in facility, originally shown in Figure 7.1. Once again, predictive confidence in the cause-and-effect

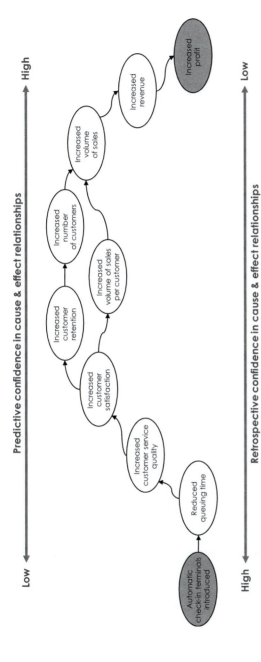

Predictive confidence in cause & effect relationships

Low ←————————————————————→ High

Automatic check-in terminals introduced

Reduced queuing time

Increased customer service quality

Increased customer satisfaction

Increased customer retention

Increased volume of sales per customer

Increased number of customers

Increased volume of sales

Increased revenue

Increased profit

High ←————————————————————→ Low

Retrospective confidence in cause & effect relationships

Figure 7.13 Confidence in cost-benefit modelling: Airline's automated check-in facility

relationships shown is low toward the cause end of the chain and high toward the effect end. It is tricky to predict how much customer service quality will rise given a reduction in queuing time. However, a given increase in volume of sales will, all other things being equal, have a relatively predictable impact on revenues. Conversely, retrospective confidence in the cause-and-effect relationships shown is relatively high toward the cause end and low toward the effect end. A sudden improvement in customer service quality in airports where queuing has suddenly shortened can confidently be assumed to be an outcome caused by the queue reduction. Conversely, it is difficult to be confident about the extent to which any revenue increase may be due to the introduction of the automated check-in facility, because thousands of factors will also indirectly affect revenue.

Hence, the best way to produce useful cost-benefit models is to combine confident *predictions* about causality with confident *retrospective tests* of causality to arrive at confident conclusions about which activities have the greatest impact on primary objectives. Before implementation, we are forced to make assumptions about what will happen if all other things are equal. Naturally, all other things never remain equal but, after implementation, we can test our original assumptions and refine them as necessary to build a model that provides a fairly robust assessment of what has happened, and informs the assumptions that may be used for similar future endeavours. Causal chains provide a context-specific framework to develop cost-benefit projections that are highly transparent, and retrospective reviews that can provide valuable feedback to inform future decisions.

Summary of key points

- Many initiatives that have strategic value and impact emerge 'bottom-up', not having been deterministically planned by senior leaders.
- Emergent strategy can complement deterministic strategizing, the plans from which are made imperfect by bounded rationality, imperfect information, and changing internal/external environments.
- Bottom-up activities can respond to unanticipated problems or opportunities and do not rely upon senior leaders' strategic planning.
- However, there is a risk that activities emerging bottom-up are seen as ends in themselves – for example, delivering project, successfully does not guarantee they are the right projects.
- Managers tend to overestimate the positive impact the activities they undertake will make, so systematic alignment of these activities with overall objectives is important.
- Causal chains, which use the same underlying methods as strategy execution maps, can be used for aligning activities and projects with overall objectives bottom-up – they link activities or the products of projects with overall objectives via a series of cause-and-effect hypotheses.

- Causal chains can depict the logic of implementing projects and other activities to help structure thinking, inform debate with stakeholders, and aid communication of plans.
- Causal chains can be difficult to construct, especially if the true strategic impact of an activity is unclear or questionable.
- Causal chains are useful to articulate how the activities of support functions will plausibly affect overall objectives, because these activities typically affect overall objectives highly indirectly.
- Causal chains inform not only *why* activities should be undertaken but also *how* they should be undertaken, through making explicit intermediate outcomes, which have implications for activity design and implementation.
- Causal chains can help to increase 'line of sight' between individual responsibilities and overall objectives, improving *ad hoc* trade-off decisions, productivity, and motivation.
- There are various problems that managers often encounter when developing causal chains:
  - Lack of strategic logic and clarity
  - Leaps of causal logic (between means and ends)
  - The use of vague and/or ambiguous terminology
  - Confusion between causality and task dependency.
- Most competent leaders and project managers can identify risks that threaten the *implementation* of initiatives and projects.
- However, even perfectly delivered initiatives or projects may suffer from two types of *post-implementation* risk:
  - Failures of intended outcomes – whereby hypothesized causal relationships fail to materialize as expected
  - Negative unintended effects – whereby undesirable side-effects appear alongside intended effects.
- Causal chains are useful for identifying both types of post-implementation risks, thus enabling their proactive management (and usually altering the business case for initiatives and projects as a result).
- Performance measures provide 'feedback' that can inform future decisions and generate 'feedforward' by affecting people's behaviour through focusing attention on particular performance variables.
- It is important to identify both lagging measures (pertaining to ultimate objectives) and more forward-looking leading indicators (pertaining to the activities that plausibly affect ultimate objectives).
- Strategy execution maps are ideal frameworks for developing a hierarchy of leading and lagging performance measures that are appropriate to the unique objectives, strategies, activities, and situations of organizations.
- There are serious risks with adopting prescribed performance measurement frameworks, as these do not necessarily reflect the unique objectives, strategies, activities, and situations of particular organizations.

- Causal chains can also be used to identify measures for all the performance variables affected by an activity, project, or initiative.
- It is important to develop measures that are accurate and balanced – using triangulation where necessary and appropriate time horizons to generate representative data samples.
- Causal chains with associated performance measures can also be used to build cost-benefit models for predicting and retrospectively evaluating the strategic impact of activities, projects, and initiatives.
- Retrospective analysis can be combined with predictive models to enhance assumptions and produce robust cost-benefit evaluations.

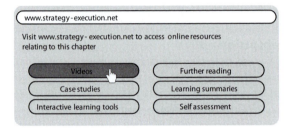

www.strategy-execution.net

Visit www.strategy-execution.net to access online resources relating to this chapter

Videos	Further reading
Case studies	Learning summaries
Interactive learning tools	Self assessment

Chapter 8

Aligning organizational designs and systems

Action is the foundational key to all success.

Pablo Picasso

Organizational life is littered with cynical jokes about leaders tinkering with the designs and systems for which they are responsible while missing the bigger picture. In anxious times, they are accused of 'fiddling while Rome burns' or 'rearranging the deckchairs on the Titanic'. Many such jokes relate to leaders' apparent tendency to change the people in their teams or organizational structures when they start a new job or come under pressure for poor performance. This cynicism is not entirely misplaced; many such organizational changes are high-profile but shallow reactions to short-term pressures, undertaken without clear articulation of how improved performance will result. So how should leaders approach such issues?

Phase 2 of the inverted pyramid framework focuses on aligning organizational designs and systems, dealing with them in a logically sequential order. Of course, this sequencing is slightly idealistic – existing organizations already have processes, structures, capabilities, and so on that constrain options. However, it is still important to think about these issues sequentially to examine and enhance *alignment*.

Phase 1 of the inverted pyramid was concerned with translating the organization's overall objective into critical activities. As we have seen, doing this required some effort, but this hard work is well worthwhile. The critical activities identified are the essential ingredient to ensure that effective decisions can be taken in relation to aligning organizational designs and systems. The organizational designs and systems of key importance to strategy execution are included within phase 2 of the inverted pyramid framework, highlighted in Figure 8.1.

In particular, critical activities can be used to resolve common dilemmas relating to organizational designs and systems. For example, most managers will have been involved in debates about the right degree of centralization or decentralization in their organizations. Those making organizational design decisions often struggle to find the right answer to this dilemma. Naturally, the right answer depends on the context but, in particular, it depends on the nature of the critical activities. Different levels of centralization or decentralization will support or hinder different critical activities. In fact, an examination of critical activities can make the question seem poorly framed. The answer might be that some parts of an organization should be loosely controlled, whereas others need to be dominated by centralized controls.

In most organizational design and systems decisions, there are arguments in favour of different solutions and of trade-offs that must be made between mutually exclusive options. Critical activities help to resolve the dilemmas as the dominant factor that should drive the decision. Specifically, decision makers can frame questions about organizational designs and systems around the five Cs by asking if they will help the following:

- ensure that the critical activities *cause* the strategy to be realized
- maintain focus primarily on the *critical* activities
- ensure *compatibility* between the critical activities
- ensure *continuity* in the execution of the critical activities
- increase *clarity* of the critical activities and the 5Cs.

Organizational designs and systems play a vital role. Just because critical activities have been identified, it cannot be assumed that any of them will actually occur as intended. Inevitably, many people will have had limited or no involvement in shaping critical activities and, therefore, restricted commitment to executing them. Even those intimately involved in the hard intellectual exercise of establishing

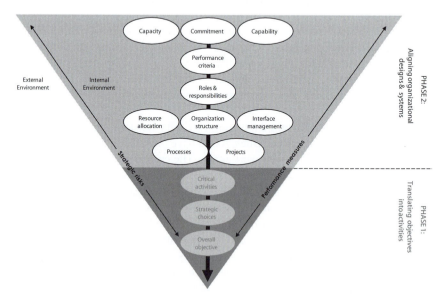

Figure 8.1 Aligning organizational designs and systems highlighted in the inverted pyramid

critical activities will be subject to numerous other pressures and influences. There can be no assumption that the organization will possess the appropriate structure, information, resources, capabilities, or capacity to undertake particular critical activities. Unless managers can align organizational designs and systems with critical activities, they are extremely unlikely to occur.

This job is made much easier by the effective identification of activities. (In contrast with trying to align organizational designs and systems with something as vague as a conceptual strategy – a remarkably common but usually doomed endeavour.) This highlights the importance of putting what was covered in Chapters 6 and 7 into practice properly.

There is some evidence that senior leaders tend to assume that lower parts of organizations will fall into place behind strategies that have been developed. They perhaps assume that systems will be realigned and the tweaks made to ensure that all-important strategies are implemented. However, as we have discussed, many strategies fail, apparently because all kinds of organizational designs and systems are not suited to the demands made of them. Organizational realignment is a complex and difficult challenge.

Chapter 1 made important distinctions between strategy execution and change management – pointing out that important though it is, change management is not necessarily strategic. This chapter starts to move the discussion toward the world of change management but carrying the vital point that it is this alignment to support critical activities that can link change management with strategy – and makes it 'strategic'.

A great deal has been written about change management, and it is not the role of this text to reiterate it. Rather, the proceeding discussion will explore how this alignment with critical activities can be achieved in relation to each of the remaining elements of the inverted pyramid framework. Critical activities, as with all activities, can be undertaken in an organization in two ways – as part of a project or a process. Both are discussed next.

Projects

The value of projects to strategy execution

All organizations undertake projects, regardless of whether they are labelled as such. Informal changes can usefully be thought of as a project. Initiatives are usually projects. Programmes are usually clusters of related projects.

A project can be thought of as a one-off series of related activities, with a defined start and end and performed to achieve a particular objective.

Obviously, this potentially incorporates a wide range of activities, from small and quick exercises through to much more complex, costly, and time-consuming undertakings. Projects are of interest because they are useful containers to manage the delivery of activities. A substantial body of knowledge, tools, and expertise has developed within the project management field, offering a disciplined task execution method.

Projects are also an effective mechanism for overcoming some of the constraints created by the way organization structures tend to operate. Most organizations and the managers in them are victims of 'silo-based' thinking and inter-functional mal-coordination and conflict. However, projects can be run right across structural boundaries, bringing together expertise and resources from many disciplines and subunits. For these reasons, and with some important caveats, project management is an ideal framework to ensure critical activities happen.

What really matters, in relation to strategy execution, is ensuring that the projects an organization undertakes are, first and foremost, oriented toward properly executing critical activities. This is not as a simple as it may sound. Most large and complex organizations are simultaneously undertaking huge numbers of projects – often so many that even counting them is practically impossible. This is typically because many pressures and influences lead to projects arising. As Chapter 4 demonstrated, many initiatives and projects arise almost as if from the ether, because of perceived organizational problems. Performance dips, complaints, risks, and personal frustrations all give rise to reactions that rapidly evolve into projects that then soak up time, money, and resources. Equally, perceived opportunities also create excitement and momentum that can quickly lead to formalized projects. In other words, not all projects result from a systematic process translating strategic objectives into critical activities. Many – and often the substantial majority – arise bottom-up from more evolutionary sources that are typically less carefully controlled. As Chapter 4 also demonstrated, many of these projects, though usually arising from good intentions, are simply the wrong ones – suboptimal responses to poorly framed problems and opportunities.

These bottom-up projects – both 'good' ones and 'bad' ones – inevitably compete with projects determined through the strategy process. Organizations rarely have the resources or physical scope to undertake all proposed projects – they are forced to choose between them. Making selections of this sort is clearly a complex challenge, and insofar as it is not done ideally, suboptimal project selection results, threatening the execution of strategy.

In summary, from a strategy execution perspective, there are two challenges in relation to projects:

- effective screening of emergent projects to ensure alignment with overall objectives

Box 8.1 Project definition
A *project* is a one-off series of related activities with a defined start and end and performed to achieve a particular objective.

- Effective prioritisation of all projects to ensure maximum impact on overall objectives, given available resources.

These issues underlie a distinction that we can draw between project management and strategic project management. Managing a given set of projects effectively is important but a secondary concern to selecting the right projects to manage in the first place. The way in which projects arise and are selected in organizations needs to reflect this subtlety. A consistently applied alignment framework can be enshrined in an organization's project management processes. Exactly how is discussed in the sections that follow.

Doing the right projects

Counter-intuitively, a major challenge facing large and complex organizations is preventing projects from ever happening. More precisely, organizations need to stop in their tracks emerging projects that will contribute little or nothing toward the achievement of overall objectives. This is crucial if limited time, money, and other resources are to be directed toward genuinely critical activities. Building on the insights provided in Chapter 4, a critical issue is if and when an idea or proposal becomes a project. Organizations need to ensure that problems and opportunities that have not been properly diagnosed do not become projects – consuming time, money, and other resources – without reasonable confidence that they are valid means of achieving strategic objectives.

Many project management processes are designed to start being used once a project has actually been conceived; however, this is really too late. By the time related activities are being called a project, they have a well-developed frame of reference and are typically difficult to unwind. Ideally, project management processes should incorporate an early stage that stipulates a requirement for diagnosis of the perceived problem or opportunity. In fact, good project management processes can positively support effective diagnosis by incorporating a quick and simple mechanism for managers to secure the necessary resources to conduct diagnosis properly. Although diagnosis activity can often be done quickly and easily through good thinking and discussion alone, sometimes research or trialling is necessary, and that may require that resources be allocated. This step ensures that projects are the right ones – and done right. Figure 8.2 depicts five stages in a well-designed project management process, incorporating issue recognition and diagnosis ahead of the more conventional stages in a project's lifecycle.

Handling projects at the right level

Another consideration that organizations must make in designing project management processes is which projects are sufficiently significant to be authorized and monitored formally and by whom. Because organizations undertake so many projects and managers have limited time and attention, their focus must be on substantial projects that deliver critical activities or in some other way might significantly affect performance. A 'governance framework' that defines the conditions a project must meet to be worthy of such attention helps ensure that a project management process does not become a pointless bureaucracy. As a rule, the more significant the project, the more senior those approving it should be and the more widely the project's progress should be reported, to ensure it has sufficient visibility. The factors that make a project significant vary from one context to another, but typical criteria include the following:

- strategic impact
- budgetary requirements
- length of schedule
- level of risk foreseen
- level of cross-functional/divisional cooperation required
- extent of dependence on external sources
- seniority level of key stakeholders/project sponsorship
- extent that other projects/subunits depend on project delivery.

Broadly speaking, the higher each of the foregoing, the more significant a project is and more intensely it should be examined before approval and tracked when underway.

Enshrining strategic alignment in project processes

As well as omitting a diagnosis stage, many project management processes also are deficient in terms of their focus on strategic impact. As already discussed, project management processes typically reflect the concern to deliver projects within planned timescales, budget, and specifications. The governance mechanisms and documents used for projects are typically light on the issue strategic impact. Usually, there is a requirement to consider objectives, and these are listed, but often they reflect more closely the products of a project (i.e. the physical changes introduced by the project) or highly specific outcomes that are not explicitly

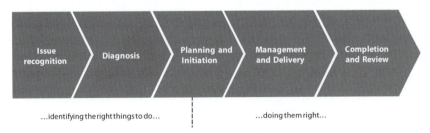

Figure 8.2 Diagnosis as an early stage in the project management process

related to strategic or overall objectives. This is unsurprising, given the challenges in aligning activities with strategy discussed in detail already. An obvious potential improvement to most project management processes is the inclusion of causal chains of the sort introduced in Chapter 7. These clearly tie the products of projects to overall objectives and, of course, enable post-implementation risk identification and support both performance measurement and cost-benefit modelling – all important steps in the project planning cycle.

Embedding project products

There are many other areas in which project management can generally be improved to help bring about change more effectively and reliably. One last area deserves mention here because of its relevance to strategy execution success – the embedding of project products. As Chapter 4 made clear, it is easy for organizations to slip into reinforcing cycles of symptomatic problem solving that do not tackle underlying causes of problems and then go on to continue constraining performance. This often happens when projects are used to create temporary performance improvements though their products are not embedded for a lasting impact.

An example makes the point well. Several of the organizations I have worked with have suffered from high levels of absenteeism among particular groups of employees. Absenteeism has a significant impact on performance through generating significant costs and constraining revenue generation. When absenteeism has risen particularly high, these organizations have launched projects aimed at reducing it. Analysis is conducted, managers are trained in managing the problem, long-term absenteeism cases are reviewed thoroughly, and policies are enforced more tightly. The result is usually a fairly substantial reduction in absence, with a corresponding improvement in operational and financial performance. However, the benefits are typically short-lived. Once the project is completed and project team disbanded, the spotlight shifts elsewhere and, before long, absenteeism rises again. Eventually, it peaks at an unacceptably high level, and a new project is launched to tackle the issue again. Those with reasonable tenure in relevant roles can testify that these organizations go through a seemingly never-ending cycle of sorting the problem and then seeing it reappear a year or two later.

This pattern, observable in all kinds of organizational areas, is dysfunctional. Projects are not efficient vehicles for what should be ongoing activities – they are inherently disruptive and costly and are best used judiciously. Though projects may be ideal for analysing problems and developing solutions, these solutions can be embedded such that they continue to function once the project is complete. The products of many projects can to be embedded as efficiently managed ongoing activities. Hence, we shortly turn to the next element of the inverted pyramid framework – processes.

Problems with projects

It is important to acknowledge that projects are not a panacea – they have downsides. Projects are inherently disruptive, pulling people away from primary roles and interrupting smoother-running processes. Project teams take time to become productive, often having to overcome different perspectives and sometimes conflict. Not all organizations are good at enabling and supporting projects, often failing to resource them effectively and in a timely fashion. If projects are not governed well, they can run too long or not deliver positive long-term effects.

From the perspectives of those working heavily in projects, life can be difficult. Comfort with ambiguity and uncertainty are prerequisites for such roles. When projects come to an end, there is rarely the certainty of an appropriate role being vacant for all those looking for one. Career paths for project managers are sometimes vague and active career development support limited. Some organizations do not develop project management capabilities actively and are content to rely on project managers' looking after themselves (which they often do quite well!).

Processes

The role of processes

A process is a series of related activities that is repeatedly undertaken to generate a specific output. In an organizational context, such outputs could include anything from finished products to the production of invoices or the selection of a new recruitment candidate. All organizations of every size and shape use processes – they are formed, however informally, when sequences of activities are repeated to create something. That is not to say that all processes are the right ones or are performed effectively and efficiently.

Processes are important for strategy execution because some critical activities are ongoing – they need to be performed repeatedly for the foreseeable future. Let's take the example of a low-cost airline that relies upon fast turnaround of aircraft on stand at airport terminals, to maximize aircraft utilization and maintain a reliable schedule for passengers. Cleaning the aircraft properly but quickly is a critical activity – an essential means by which the airline's overall objective will be achieved. Selecting the best way to clean aircraft (e.g. training the cabin crew to do it, rather than using external suppliers), designing an efficient cleaning method, and establishing how to supply cleaning materials might all be within the scope of a project. However, once established, cleaning becomes a process (albeit a critical process) – repeated for every aircraft on every stand for the foreseeable future.

Like projects, processes have some advantageous features. They can run across organizational subunits and help to counter the tendency toward silo-thinking and inter-functional conflict. Processes inherently join together for the purposes of analysis and design sets of related activities that, if undertaken in isolation, may contribute little. Most people with experience of organizations will know of amusing or alarming examples of process dysfunction because effective analysis and design have not occurred. It is not uncommon for senior leaders to remain blissfully unaware of dysfunctional processes as their juniors struggle to find 'workarounds' or put up with poor performance, unable or unmotivated to see how improvements can be made.

Process design and improvement

Process design and redesign are vital and probably underrated as capabilities. Perhaps too many managers see process design as a commoditized function, safely left to armies of junior staff or short-term contractors. Given the performance implications of activities that are being repeated regularly, it seems unwise to leave good process design in part to chance. The operational performance of organizations that rely firmly on slick processes underlines the opportunity to improve things. In particular, technology-based businesses such as Amazon, Dell, and eBay offer an insight into how well-devised processes can produce a low-cost base, a product offering hugely attractive to many consumers and (usually) seamless customer experiences.

One of the other effects of the rather inattentive attitude some leaders have towards processes is that even important processes can have low visibility in organizations. At a minimum, core processes might be identified and listed so all important stakeholders can recognize them and how they fit together. Ideally, they should also be carefully mapped. Mapping processes has various potential advantages:

- Processes can be identified clearly (more so than only having been named).
- Processes can be analysed in detail to support their enhancement.
- Relationships between processes can be identified – particularly dependencies and impact between them.
- Important stakeholders can both be identified and acknowledge themselves.

Box 8.2 Mobile network process failure
A researcher was recently examining customer-facing processes at a major mobile phone network operator. She ordered a new handset successfully but, shortly after it arrived, found her account had been blocked and she could make no phone calls. Upon calling customer services, a quick investigation revealed that the account had been blocked because the cost of the new phone, which was charged to the account, had caused the account balance to exceed the approved credit limit. The researcher asked if this was a common problem. The customer services agent explained, "It happens all the time."

- The impact of other organizational changes (e.g. restructuring) on processes is more easily established and thus better managed.
- Mapping is an important step toward automation or computerisation, if this is viable and attractive.
- The skills necessary not just for undertaking activities but also managing related activities effectively can more readily be identified and developed.
- Risks related to processes can more easily be identified.

In recent decades, a series of approaches to improving processes and related operations have appeared, including:

- enterprise resource planning (ERP)
- total quality management (TQM)
- business process re-engineering (BPR)
- lean management
- Six Sigma

Each of these approaches shares many commonalities but offers different philosophies and methods to improve process-based operations. As operations management expert Nigel Slack notes, each approach is more or less appropriate under different circumstances – depending, for example, on the speed of change sought and whether a prescriptive or facilitative approach is preferable.[1]

Integrating process design

From a strategy execution perspective, it is certainly preferable to take an *integrated* approach to the development and refinement of processes. Unnecessary organizational complexity is the enemy of successful strategy execution, and perpetually adding and changing business processes in an isolated fashion usually adds to this complexity. In many organizations, including some of those studied in my own research, there is a tendency to tackle problems and pursue opportunities through 'bolt-on' developments. For example, recognition of inadequate risk management may lead to the creation of a dedicated risk management function, or a wish to exploit the Internet as a channel might lead to the development of a new 'online' division. Bolting on new parts to an organization can give the sense of rapid progress in developing new capabilities. Sometimes this is fine, but often such progress comes at the cost of leaving behind the other parts of the organization and the processes managed by them. Risk is a good example of an issue that usually has to be managed in an integrated fashion by many stakeholders in an organization. Lots of existing processes need to be designed with risk in mind, and it is, therefore, difficult and unsustainable to compartmentalize risk management. This problem closely reflects the findings from my research reported in Chapter 6, whereby many developed strategies relate to planned changes only – and are not integrated with existing business models.

Box 8.3 Process feedback in outsourced HR

A large manufacturing company recently decided to outsource all its administrative HR activities – including processes such as payroll, volume recruitment, training administration, and so on. A great deal of time and money had been spent analysing processes, determining requirements, selecting a lead supplier, forming service-level agreements, migrating activities and staff to the supplier, and communicating changes to employees using the services. The head of department responsible for the project proudly told the story to a researcher, who asked about what kind of management information the supplier was producing as a result of managing all the services. The worrying answer was, "Well ... I suppose we can get whatever we want ... but we'd have to pay for it ..."

Feedback from processes

A final major concern about processes, from a strategy execution perspective, is to ensure that they are designed in such a way as to generate useful feedback. Processes can produce vitally important performance measures that help to inform whether the causal hypotheses baked into strategies and their breakdown are valid. However, often measures are easy to generate if considered early on in process design and difficult to produce once processes are established. This has become more of an issue with increased process automation and computerization. Countless business analysts have come to regret not asking managers about the measures they would like IT systems to produce at the planning phase. Systems that automate workflow but do not provide meaningful management information are really only half complete (see Box 8.3).

Organization structure

The basics of structure

As was discussed at the beginning of this chapter, leaders like changing organization structures. In most large organizations, structure changes are common – especially after the arrival of new leaders and when performance is suffering. There seems to be a common assumption that structural changes can improve organizational performance – that if a particular structure isn't really delivering the goods, moving to its logical alternative will do the trick. Some organizations and subunits seem to bounce between one structural model and another over the years, never really finding out how to make either work but causing a great deal of turmoil with every change.

Very small organizations need little formal structure. However, larger organizations normally need hierarchies of leaders acting as 'span-breakers' to facilitate decision making and general management. Operational complexity also necessitates more complex structures. A business with more products, operating in different geographies, using different channels, and serving different customer groups is more likely to see sense in having separate structural units focused on these different aspects, each of which requires leaders and hierarchies themselves.

Organization structures can be thought of as modules arranged in a particular way. The modules may be focused on the following:

- functions (based on a technical specialty)
- products/services
- channels (for communication, sales, and distribution)
- markets/segments (based on a geography or customer type/need).

In large organizations, such modules with a functional focus are typically known simply as *functions*. Modules with a focus on products/services, channels, or markets/segments may be called *divisions*. All these modules reflect the nature of strategy discussed in Chapter 2 – functions representing resource-based interactions and the remaining three reflecting market-based interactions.

These modules can be configured in many different ways. An organization might be made up of both divisions and functions operating in a 'matrix' structure. Divisions may sub divide into functions. Both divisions and functions may sub-divide into smaller subunits such as departments and teams.

More complex decisions arise for leaders making structural decisions when there is the possibility of duplications appearing. For example, if two divisions need to undertake marketing activities, should they do this independently, share some level of resources, or both be served by a centralized marketing function? Independence fosters absolute focus on specific products/services, channels, or markets/segments and is likely to maximize market orientation. Centralization fosters focus on internal activities and is likely to maximize efficiency through increased task specialization and economies of scale.

These relationships are not hard and fast. There are many ways to increase market orientation or efficiency besides using conventional structural configurations, though particular choices are likely to make certain outcomes more probable. Therefore, structure choices need to be driven by a detailed examination of context and objectives.

Small and simple businesses are unlikely to need complex structures.[2] Those with only one product line, serving only one market through one channel, are likely to find a functional structure adequate. Conversely, those with lots of different products in many materially different markets and using multiple channels will likely need a more market-orientated structure. Most large organizations lie somewhere between these two extremes, making the choice a more balanced one.

Box 8.4 A different approach to organization structure at Gore[3]

Not all organizations approach structure in conventional ways. Privately held firm W. L. Gore & Associates designs and manufactures a wide range of products, from clothing and fabrics to medical devices and guitar strings. Almost all of its thousands of products are based on expanded polytetrafluoroethylene, a polymer discovered by Bob Gore in 1969.

Gore is famously unusual in the way it is organized. Since it was founded, it has deliberately retained a very flat structure to encourage individual employees to act creatively. The firm does not issue traditional organizational charts and has no conventional command hierarchy or even formal communication channels. It values informality, trust, and direct communication. Gore does not have employees but rather appoints 'Associates' who all become part-owners in the business through the company's Associate Stock Ownership Plan.

Gore relies on Associates and the multi-disciplinary project teams within which they work to manage themselves and coordinate with others in the business as they see fit. The company sees this flexible and empowering approach as being essential to nurture creativity and create the kind of environment in which Associates will thrive, enjoy their work, and choose to stay. The company recruits Associates for broad areas of work and relies upon their Sponsors (Gore does not have line managers or bosses in a conventional sense) to guide them in their work. Rather than select individuals for promotion, the firm allows leaders to emerge naturally, as Associates choose those who inspire them and follow their ideas and suggestions.

Gore's unusual structure does, it seems, successfully drive innovation. The company has been awarded more than 2,000 patents worldwide and has annual revenues of more than $200m and over 8,000 Associates.[4] It is perhaps important to note that Gore's structure and the way it works is not an emergent phenomenon – it is carefully maintained through deliberate decisions about what is important for success.

Determinants of structure

It is obvious that strategic choices about products, markets, and channels naturally affect structure choices. So, too, do decisions about strategic positioning (drawing upon the discussion in Chapter 6). Organizations adopting differentiated strategic positions are more likely to benefit from market orientation and likely to tend toward divisional structures. Conversely, low-cost competitors need high levels of efficiency and are more likely to pursue specialization and economies of scale through functional structures.

If an organization does determine that a divisional structure is preferable to a predominantly functional one, it must of course select an appropriate product/service, market/segment or channel focus. These are not always mutually exclusive options. For example, some products are so heavily adapted for different markets that a natural division along both product and market lines is logical. In addition, divisions can, of course, be subdivided for a secondary purpose besides function – though this is likely to further reduce scope for efficiencies. For example, a large multinational business may have a North American division with consumer, small business, and corporate subdivisions.

When such levels of complexity are reached, many organizations opt for a matrix structure. In a matrix structure, functions and divisions typically hold roughly equal status, with their leaders represented at the same levels. Functions may be fully or partially centralized to pursue specialization and economies of scale, whereas divisions are orientated toward their respective product/service, market/segment, channel, or combinations of these. Inevitably, matrix structures are complex and have a reputation for being difficult to manage effectively. However, as the world's largest organizations have grown bigger and expanded into new markets, launched many new products, and adopted new channels, matrix structures have become more necessary. It seems that with the right integrating mechanisms, they can be made to work reasonably well where circumstances require it.

From a strategy execution perspective, the critical consideration when selecting an organization structure is how it will adequately ensure that critical activities are undertaken as intended. Critical activities are a more-refined unit of analysis than strategic positions for informing structure decisions. If the majority of critical activities are oriented toward securing efficiencies, a functional structure may be more suitable. Conversely, if critical activities reveal the need for an organization to compete via the best products or tightest segment-focus or leadership using a channel such as the Internet, a particular divisional form may be ideal. The devil of such decisions lies in the detail, and critical activities can perhaps provide that detail much more reliably than broad strategic positions or rules of thumb about organization structure.

Perhaps just as important, the obsession that many leaders have with organization structure is probably unwarranted. Organization structure decisions can be quite finely balanced, so adopting structural configurations that are broadly appropriate to critical activities is probably an adequate first step. The really important (and often relatively ignored) next step is making these structures work well. Well-defined projects and processes help structures to work. So, too, do well-designed resource allocation systems and the effective management of interfaces, each of which are discussed next.

Resource allocation

The prioritization imperative

In organizations, resources include a wide variety of entities that can be used or help to undertake activities and produce outputs. Obvious examples include people, finances, materials, equipment, information, intellectual property, and other legal rights.[5] No activities can be undertaken without some level of resources; even the most automated processes need to be developed, supervised, and maintained. Leaders exercise huge influence via their power to allocate resources – they enable or disable the performance of activities through determining when and where particular resources are deployed.

The effective and efficient allocation of resources is rarely easy. Demand for resources is typically much higher than their supply. Few organizations are short of things to do, with an endless series of activities identifiable that might just help to achieve overall objectives. Similarly, it is rare that an individual manager reports he or she has enough resources or is even willing to give some up. Managers often want to grow their roles in their organizations – after all, who would tell their bosses there is no need to improve things? Managers also tend to overstate the resources required to undertake any given activity when negotiating resource allocations with their superiors. Naturally enough, they are keen to secure a contingency or 'cushion' to make certain they will deliver desired performance (especially if stretching targets have been set). These pressures mean that senior managers must have effective means of prioritizing resources. They ideally need to concentrate resources on undertaking activities that will result in the greatest impact on their organizations' overall objectives. Various challenges exist to achieving this.

First, these senior managers have to know which activities will plausibly create the most attractive outcomes. Of course, this is where many of the tools we examined in Chapters 6 and 7 are useful. If critical activities are being systematically tackled via projects and embedded via processes, this is a great start. However, such rigour is rare, and other factors can mean that even critical activities are not resourced properly. As Chapter 4 showed, proposals for initiatives emerge continuously as a result of perceived problems, apparent opportunities, and new ideas. Some of these proposals will be valid ways of achieving overall objectives – perhaps even superior to critical activities identified as part of a systematic strategy breakdown. However, emergent activities are rarely as well planned and articulated, and many are in fact products of symptom-focused problem solving. Organizations need to ensure that ideas emerging outside the strategy process are still evaluated carefully, not least to support prioritization and optimal resource allocation.

The influence of time horizons

A related issue for many organizations is that of time horizons. One of the challenges of aligning activities with overall objectives is that many activities can plausibly affect overall objectives but over markedly different time horizons. For example, drastically reducing prices may attract many new customers, increasing sales volume, revenue, and (perhaps, depending on cost structures) short-term profit. However, in the longer term, aggressive price competition may lead to competitive reactions that reduce returns for industry players. In the long run, steady investments in product quality and brand development may be options superior to price cutting. In other words, the time horizon over which leaders assess investment options radically affects how they may be valued, correspondingly prioritized, and thus resourced. Various pressures can make managers aim for quick wins at the expense of longer-term sustainability, and these are discussed in depth later.

Regardless of such pressures, all managers must balance apparently urgent challenges with important longer-term agendas. Focus too much on solving today's problems and managers get swallowed-up by the minutiae of tiny details; ignore today in favour of blue-sky thinking about the really important long-term issues and there is a risk of operational breakdown. These dilemmas directly affect resource allocation decisions and explain why knowing what the critical activities are is not all that is needed for wise resource decisions. Organizations and the managers in them are quite good at dealing with these dilemmas when they are clearly identified. Where they are not, managers often make decisions with best intentions but get the balances wrong.

Resourcing projects and operational processes

Obviously, resources can be allocated both to projects and ongoing processes bound up in day-to-day operations. With well-designed project management processes such as those described earlier, the allocation of resources to projects can be dealt with relatively simply. Where causal chains are used to tighten alignment between projects and objectives, identify risks, establish measures, and build cost-benefit models, the prioritisation exercise needed to make resource allocation decisions is a relatively small additional step.

Allocating resources to the operational subunits that undertake ongoing processes is made simpler by the fact that processes are repeated and therefore easier to analyse than projects. However, these operational subunits also conduct some non-critical activities, which are not worthy of the sophisticated cost-benefit analysis that supports optimal resource allocation. This inevitably leads organizations into difficult decisions about how to analyse and manage overheads that are not explicitly tied to critical activities. It is certainly not a simple matter of allocating resources on a proportional basis. For example, in many business, facilities management subunits will be responsible for few if any critical activities but, by necessity, will typically manage huge budgets relating to buildings and physical assets. The good news is that tricky though these decisions are to 'optimize', they don't matter nearly as much as decisions about critical activities and are likely to have much less influence on long-term organizational success. It is important that employees get mobile phones to help communication and that buildings offer a pleasant work environment. However, within reasonably easily achieved parameters, performance in delivering these will not strongly affect overall objectives unless for some special reason they are critical activities.

Additionally, of course, senior managers must make choices between projects and ongoing processes. Despite some of the sophisticated techniques we have introduced that support prioritisation, comparing projects and processes and trying to estimate the relative value of investing in each remains awkward. Once again, time horizons become important – processes keep production levels and quality up within established parameters, whereas projects may fundamentally change the organization, its processes, and these parameters. Knowing what level of change is necessary comes from good strategy development and breakdown into critical activities – and is probably reliant on a fair bit of subjective assessment.

Natural selection via resource allocation

When organizations get resource allocation right, they create intelligent feedback systems that naturally encourage and support positive activities that are planned effectively and plausibly help achieve overall objectives. Leaders and organizational subunits that approach the challenge of aligning activities with strategic objectives intelligently and demonstrate the capability to manage the five Cs effectively benefit from being allocated greater resources – and thus can make greater progress with activities and justify undertaking more of them to build upon successes. Conversely, areas that cannot demonstrate that their activities deliver results are prone to shrink and do less. This process, akin to natural selection, is an attractive outcome in that it leads to a certain level of passive evolution without managers having to place big bets on which parts of the organization deserve to live or die. It is perhaps a rarer but more sensible approach to re-shaping organizations than deliberate and speedy structural changes that can cause so much disruption and might achieve little.

This kind of approach can be an attractive option in cases situations in which entrenched organizational problems, perhaps rooted in leadership and cultural inflexibility, make positive changes seemingly impossible to generate. Some organizations inevitably become so technically and socially complex that they cannot respond effectively to their environments. In the private sector, these businesses usually suffer fairly swift deaths unless operating in some peculiar monopolistic or oligopolistic situation. However, in the public sector, such problems are perhaps more common. Politicians and senior public administrators must take the decision about whether it is worth trying to change the way some organizations operate or instead progressively reduce the resource allocations made to them while switching responsibility for particular activities to other better performing agencies or brand new organizations that do not have the same 'baggage'.

Sharing resources

In a similar vein, senior managers can sometime use resource allocation to encourage (or perhaps force) better inter-functional and cross-divisional coordination. The surge toward developing shared service centres that centralize similar processing for support functions (such as human resources and finance) demonstrates this resource sharing in action.

Making subunits share resources and associated objectives necessarily draws them together. Conflict may (and often does) result, but if it can be overcome, bonds can develop that improve the interfaces between structural subunits. The next section focuses explicitly on this issue.

Interface management

Overcoming structural limitations

Fans of *Star Trek* will be familiar with the terror that is the 'Borg' – a group of cybernetic humanoid drones that use their 'hive mind' to act as a 'collective' without the need for communication. In the fictional space adventure, the Borg think as one organism and thus adapt incredibly quickly to their environment, making them a formidable adversary for Captain Jean-Luc Picard and other *Star Trek* heroes. No organization is like the Borg in its ability to 'think as one', but this ability would really help with strategy execution. Organizations need to operate as a 'collective'.

Box 8.5 Resource allocation through strategic commissioning
In the last few years, the UK government has introduced to public sector agencies the notion of 'strategic commissioning' in an attempt to improve the impact they make. Strategic commissioning aims to change how public sector agencies work and responds to the following problems:

- Citizens do not see divisions between government agencies as important or easy to understand. They thus become frustrated when the agency responsible for a particular issue cannot readily be identified.
- Citizens are frustrated at having to 'join up' government because agencies do not share information effectively, and treat them as individual customers.

- Many problems are highly interrelated and cannot be solved by one agency working alone – for example, poor health may be caused as much by poor housing and poverty as it is caused by inadequate access to health care advice and services.

To tackle these problems and discourage public-sector agencies from working in isolation, the government first initiated various partnerships structures that essentially acted as forums for public service providers to get together and determine how to act in concert – particularly in areas in which there was significant deprivation caused by interrelated social problems. These partnerships relied heavily upon the energy and commitment of agencies to pull together. Although special funding was available in severely deprived areas to support initiatives, many of these partnerships struggled to make substantial progress because the bulk of local government finance was still provided to individual agencies.

With strategic commissioning, the government started to formalize the partnership approach for a much wider range of public services – and associated budgets. Strategic commissioning requires agencies to follow a logical decision-making process that does not respect historical agency distinctions. It requires decision makers to:

- explicitly focus on the real needs of 'end customers' (citizens) and develop detailed definitions of their needs – based on good evidence rather than assumptions;
- design the solutions/services required – orienting them to have an impact on outcomes (not outputs);
- stay focused on a limited number of critical priorities – to ensure efforts are not spread too thinly to be successful;
- procure the solutions/services – internally or externally and from the most appropriate provider, whether or not that is a public sector agency; and
- ensure solutions can be mainstreamed and are sustainable and are good value.

These changes have significant implications. Decision makers now must demonstrate that proposed solutions will plausibly cause their objectives to be achieved. They also must appoint the best-placed providers to deliver solutions, without regard for convention or what some agencies might traditionally see as their 'territory'. Also, because the solution comes first (not the agency or its strategy) citizens' needs will often have to be met by multiple agencies working in partnership.

Special agreements have been formed through which central government can effectively incentivize public service providers to work effectively together – and punish them if they fail to do so. These are formal multi-year contracts between agencies and central government. They require the identification of problems and the development of plans to tackle these problems. Central government funding is provided if satisfactory cases are made to show how this money will be spent and how it will make a difference. Partners must show how they will work together and agree to achieve stretching targets to secure funding. Significant funding penalties are expected when targets are not met.

As discussed earlier, all but the smallest of organizations need some structural subunits to avoid being an uncontrollable mass of people with no chains of authority. However, as soon as any given structure is chosen in pursuit of its advantages, certain disadvantages of that structure also arise. Hence, functional organizations may be efficient but not customer-oriented. The divisions of geographically segmented business may understand their markets well but have unwieldy, inefficient, and uncoordinated operations that undermine the value of their common parentage. Interface management is the primary mechanism through which organizations can seek to compensate for the disadvantages of any given structure and seek to make whatever structural model they have chosen work as well as possible. For organizations to act as much like one organism as possible, the people and groups of people within them must communicate information and coordinate their actions effectively.

Of course, much of what has been covered in previous chapters is relevant here. Clear overall objectives are important, as is the use of tools such as strategy execution maps and causal chains that articulate plausible means by which these objectives will be met. These tools help with causality by linking actions and outcomes with criticality by focusing on the actions that matter most and with compatibility by enabling checking across critical activities to ensure they work well together. Interface management is particularly important for the other two Cs – continuity and clarity.

Continuity can be thought of as the link between a strategy execution map on paper and the actual division of labour to undertake the critical activities within the structure. Because many critical activities need more than one part of the organization to cooperate and act in unison, it is vital that the interfaces between these areas are managed well.

Clarity is also ensured by active management of the links between structural subunits. As was discussed earlier, in large and complex organizations, it is not always possible to have one unifying strategy execution map. Often, there are simply too many markets, products, channels, and subunits in the organization for them to logically articulate how their activities relate using a tool such as a strategy execution map. A web of maps may be necessary, explaining the business models for different 'units of analysis'. Even without such complexity, the detailed planning of activities and projects necessitates planning and articulation of ideas that cannot be crammed onto a shared strategy execution map. Subunits must share this information to properly understand everyone's objectives and activities.

Stakeholder management

A good starting point for any subunit is to actively consider stakeholders. Stakeholders can be identified and analysed for any unit of analysis – a task, a process, a project, a programme, or any organizational subunit. What is important is that the unit of analysis is clearly articulated. Care when defining the unit of analysis is important. For example, there may be major differences in the stakeholders who should be considered if one is concerned with a project having its intended outcome rather than simply delivering it successfully. For an organizational subunit, it usually makes sense to think about stakeholders relevant to the successful achievement of the subunit's overall objective.

With the unit of analysis as the starting point, it is useful to think about stakeholders widely. Hence, we can define a stakeholder as any individual or group who, now or in the future, is important to the achievement of objectives. It is worth bearing in mind that some stakeholders become important by virtue of their own interest in these objectives or their means of achievement – as interested stakeholders may interfere in activities, even if their involvement is not deemed necessary.

With these caveats, most subunits will be able to identify their stakeholders relatively easily, perhaps using the following tactics:

- Review the organization chart and similar documentation.
- Invite colleagues to give suggestions.
- Invite each stakeholder to identify others.
- Enable stakeholder self-selection by inviting 'notes of interest'.
- Ask experts to advise on relevant stakeholders – especially in new situations.
- Conduct or examine relevant research to uncover stakeholders.
- Check records of stakeholders for similar situations.
- Identify logical groups of stakeholders and then individual stakeholders within the groups.

Although stakeholder identification is the first step in the stakeholder management process, it is never entirely complete in that new stakeholders often emerge over time. Any subunit should revisit its stakeholder identification work at least every 6 or 12 months to ensure it is up to date.

With stakeholders identified, a common second step is analysis and mapping. Various criteria are commonly used to map stakeholders, such as level of interest

> *Box 8.6* Stakeholder definition
> A *stakeholder* is any individual or group who, now or in the future, is important to the achievement of objectives.

(in the unit of analysis), level of power to influence (the unit of analysis – not necessarily equivalent to general organizational power), and predictability.[6] Stakeholders can readily be mapped against these dimensions using simple graphs. Such exercises are useful, particularly when done in a diverse group setting, in which many views and perspectives can be shared. However, stakeholder mapping is most useful because it typically triggers intense debate about *why* stakeholders vary in terms of their interest, power, and predictability in relation to the unit of analysis. It is often this discussion (rather than the eventual maps) that is of greatest value – and capturing the logic of mapping decisions is crucial (but often missed in favour of focusing on the simple stakeholder maps). Specifically, the differences between a stakeholder's default position in relation to a subunit and the subunit's preferred position of the stakeholder should be examined. It is this that leads purposefully from analysis, which can be rather conceptual, to specific actions that can be undertaken to better manage stakeholders. As with strategy in general, analysis is of use only insofar as it is translated into action (or deliberate maintenance of the status quo). Subunits conducting systematic stakeholder analysis typically identify new stakeholders they had not properly considered before, establish numerous activities (many of them quick and resource-light) that will plausibly manage stakeholders much more effectively, and materially aid the achievement of their overall objectives. Many managers will claim to be brilliant stakeholder managers 'in their heads' – never having actually conducted a systematic exercise as described – but my experience is that they almost always gain useful new insights when working with a group of colleagues in this way.

A related and also useful analytical approach is to examine alignment between stakeholders – particularly individuals or subunits that need to work closely together. This is helpful when evaluating continuity and clarity – both elements of the five 5Cs. Examinations of stakeholder alignment can centre on any issue, provided it is broken down meaningfully. Table 8.1 shows a stakeholder alignment analysis matrix for a local government agency. It examines five key stakeholders (the members of the executive management team) using key elements drawn from the inverted pyramid. It highlights important differences in the perspectives of the five individuals and points to likely conflicts with the way they manage their parts of the organization. People watching leaders in organizations are usually highly sensitive to differences between them – picking up the nuances of their language and signals given through focusing on particular issues. Senior managers can expect employees to be disheartened by such misalignments and perhaps to exploit them too. Various differences in perspective are made clear by the analysis in Table 8.1, and such differences helps explain divergent behaviour in teams that need to cooperate.

This kind of analysis can be performed for any group where sufficient qualitative information can be gathered – for example, via interviews – to populate a similar matrix within meaningful data. The implications for actions managing stakeholders are often numerous and, depending on the context, might include challenging the group involved to explore and resolve different perspectives.

Communication

Many stakeholder management actions identified relate to communication. It seems that internal communication is rarely adequate in organizations and leads to all sorts of problems. Indeed, in the *Economist Intelligence Unit* survey mentioned in Chapter 1, communication was ranked as the most significant strategy execution barrier. Once again, subunits can rely heavily upon tools such as strategy execution maps and causal chains to enhance their critical communications about overall objectives and means of achievement. It is particularly important that stakeholders understand how subunits add value, the critical activities they undertake, and how the activities of subunits fit together within the broader organization.

Participation

Communication between subunits can be substantially enhanced by the involvement and participation of subunits in the activities of others. At a basic level, this might mean inviting colleagues from other departments and functions to relevant meetings and events. More proactive involvement can take the form of dedicated partnerships to plan and implement specific changes and projects. In the subunits of many organizations, involving 'outsiders' is something managers naturally shy away from doing. There is often a sense that it will complicate things and slow down progress. However, the research suggests effective involvement of stakeholders can often lead to greater success in the longer-term. Not only are the additional perspectives provided invaluable but stakeholder resistance is typically much reduced where involvement has been high.

Reporting

It is tempting to think of reporting as something that should happen only 'upward' toward higher authorities. This is a dangerous mindset, discouraging the sharing of information horizontally in an organization structure. It's really important for subunits to share plans, activities, and performance reporting. Besides general information sharing, it is in the interests of any subunit to systematically exchange information relating to two key things – 'upstream' dependencies and 'downstream' impact. Dependencies and impacts arise in project and process management – essentially, they are important wherever cooperation is important

Table 8.1 Stakeholder alignment analysis matrix

Framework elements	Chief Executive Officer	HR Director	Finance Director	Operations Director	Legal Director
Overall objectives	To improve quality of life for citizens and visitors in our area	To be recognized as the best Local Agency in the region	To provide value-for-money public services	To provide an efficient and effective service portfolio	To meet statutory obligations to provide effective services
Key environmental pressures	• Increasing population • Unemployment amongst unskilled citizens • Poor road transport network	• Cultural disharmony in population • Competition for quality staff	• Infinite demand for services • Maintaining control of costs • Effective portfolio management of capital projects	• Geographic dispersal of population • Lack of systems integration	• Central government interference • Patchy internal control systems
Strategic choices	• Focus on nurturing education • Focus on enabling employment	• To build organizational capability to support education and employment	• Nurturing employment and tourism to increase wealth	• Lean thinking • Operational effectiveness • Systems integration	• Holistic approach to health, wealth and social issues
Strategic performance measures	• Quality of life index • Unemployment rate • Educational attainment	• Staff satisfaction • Time to fill vacancies	• Debt control • Financial audit rating	• Customer service index • Efficiency metrics	• Strategic risk audit • Outstanding claims

to undertake a task *or* a series of related tasks. Upstream dependencies arise where one subunit relies upon another for input – perhaps information or a finished product of some sort. Downstream impact occurs when the activities of one subunit have implications for another – such as handing over responsibility for executing planned tasks or processing information. A great many problems are caused whereby subunits do not collaborate to give one another better sight of how they handle and are progressing and performing in relation to dependencies and impacts. Anyone with experience of large organizations will be familiar with the conflict that arises when such coordination breaks down. Accusations often fly around – 'this is the first we've heard of it' and 'we've been left high and dry because they haven't delivered what they promised' are two of many common complaints. It seems as if such complaints arise as often because of communication breakdowns as because of general operational failures.

There are lots of ways to increase participation, and organizations must look for what will work in their unique situations. Secondments are useful as a general tactic and, at a deeper level, career path management can ensure senior managers have experience of a reasonable range of different organizational subunits before they are asked to lead one of them. In some organizations, senior managers are regularly rotated between functions and divisions to broaden their business knowledge and foster understanding and cooperation between subunits. In these organizations, an HR director might move to being a marketing director. There are some constraints on this policy – particularly in heavily governed roles such as finance, risk, and audit. However, the approach is still a valid option for many organizations, especially in middle-management ranks.

Roles and responsibilities

Conventional role definition

So far, in examining how organizational designs and systems can ensure that critical activities are carried out as intended, we have established that:

- activities can be segregated into one-off projects and ongoing processes;
- all but the smallest organizations must be structured through establishing manageable subunit groups;
- resources must be allocated effectively across projects and process being undertaken by these subunits; and
- subunits must effectively manage the interfaces between them to compensate for the weaknesses inherent in any given structural model.

The next considerations in the inverted pyramid framework are roles and responsibilities. Of course, both roles and responsibilities can and should be assigned to organizational subunits, but they become increasingly meaningful when assigned to small teams and individuals. It is this that gives shape to the

Box 8.7 Mini case study – Building cooperation through reporting and involvement

Some of my own case study research involved examining the relationships between the divisions of a large multinational company and its central support functions. As is often the case, relationships between these groups were strained. The business divisions disliked the 'one-size fits all' approach they claimed the central functions used and regularly complained that central initiatives were not oriented to meet the business goals they were pursuing in their divisions. They further complained that the support functions did not provide adequate support for the projects they were hotly pursuing to deliver their business results.

Conversely, staff in the central functions complained that their divisional colleagues had too little regard for the wider needs of the organization to develop efficient support operations and observed that divisions claimed to be unique in respect of their needs when in fact they were not.

The research revealed that although these subunits complained a lot about one another, they appeared to be doing little to solve the problems they identified. Staff in the divisions agreed that to support them properly, their colleagues in central support teams would need good information about the divisions, their strategies, and their activities. Upon reflection, they realized they were not really providing it – if anything, they tended to hide information from centralized support functions. Equally, the central support functions acknowledged that they should be developing their initiatives with the cooperation of divisions and giving them early visibility of intentions to allow for joint development of implementation plans if these initiatives were to be successful.

As part of an action research phase within the case studies, the divisions were encouraged to start systematically sharing information about their objectives, strategies, and critical activities. They also started reporting planned and ongoing projects to the central teams, highlighting where they had upstream dependencies on these support functions, and were thus relying upon them to deliver successfully.

The initial reaction from the support functions was negative. Although they appreciated general information about divisional strategies and activities, the project reporting put them under pressure. Some central teams complained that they had not agreed to deliver support in the way or to the timescales indicated in the project reports. However, this led to a useful round of negotiations, clarifications, and explicit agreements.

Partly in an attempt to 'get their own back', the central functions started reporting to the divisions the emerging plans they had, indicating where support would be required for successful implementation. Once again, conflict emerged in reaction to these plans. However, over time, this process settled down, and the divisional teams ended up with what they called 'radar maps', displaying the incoming waves of interventions from central functions.

Ultimately, a much more constructive relationship between divisions and central functions emerged, as they each saw the benefits of early engagement and active involvement. Representatives from corresponding areas were invited to the management meetings of others as standing members of the teams. From this position 'in the tent' and with the systematic reporting continuing, far fewer surprises arose, and a much more efficient and effective working relationship developed.

contributions that individuals make and increases the 'line of sight' between their actions and strategic outcomes – a vital step to increasing alignment and motivation.[7]

Most large organizations make use of job descriptions and role profiles. These documents seek to capture the essence of individual roles, outlining key responsibilities and reporting lines, requisite skills and experience, and so on. Such documents are often a legal necessity (either statutorily or in practice). They are also used widely for recruitment, selection, and appraisal. However, it is rare to come across employees who make regular and heavy use of their job descriptions in their everyday work. These documents tend to be formalities that only partially reflect the reality of roles and fall out of date quickly. The problem with such documents is perhaps that they centre on roles and seek to identify the activities for which role-holders are responsible. As the inverted pyramid framework highlights, activities need logically to be determined ahead of roles.

Responsibility charting

A good addition to job descriptions is responsibility charting, which establishes different forms of involvement centred on a series of activities. Responsibility charting was first developed more than 40 years ago and remains a simple and seemingly effective methodology.[8] However, it does not seem to have achieved wide application. Some managers may know its output as a responsibility assignment matrix or linear responsibility chart. It is also often called a RACI matrix, RASCI Matrix, or some other acronym reflecting the different forms of involvement specified (these acronyms are explained below). In essence, the tool requires the breakdown of a project, process, or other series of activities into specific tasks.[9] Then each task is analysed to determine how each of a specified range of stakeholders should best be involved in each task. This is charted in a matrix using codes denoting different forms of involvement. The most common forms of involvement include the following:

- accountability – the one stakeholder who must ensure the activity is undertaken satisfactorily
- responsibility – the stakeholder(s) who must actually undertake the activity
- consulted – the stakeholder(s) who must be consulted about the activity before it is undertaken
- informed – the stakeholder(s) who must be informed about the activity
- Support – the stakeholder(s) who must support those with responsibility to undertake the activity
- veto – the stakeholder(s) with the power to veto an activity being undertaken
- verifier – the stakeholder(s) who must verify that an activity has been completed satisfactorily
- omitted – the stakeholder(s) who must *not* be involved (e.g. to maintain confidentiality).

Of course, other forms of involvement can be designed, and any combination of the foregoing can be used in practice. However, it is important to keep the matrix reasonably simple so it is easy to develop and interpret – and, of course, codes used should be clear to prevent potential confusion. Table 8.2 shows an example of a high-level responsibility chart for an information technology project, using the designations for accountability (A), responsibility (R), consulted (C), and informed (I).

A few clarifications are worthwhile:

- Stakeholders can have more than one form of involvement – for example, it is common to be both accountable and responsible for a particular task.
- However, usually it is important that only one stakeholder is accountable – otherwise confusion arises as to 'where the buck stops'.
- It is vital to check that for each activity there is one stakeholder accountable and at least one stakeholder responsible for actually undertaking the task.
- It is important that the assigned responsibilities are realistic and appropriate – for example, those accountable for results must have adequate authority, resources, and opportunity to bring them about.

The most common problem in applying responsibility charts is that it can be difficult to assign the different roles logically – sometimes, it seems as if everybody is doing everything, which is no use. This is most likely because the activities have not been broken down into enough detail. Remember, you cannot assign responsibilities for a strategy or a project – but you can do so for activities that together will plausibly realize the strategy or together deliver the project.

Table 8.2 Example responsibility chart for an information technology project

Activity	Project Sponsor	Project Manager	Business Analyst	Developer	End users	Launch team
Define core business requirements	C	A	R		C	I
Establish major options for solution	C	A/R	C	C		I
Select preferred solution	C	A/R	C	I		I
Define detailed business requirements	I	A	R	I	C	
Produce detailed system specification		C	A	R		C
Validate cost-benefit analysis	I	A/R	C	C		
Complete beta application build		A	C	R		C
Conduct beta testing	I	A	R	R		I
Complete bug fixes and tweaks from beta testing		C	A	R		I
Conduct user acceptance testing	I	A/R	R	C	R	I
Complete final bug fixes and tweaks		C	A	R		
Approve final application for launch	C	A/R	R	R		C
Hand over to launch team	I	A/R	R	I		R

Responsibility charting does not just bring clarity to roles. It also helps to analyse them. For example, in Table 8.2, it is possible to examine each stakeholder and his or her role within this particular project. It is fairly easy, for example, to establish that the project manager is the primary leader of the project. We would expect him or her to be in control of the project budget and ideally come from the subunit 'owning' the project. Examining charted responsibilities across many projects and/or processes enables a rich articulation of the kinds of activities in which any given stakeholder is involved. This is a useful complement or input to a job description or role profile.

This kind of analysis also has a wider use – to examine and validate structure and resource allocation decisions. Responsibility charts suggest logical divisions of labour that may or may not reflect the structure and resource allocations of the organization. If particular critical activities (which should, of course, be the dominant focus) are frequently being assigned in terms of responsibility for action to certain stakeholders, it may suggest that a particular structural model (and consequential resource allocation pattern) will fit the pattern of critical activities. For example, if an IT function boasts an army of project managers, but responsibility charts repeatedly assign project leadership roles to project managers from within subunits where end-users are located, it may be because for such projects, domain experience trumps IT experience. There are complicating factors, of course, but responsibility charts are useful diagnostic tools to uncover and explore such design and system misalignments.

Performance criteria

The need for performance criteria

Chapters 6 and 7 explored strategic performance measurement and showed how measures can be developed around the performance variables plausibly affected by critical activities and affecting overall objectives. Performance at the individual and team level (even for non-critical activities) is also important to strategy execution. The last section looked at how roles can be clarified for individuals and teams within large organizational subunits. The next logical concern according to the inverted pyramid framework is performance criteria because beyond articulating what a role involves, it is important to define what constitutes good performance within that role. Not only must role holders know this but so, too, must their leaders.

Performance management is currently a hot topic. Lots of organizations are focusing on developing 'high-performance cultures' and adopting more proactive approaches toward managing the performance of individuals. There is little doubt that organizations can manage performance of individuals and teams better – all insiders in large and complex organizations can identify examples of slack performance, needless organizational 'fat', and individuals who could work harder and smarter. However, performance management is an area full of dilemmas and risks – not all of which are immediately apparent. Perhaps the greatest challenge is that effective performance management relies heavily upon effective performance measurement. Without knowing how well employees are performing, how can their performance be managed?

Individual performance assessment

The assessment of individual employee performance has long been a tricky art. Of course, the framework within which individual performance standards are defined can ideally be developed only from an organization's overall objective and mechanism by which that is translated into activities individuals can undertake. As we have seen throughout this book, that is a huge challenge in itself and, where it has not been done well, the alignment of all individual performance criteria is jeopardized. What is the point in being able to measure individual performance without confidence that it is being measured against valid criteria? However, we have laid out a systematic methodology for translating overall objectives into critical activities and structuring an organization into subunits and roles. Hence, we can now look at how to measure and thus enable management of individual performance, assuming performance criteria can be established adequately.

Even with clear performance criteria, individual performance measurement is dogged by problems including assessor subjectivity, the influence of negotiation skills, and low line manager commitment to the task. As a result, at present we perhaps know more about what does not work than what does. For many organizations, a potential solution to these problems is the use of forced distribution- ranking systems, which require assessing managers to differentiate performance of their employees, usually according to a predetermined statistical distribution. High performers can thus be recognized and rewarded, whereas underperformers can be pinpointed and dealt with, via remedial support and, if necessary, dismissal. Forced ranking was made famous – and perhaps palatable – by Jack Welch, who as CEO of General Electric went so far as to fire the poorest performing 10 per cent of his workforce.[10] Various theorists have also championed the use of these 'rank-and-yank' systems.[11]

Many organizations have been attracted to forced rankings by the apparent financial control offered. Defining performance assessment patterns offers greater control over related rewards (such as salary increases and bonus distributions) and allows some advance signalling of the rewards on offer for specific performance levels. In the United Kingdom, forced-ranking systems are growing in popularity. According to one survey, 45 per cent of managers are required to rank employees' performance using a predetermined distribution.[12] However, in the United States, there are growing legal concerns about forced ranking. Some time ago, one major company lost an unfair-dismissal case on the basis of age discrimination, being unable to show that its forced-ranking system produced a valid assessment of individual performance.[13] More recently, class action lawsuits have reportedly been filed against numerous others.[14] Many firms in the United States have abandoned forced ranking, perhaps as a result.

Aside from the legal issues, questions are being asked about whether forced ranking actually works as intended. A recent survey of HR professionals suggested there are widespread concerns about the practice.[15] Another survey of U. S. firms suggests that the use of forced-ranking systems is associated with lower effectiveness of performance appraisals – particularly if routine dismissals follow.[16] Despite some claims to the contrary, there is currently no sound empirical evidence supporting the use of forced-ranking systems.[17]

One issue to consider is the ongoing benefits from using rank-and-yank systems. Common sense would suggest that the better organizations are at removing underperformers, the fewer underperformers they will have. A law of diminishing returns must set in.[18] This implies that if rank-and-yank should be used at all, it should be used only for short periods and under specific circumstances. It sounds impressive to say that organizations should keep 'raising the bar', but this can ignore the realities of the labour market and hard financial implications of staff turnover. Organizations that keep cutting the bottom 5 or 10 per cent of their workforce are in time likely to start dismissing capable employees, with no certainty that their replacements will be any better – let alone so much better as to justify the costs, disruption, and productivity losses caused by enforced turnover.

There are other regularly cited problems with the practice. 'Survivor guilt' can affect those who escape workforce culls, and any perceived unfairness in systems used is likely to invoke anxiety among survivors and those dismissed. Perceived unfairness in forced-ranking systems is common and, of course, affects even those organizations that do not routinely dismiss lowest performers but use ratings to drive development, promotion, and reward decisions. The unfairness perceived in forced-ranking systems is probably underestimated. Behavioural scientists have known for years that we consistently underestimate contextual influences on individual performance and correspondingly give individuals too much credit or blame for their successes and failures.[19] Forced-ranking systems and many other performance assessment tools do not acknowledge organizational performance constraints and arguably even discourage diagnosis of them by providing the illusion of control via measurement. Being forced to differentiate employee performance is not a substitute for improved accuracy of performance assessments. Using rankings is neither a prerequisite to identifying clear assessment criteria (as some suggest[20]) nor does it overcome assessors' tendencies to be influenced by factors that do not relate to job performance. Being fallible humans, managers are prone to give high ratings to people like themselves, people they like, people they hired, good negotiators, those who have performed well recently, and so on, regardless of the mechanism used to distribute their assessments.[21]

Comparative performance evaluations have another disturbing feature in that often neither organizations nor employees can tell whether individuals' performance is improving, stagnant, or declining from one year to the next. Without absolute performance benchmarks, there is no way to tell – and that throws into doubt efforts made to improve individual performance. This is a particular problem in senior roles and complex ones, in which hard performance data (such as sales made or applications processed) are rarely available.

Ironically, motivation problems are common with forced ranking.[22] The system leads organizations to regularly tell the vast majority of their people they are average or worse than average. There is a wealth of evidence that such 'labelling' and beliefs about personal potential are self-fulfilling prophecies.[23] Tell people they are doing well and have plenty of potential and they will generally prove you right; tell them they are failing and you'll probably come to be right about that, too. Of course, leaders don't need sophisticated research to tell them this; it is partly why they prefer to avoid giving poor evaluations.

Forced-ranking systems have caused leaders to develop numerous tactics to compensate for these deficiencies. Many distance themselves from the process, explaining that they do not like or agree with it, reinforcing resentment over its use. Some leaders – particularly those who have to perform regular evaluations – rotate employee evaluations to restore a sense of equity. Others retain serious underperformers for prolonged periods to ensure they have candidates for low ranking come appraisal time. Equally, sometimes underperformers are not dealt with because they fall too high up the ranking and escape attention. Managers also tend to give similar ratings to most employees because they recognize another danger – that forced rankings can create unhealthy competition between individuals. For organizations that require good teamwork and cooperation between people, forced-ranking systems that will affect rewards, promotions, and even organizational survival are risky choices. Internal conflict over perceived unfairness can result from distribution patterns' being applied to different structural subunits. If a company's marketing function is performing brilliantly and attracts high performers but its IT function is a dismal failure, is it appropriate for the good but lowest performers in marketing to be punished and the poor but top performers in IT to be rewarded?

Forced-ranking systems also direct the attention of employees to their performance evaluations rather than their development needs. The more significant the implications of a specific ranking, the less likely it becomes that employees will approach managers to discuss skill gaps or request developmental support – doing so may simply make them more likely candidates for the 'underperformer' label.

There are signs that organizations are recognizing the extent of these problems. Microsoft recently abandoned its forced-ranking system, wanting to encourage more open conversations between managers and employees about performance and boost morale. At the same time, it introduced a wide range of new benefits oriented to make its employees' busy lives a little easier. Even General Electric, in the wake of Jack Welch's departure, has softened its use of forced rankings. Managers no longer have to stick rigidly to the 20–70–10 percentage split introduced by Welch (the bottom 10 per cent being termination candidates), and underperformers are given considerably more support than previously.[24]

Misaligned performance measures

Chapter 6 touched on the feedforward effects of performance measurement – summarized so neatly by Drucker's warning, "What gets measured gets managed". The effects of misalignments between strategic objectives and performance measures can certainly be seen at the organizational and subunit level – entire departments, functions, and divisions can quite clearly be seen focusing on the 'wrong' things when the measures tracking their performance are malformed. However, these patterns almost always have roots at the individual level. Strategic performance measures do not come out of thin air – they are often designed and almost always approved by senior leaders who themselves are subject to individual performance measures. Leaders, quite naturally, tend to take their own performance measures and targets and cascade them to the subunits for which they are responsible. That is what they are expected to do.

Such is the nature of measurement that the misalignments created can cause organizations to systematically 'march off cliffs'. It is important to note that though explicit targets and performance-related rewards can exacerbate this effect, they are not required to influence behaviour – so strong is the feedforward effect that performance measures alone are highly potent. As a result, many organizations face a dilemma managing the balance between good performance and clear accountability. The drive toward strong accountability, though motivated by fair concerns about managing individual performance, in practice directly conflicts with balanced measurement. Clear accountability requires the identification of a limited range of performance variables over which individuals have delegated and reasonable control. It also requires measurement of these variables to drive performance evaluation and management. These are exactly the conditions that foster self-interested trade-off decisions and associated organizational conflict.

Figure 8.3 provides an example of this and demonstrates how strategy execution maps are useful for identifying and examining conflicts between accountability and performance measures. An IT firm that supplies hardware and software solutions to corporate customers had determined that different skills were required to secure new accounts than were required to look after existing customers. Hence, it had split these roles between 'new business managers' and 'account managers'. Figure 8.3 uses a partial strategy execution map to highlight the performance variable that reflected the primary objective of new business managers – increased customer acquisition. These managers were thought of as 'hunters' – charged with getting new customers and little else. Account managers, conversely, were thought of as 'farmers' – responsible for looking after customers, developing ongoing relationships, and associated business development. The new business managers had clear accountability – one major objective on which they could focus was easily measured and for which they could be held directly responsible. However, Figure 8.3 highlights the potential problem caused by this clear accountability and focus on new customer acquisition performance measures for these managers. By implication, these managers did not have to concern themselves with increasing customer retention, sales volume per customer, price, or costs – despite all of these performance variables heavily affecting the overall objective of increased profit.

The strategy execution map was used to diagnose the performance of the business, and the role of new business managers was examined in detail. It revealed that they systematically exploited their lack of accountability for these other performance variables, for example by the following:

- ignoring likely retention of customers, even promising customers they would not be contacted by account managers after buying a product;
- ignoring likely sales volumes to customers, failing to explore their possible future needs – and as a result making some inappropriate initial purchase recommendations that customers later complained about;
- securing first sales by offering products at ludicrously low prices, creating marginal losses without any confidence that these would prove worthwhile in the long-run (and often setting an untenable precedent for account managers, damaging customer relationships);
- incurring substantial costs that were not proportionate to potential revenues, within their own budgets but also especially by pulling in resources from other areas of the business (e.g. the marketing function).

Figure 8.3 throws up an ironic risk with strategy execution maps. Though they are used to establish narrow accountabilities for particular roles, they can conceivably also be used to systematically identify opportunities to maximize performance in respect of one performance variable by trading off performance in other areas. In many ways, this emerging dilemma only increases the potency of measurement. Strategic performance measurement systems may have to be even more finely tuned to the specific needs of organizations to ensure that strong accountability does not create destructive dysfunctions. Both the selection and design of performance measures will become even more crucial tasks, given the reliance placed upon them by stronger accountability.

Key implications

Lots of problems with individual performance measurement have been discussed here, and this reflects accurately the state of the science in the area. There are perhaps two lessons worth drawing out in summary – both of which reflect the discussion in Chapter 4. First, in terms of feedback, measures never tell all. Even the best-designed performance measurement systems are constructed without perfect foresight, and cannot explain all performance variations. Situations change, people behave unpredictably, and organizational systems clash in unintended ways. So, diagnosis remains a critical art, and existing measures might best be seen as 'diagnostic triggers' – points of entry to deeper investigation of apparent problems or successes. Second, in relation to feedforward, how leaders use measures is critical to how others view them. If sound approaches are used to select and design a range of performance measures but leaders pay attention to only a few specific results, problems will arise. If people are punished as soon as a bad result appears or no effort is made to understand the dynamics underlying the problem, measurement is almost pointless. Wise leaders see measures as helping them ask the right questions rather than producing all the answers.

Of course, individual and team performance measurement is intimately bound up with goal setting and reward, and these are both explored shortly in the section on commitment.

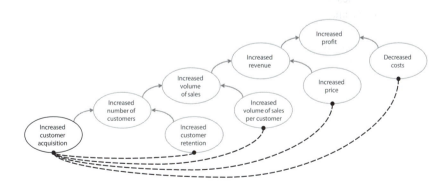

Figure 8.3 Examining accountability conflicts using strategy execution maps

Capacity

Interrelationships with other elements

Capacity management is an established part of operations management and is covered well by experts in that field.[25] However, it is also an important element within the inverted pyramid framework because it is closely tied to many of its other elements. Most obviously, capacity must be considered – both when diagnosing and planning – as being intimately tied up with commitment and capability (both discussed shortly). Ignoring capacity when examining commitment or capability leads to misdiagnosis and imbalanced plans.

These three performance variables – capacity, commitment, and capability – tend to substitute for one another in the short term and reinforce one another in the longer term. For example, if capacity is too low for a short period, highly committed and capable staff will usually overcome the challenges presented. However, in the long run, if capacity remains too low, commitment and capability will also fall away. Similarly, if capability is limited, high levels of capacity and/or commitment will offset the impact of this. However, in the long term, capability must rise to feed motivation and improve capacity management so as to control associated costs.

Capacity is also closely tied to resource allocation in that it involves using the right level of resources in the right place. However, capacity is more than the allocation of units of resources. It also relates to the effective management of allocated resources. For example, it is possible to change the capacity of individual employees, not by making them work harder but by changing the way in which they work to make them more efficient and effective. Similarly, the capacity of a team is a function not only of the number of team members but of the way in which the team operates and, thus, its potential output. Hence, project and process management also dynamically affect capacity. So, too, does organization structure, which through specialisation and division of labour influences the productivity of individuals and teams.

The mechanics of capacity management is complex, inevitably involving skilful analysis and predictions relating to supplies, operations, and demand. From the strategy execution perspective, the key concern is ensuring that capacity requirements for critical activities are prioritized, developed, and protected. This is easier said than done, and a range of common problems results when critical activities have not been identified and adequately considered with capacity management decisions.

Change responsibility and absorbability

First, managers are frequently asked to manage changes that will realize strategy on top of their 'day jobs'. This is ironic and dangerous. It is ironic because there can be few things more important than executing strategy – yet it is often given a low priority by managers who do not view delivering change as part of their primary roles. It is dangerous because change is typically managed slowly and badly when it is not a dedicated responsibility that is properly supported. As a rule, those managing areas in change should either have a reasonable proportion of their time explicitly committed to managing changes or be supported by dedicated change/project managers. Often, some combination is appropriate but, in most organizations, it is preferable to engage all managers in planning and executing strategy in some way – and build this into their roles.

A second major issue to consider in relation to capacity is 'absorbability' – in other words, the capacity of the organization and its subunits to cope with changes generated to implement strategy. Many organizations suffer 'change fatigue' – a sense of frustration and exhaustion after seemingly endless waves of changes that cause operational disruption and emotional stress. Change fatigue leads people to care less about change and work less enthusiastically to make it successful. Some executives delight in causing perpetual and substantial change – viewing it as a way to 'keep everyone on their toes' and foster a culture of continuous improvement. There is some merit in this approach but only up to a point. If the pace and extent of change exceed the absorptive capacity of an organization by too much for too long, the law of diminishing returns sets in. As Chapter 4 highlighted, a high proportion of projects and initiatives are simply the wrong ones – the results of flawed diagnosis. As was observed in Chapter 1, around half of strategies fail catastrophically, and only a small minority achieve all their objectives. This is further evidence that much of the painful change people endure in organizations is wasteful and futile. In general, there is a strong case for less, steadier, and better change that is more closely matched with the absorptive capacity of organizations.

Commitment

The potency of reward management

One might expect that managing the commitment of employees would be outside the domain of strategy execution – it is not obviously an inherently strategic task. However, commitment is strongly influenced by the various forms of reward on offer to people through their employment, and the emphasis placed by so many organizations on financial rewards makes two specific issues of great relevance to strategy execution:

- Because chief officers and other senior managers have significant power over organizations, the alignment of their financial rewards with the organization's needs has a huge impact on strategy execution.
- Performance-related pay (at all levels) has proven to be a high-risk area for strategy execution – in which misalignments can create serious problems.

This section, therefore, explores performance-related pay in some detail and explains how strategy execution is impacted by it. There can be few more intuitively appealing ideas in management than linking pay to performance. It conjures up all the right notions – leading edge, logical, wise, prudent, and equitable. Plenty of organizations seem to agree. For example, more than 80 per cent of the U. K. workforce is eligible for some form of performance-related pay (PRP) – a figure that is growing fast.[26] PRP is being introduced to an increasingly diverse range of jobs – including an increasing number in the public sector. Not only is PRP becoming more widespread but organizations are relying upon it more than ever before – especially for the most senior roles. One survey reported that the annual bonuses of executive directors and senior executives in the United Kingdom now average more than 40 per cent of salary.[27]

Incentivizing senior executives

The corporate governance movement has fuelled the drive toward using PRP. In the United Kingdom, the Greenbury and Hampel committees both recommended that incentive compensation be closely aligned with performance.[28] These recommendations followed the concern, backed by considerable evidence, that the relationship between executive pay and company performance was very weak.[29] Indeed, chief officers' pay appears to be far more closely associated with the size of firms than the returns they generate.[30] Of course, more recent events in the financial services sector have complicated the picture. There is a wide perception that banking bonuses have been excessive and may have contributed to the failure of some institutions. However, interestingly the concern seems to be more about the scale of rewards than the efficacy of the mechanisms by which they are determined. Indeed, the argument generally posed favours pay that is more authentically performance-related.

Questions remains about whether the widespread enthusiasm for PRP is justified and whether the complex apparatus and sensitive stakeholder management required to operate PRP are worth the trouble. The research evidence is far from supportive.

Looking at chief officers first, payments under simple bonus schemes are quite closely associated with firm performance. However, of course, that is because in such senior roles firm performance usually determines them. It is not evidence that bonuses cause or are necessary for superior performance. Ironically, there is now a strong trend toward complex bonus schemes, partly to incorporate more non-financial performance measures for a longer-term view. This move is motivated by the right principles, but complex bonus schemes offer executives many more ways to manipulate their pay. Long-term incentive plans (LTIPs) don't fare any better. There is evidence that their design is easily and regularly manipulated[31] and that they handsomely reward average performance.[32] Executive share options (ESOs) might be expected to avoid all these problems. After all, they are surely directly linked to the performance of chief officers who are responsible for maximizing shareholder returns. Here, a different problem and interesting irony crop up. The more senior an executive, the more he or she is considered responsible for firm performance, having the remit to manipulate an extremely wide range of organizational variables. However, it is precisely the control over these variables that empowers executives – where they are so inclined – to make self-serving decisions at the cost of the company. We tend to forget when granting share options (a 'long-term' incentive) that often the executives receiving them will still be in control of the important levers when these options mature and tempted at that point to make short-term decisions to maximize personal rewards. It is often the dysfunctional behaviour that is delayed as well as the reward. For example, the use of share buy-back schemes, which increase share prices (but not long-term shareholder return),[33] has increased in line with the use of ESOs, and there is evidence that such incentive schemes affect stock repurchase decisions.[34] Just to add to the confusion, many executives receive share options based on a multiple of salary, so at the time of the award, a lower share price translates into a greater number of shares. This diminishes the incentive for early share price increases.

Motivation through PRP

Moving away from chief officers, we can consider whether organizations can make PRP work for those in less senior roles, who don't have the power to manipulate LTIPs and share prices. Tackling this issue is much more complex than studying the link between chief officer pay and shareholder return. A number of interrelated issues crop up.

First, there is the simple question of whether paying people more makes them work harder. It is well established that stretching but attainable goals can motivate people.[35] However, it is also known that easy or very difficult goals are de-motivating,[36] so immediately a significant challenge is created – repeatedly fine-tuning goals that are appropriate for roles and the individuals in them. It is important to note that goals can be motivating in themselves. Indeed, there is evidence that the introduction of extrinsic rewards for goal achievement can destroy intrinsic rewards and cause poorer performance.[37] When the financial rewards of high performance are stressed, attention to and interest in the actual job itself tends to diminish. As someone once said, 'You'll never score a century if you're looking at the scoreboard'. Related to this, there are concerns that PRP can crush creativity. Ironically, highly committed employees' performance can deteriorate with PRP because performance criteria are being imposed rather than shaped by strong personal values. Equally, offering PRP may, over time, attract and retain staff who little value intrinsic rewards. An uncomfortable issue arises – does any organization really want to recruit and retain the kind of employees it has to bribe to do a good job?

There are other problems with PRP. Pay is intended to reinforce goals as a motivator. It has an equally strong impact as a de-motivator when it is withheld. Line managers instinctively recognize this, which is why they try to give bonuses to average performers. Of course, with restricted bonus pots, if they manage this, the differentiation between high and mediocre performance is marginalized, undermining the PRP concept. Individual PRP can also undermine teamwork as colleagues compete against one another for limited rewards.[38] One solution to this is to use team-based PRP, but this can cause serious conflict between teams, a big problem wherever cross-team coordination and cooperation is important. Perhaps most worrying of all, PRP does not address the issue of how to improve performance. There is a risk that it is used as a shortcut for managers who do not effectively manage staff and support them in their roles. Some managers may be reluctant to go to the trouble of diagnosing problems and finding innovative solutions if they perceive that 'tinkering' with the reward system will deliver desired results.

Incentivizing people to do the right things

There are clearly many problems with making PRP motivating. However, another fundamental issue is whether it can motivate people to do the right things. The logic of PRP is based on numerous assumptions, which are generally not addressed by those designing or researching PRP systems. Economists see pay as a solution to the 'principal-agent problem'. Managers need others to undertake tasks they cannot attend to themselves, so they must find ways of making individuals' goals consistent with those of the organization. Paying people to undertake specific tasks is an obvious answer, but we must consider the assumptions this involves. The inverted pyramid framework suggests that to be sure that employees contribute effectively toward strategy execution, managers must perform as follows:

- Be very clear about the organization's overall objective.
- Understand the organization's environment and how it affects strategic choices.
- Craft a strategy to achieve the objectives.
- Break that strategy down into critical activities that can feasibly be implemented.
- Create an appropriate organizational structure, interface management method, and resource allocation system to manage these activities.
- Establish roles and responsibilities within that structure.
- Define performance criteria in each role.
- Fill the roles and create the right kind of commitment – potentially via pay – among the role-holders.

If managers can do all that complex and voluminous thinking perfectly, and the environment doesn't change too much, they might end up with a well-aligned reward system (albeit suffering from the problems with pay discussed so far). However, in most organizations, there are serious misalignments between these elements. Even well-aligned organizations will never get all of this 'perfect'.

This is a big problem. If managers can create an effective line of sight between organizational goals and individual roles, employees might have the scope to modify their activities in recognition of where they can make a better contribution, taking into account environmental changes and the needs of the organization as a whole. However, measures, goals, and PRP in particular all have the power to focus the attention of individuals on pursuing specific outcomes, sometimes at the expense of all else. If managers operate like economists – assuming that employees need to be accurately 'programmed' – they potentially prevent these employees from programming themselves, even when their altered actions would be in the organization's interest. Leaders should be in no doubt that using PRP narrows the views their employees take and reduces their focus to achieving a limited number of (often short-term) objectives. If businesses need creative, outward-looking activity to flourish, PRP is a dangerous choice.

Another major problem is that no matter how simple a job, it is difficult to create a reward system that is perfectly balanced and representative of the kind of performance desired. In particular, it is difficult to predict the manipulations of the systems that individuals might attempt. History is littered with examples of reward systems that have been 'played' to the advantage of employees, usually at the expense of their employers (see Box 8.8).

There are typically many opportunities for such game playing. As discussed earlier, individual performance measurement is remarkably difficult. Senior role holders in particular often know how to ensure controllable metrics are selected for their assessment. Goal setting is equally difficult, with the obvious problems of politics and negotiation and many other less obvious problems related to ensuring target achievement. There are various tactics that organizations can employ to reduce the likelihood of both these problems arising:

- awarding PRP on the basis of a more-rounded, subjective assessment of individual performance that allows for autonomous changes to planned activities and takes the environment into account
- emphasizing a wider organizational performance component in PRP
- extending the time horizon over which performance is assessed
- emphasizing wider team-based reward.

All of these tactics – many of which underpin the rationale for using LTIPs and ESOs – make the performance assessed more general and, therefore, easier to design and harder to manipulate. However, for all but the most senior roles, each of these solutions makes the reward criteria much less controllable and diminishes any motivating effect that PRP might offer – raising the question of whether it is worth the trouble.

Set against all these problems and the evidence for them, the popularity and persistence of performance-related pay looks confusing. Why do so many organizations insist on using a management tool that generally does not work? Undoubtedly, the industry that has grown up around the design and management of PRP systems works hard to ensure its survival. Perhaps more important, senior

Box 8.8 Dysfunctional rewards

The CEO of a major multinational company was recently made aware of the enormous costs associated with turnover among recently appointed staff. In some parts of the business, upward of 30 per cent of staff resigned within the first year of joining. With recruitment, selection, induction, and training costs amounting to the equivalent of more than a year's salary (ignoring associated productivity losses), this was a major problem. The CEO swiftly introduced tough targets for all divisions of the company to reduce new-staff turnover and made them a heavily weighted performance criterion for senior managers.

Some months later, research revealed that many senior managers across the company had not diagnosed underlying causes of the turnover problem and sought to develop long-term solutions to it. Rather, incentivized by short-term bonuses on offer for achieving their targets, they had developed a serious of tactics to reduce reported short-term staff turnover:

- Some managers quietly introduced a substantial '13th month bonus' that rewarded new employees for staying with the organization for more than a year. This did help to ensure a reduction in new staff turnover (i.e. measured by the proportion of new staff leaving within a year of appointment). However, this tactic, as well as being extremely costly, did not cause any change to turnover among staff employed for 13 months or more.
- Some managers decided to keep temporary staff (who were excluded from turnover statistics) on short-term contracts for much longer than previously to ensure that these individuals 'fitted in' before offering them permanent contracts. These temporary staff cost the company significantly more than permanent staff because of employment agency fees.
- Similarly, some managers hired temporary staff instead of permanent staff, despite the higher cost of this choice.
- Some managers systematically identified employees who might resign from the organization because they were dissatisfied or were intending to leave (e.g. students completing their studies and people relocating with spouses). Wherever possible, managers fired these members of staff before they resigned, thus ensuring the related turnover was classed as 'involuntary' and not included in the new-staff turnover measures.

The complex interplay between performance measures, targets, and reward systems used in the organization ensured that managers had ample opportunities to act in their own interests rather than those of the business. These systems allowed managers to increase their performance-related pay while delivering no real improvement in short-term turnover and simultaneously generating substantial unnecessary other costs in the organization.

leaders do find the illusion of control remarkably hard to resist and, when PRP has been so generous to them, may not have the incentive to challenge its use.

Intrinsic motivators related to strategy execution

Of course, there are many non-financial ways in which people can be rewarded for work. As was discussed earlier, goals without associated rewards are also motivating, and even measures alone (with associated targets or rewards) tend to capture people's attention and cause feedforward behaviour. These observations reinforce the point that organizations need to take care with all rewards, recognizing that they heavily influence behaviour and not always in intended ways. The prospect of promotion or even simply praise is sufficient to focus the attention of employees tightly on too-narrow a range of performance variables.

As already discussed, involvement in developing executable strategy is inherently motivating for employees. So, too, is having a clear 'line of sight' between individual responsibilities and organizational objectives. These are important ways in which the approaches organizations take toward strategy execution themselves impact on commitment of staff.

Capability

The role of capabilities

The final organizational design and systems element in the inverted pyramid framework is capabilities. Organizational capabilities are a function of how all of the elements of the framework operate together so, at this level, we are concerned with the capabilities of individuals and teams with roles and responsibilities within the structure selected. Once again, it is not immediately obvious that capabilities are a strategic issue and, therefore, within the legitimate domain of strategy execution. However, several factors make capabilities worthy of inclusion in the inverted pyramid framework.

First, as discussed earlier, capabilities are a close cousin of capacity and commitment. When diagnosing performance problems (a challenge described in Chapter 4), it is often difficult to tease apart capacity, commitment, and capability causes. It is rarely immediately clear whether a performance problem is a case of 'can't do', 'won't do', 'don't have time to do' – or something else entirely. It is right to think about capabilities alongside these other elements, both in diagnosis and planning.

Focusing capability development

Capabilities are also relevant to strategy in that the knowledge, skills, and competencies of individuals are vital underpinnings to all organizational actions, strengths, and performance. Ability to take decisions and deliver the right activities in the right way affects everything – from the strategy chosen to the measures adopted and from the product design to after-sales customer care. Inducting, training, educating, and developing employees are typically major investments – consuming substantial time and resources. Yet, rarely are these investments properly driven by an approach that is intimately developed as part of organizational strategy. Investments in capabilities are rarely determined via serious planning and associated business cases. In part, this is because capability development is widely seen as being very 'soft' and a highly indirect way of achieving overall objectives, which is difficult to articulate and quantify. Many organizations talk of having to make a leap of faith when deciding about what capability development activities to undertake. However, arguably the highly indirect way in which development activities impact overall objectives makes it all the *more* important that they are explicitly linked to these conceptual outcomes. As we saw in Chapter 7 in the sales management training example, it is possible not only to develop explicit causal chains linking capability development activities to overall objectives (see Figure 7.3) but also to use these causal chains to develop sophisticated cost-benefit models to project and track investment returns (see Figure 7.12).

For some time now, advanced organizations have talked about making more strategic investments in people development. They have voiced the intention to move away from a 'shotgun' approach to development, spreading available resources widely across all employees and a wide range of skill development areas. The idea has been to pick a limited number of areas in which skill development would make a real difference and focus upon these. However, this philosophy has not seen widespread application. Almost certainly in part to blame is the difficulty organizations have had in translating strategy into people-development–related activities. We might hope that the foregoing chapters have provided a framework to aid this leap.

Strategy execution capabilities

Finally, developing some specific capabilities is of relevance to strategy execution. We saw in Chapter 1 that strategy execution is a huge challenge, with a very high failure rate. It is a crucial challenge for organizations pursuing high performance and competitive advantage. Chapter 4 outlined many of the barriers facing managers seeking to implement strategy and showed how effective diagnosis is central to successful strategy implementation. In the last few chapters, we have explored how the gap between strategies and action can be closed – by translating objectives into critical activities and aligning bottom-up activities with objectives. Finally, we have explored how organizational designs and systems can be aligned with strategy to ensure successful delivery of critical activities. All of these areas require managers to have substantial knowledge, skills, and abilities – managers need strategy execution capabilities. All of the evidence points to this being an underdeveloped area – the strategy execution failure rate, the dearth of guidance in the area, the tiny number of business schools offering programmes in the area, and so on. In summary, to implement strategy, organizations need better frameworks to pull together and harness more effectively their existing resources. To develop and apply these frameworks effectively, they need to develop strategy execution capabilities at the individual level.

The environment, measures, and risks

As already noted, three elements of the inverted pyramid are relevant to both phase 1 and phase 2 – being important for translating objectives into action and for aligning organizational designs and systems. These are:

- the analysis of the internal and external environment,
- strategic risk management, and
- strategic performance measurement.

These have already been discussed in some detail, but it is worth summarizing their relevance to aligning organizational designs and systems.

Internal and external environment

As discussed previously, the environment conditions cause-and-effect relationships – including those captured in strategies, their breakdown, and organizational designs and processes. For example, an organization structure should be chosen that will enable sound delivery of critical activities. Employee commitment should be developed in ways that will support the delivery of critical activities and not create dysfunctional unintended effects. The environment is what determines whether these anticipated outcomes will in fact arise. The aspects of it relevant to each organizational design and system need to be analysed to inform related decisions. For example, an employee opinion survey provides insights about staff commitment. A process for introducing reward systems that incorporates a systematic review seeking evidence of any unintended effects informs the design and re-design of such systems. The environmental factors worthy of analysis and ongoing tracking do vary from one situation and organization to another. However the inverted pyramid provides a framework to guide this thinking and development of the right approach.

Strategic risk management

In Chapter 7, we explored how causal models linking objectives with actions can be used to identify post-implementation risks, augmenting the more straightforward identification of implementation risks. Exactly this approach can be used to establish foreseeable risks for a proposed change to organizational designs and systems. Indeed, if this kind of risk identification is an established part of project planning, any project related to organizational designs and processes should naturally incorporate appropriate risk management. Risk identification can also be incorporated with all processes for which it is required. Most organizations familiar with risk management build the checks and balances into processes to pick up certain risks. Three additional considerations are important:

- augmenting implementation risks with post-implementation risks (focused on outcomes rather than outputs)
- elevating risk identification and management for organizational designs and systems tightly related to critical activities
- paying special attention to risks arising from the way processes interact – that is, taking an integrated view

Strategic performance measurement

In a similar fashion, it is important to develop performance measures for organizational designs and processes. For example, measures can inform the following areas:

- the extent to which a project management process is operating as intended
- the efficiency and effectiveness of processes
- how well a structure is operating – for example, in relation to decision-making speed
- levels of utilization of resources allocated to different projects and subunits
- how well stakeholders think interfaces between subunits are being managed
- how well roles and responsibilities are understood
- whether individual employee capacity is increasing through improvements in work methods
- the level of commitment demonstrated by employees – for example, via surveys or unenforced turnover rates.

None of these measures are new or inherently different to the metrics that most large and complex organizations collect. What the inverted pyramid does is provide a framework to establish what measures are vital (given critical activities) and how they can be logically related to aid diagnosis and cost benefit modelling for projection and tracking.

Summary of key points

- Phase 2 of the inverted pyramid framework relates to aligning organizational designs and systems, which need to be aligned with critical activities to ensure their effective delivery.
- Critical activities can resolve many dilemmas leaders face in relation to designing organizations and their systems.
- Leaders may assume that organizational designs and systems will be realigned in response to the strategies they develop; however, this is not consistently or easily done by middle managers.
- It is important to ensure that emerging projects are the right ones and that they will plausibly contribute to the achievement of overall objectives.
- Conventional project management processes typically do not incorporate diagnosis and testing of the alignment of projects' products with organizations' overall objectives – causal chains are useful for this.
- Successful strategy execution relies upon adequate embedding of projects' products where appropriate.
- Ongoing processes magnify efficiencies or inefficiencies, so designing them effectively is important, as is taking an integrated view of process to minimize unnecessary organizational complexity.
- Processes can provide invaluable performance measurement data if such feedback mechanisms are designed into them.
- Most organization structures are made up from subunits focused on function, products/services, channels, and/or markets/segments – arranged in a particular way.
- Strategies can inform structures, with differentiated strategies favouring predominantly divisional structures and cost leadership strategies favouring predominantly functional structures; however, critical activities provide a more reliable indication of what structures will best support effective strategy execution.
- Leaders must prioritize resources because demand for them is typically high and although difficult to compare, some projects and processes contribute more than others to the achievement of overall objectives.
- The different time horizons over which investment decisions are assessed substantially complicates resource allocation decisions.
- Leaders can use resource allocation to strengthen or weaken organizations/ subunits and to force them to coordinate their activities more effectively through resource sharing.

- Any structural configuration comes with disadvantages, and management of subunit interfaces can help to overcome these.
- Organizations typically have difficulty in operating in a collective fashion because of structural divisions, communication problems, divergent agendas, and internal conflict.
- The identification, mapping, analysis, and management of stakeholders can help to support improved inter-subunit communication, coordination, and cooperation.
- Communication and systematic reporting of information between subunits can substantially increase their performance where there are significant dependencies and impacts between their projects and processes.
- Responsibility charting is a simple and effective tool for identifying and agreeing on different forms of involvement across stakeholder groups in all kind of projects and processes; it can also be used to inform and validate organization structure decisions.
- Measuring the performance of individuals and teams is important to enable effective performance management; however, individual performance assessment is fraught with difficulties and risks.
- Forced-ranking systems, which require distribution of individual performance ratings, are highly divisive, cause numerous problems, and remain unsupported by empirical research into their effectiveness.
- Narrowly defined individual performance measures, although popular to enforce clear accountability, create significant risks by encouraging self-serving trade-off decisions to maximize apparent performance.
- Strategy execution maps are useful for identifying these risks (but also for exploiting them).
- The way in which leaders use performance measures has a significant effect on their value or riskiness.
- Capacity is a function not only of volumes of resources but of their combined productivity.
- Ensuring capacity to manage and absorb change is important for successful strategy execution.
- Targets and formal rewards exacerbate the tendency of performance measures to direct attention of people toward a limited range of performance variables.
- The use of PRP to increase commitment and better match rewards to results is widespread and increasing; however, there are numerous problems with PRP in relation to its motivating effects and, more significantly, predicting and controlling the behaviours it motivates.
- Capability development can usefully be focused around critical activities to ensure it makes the greatest possible impact on organizations' overall objectives.
- Organizations can enhance strategy execution by improving specific individual and team capabilities related to the implementation of strategy.

- Decisions about organizational designs and systems should be informed by analysis of specific relevant elements of the internal and external environments.
- Both performance measures and risks with implications for strategy execution can be identified for all key organizational designs and systems.

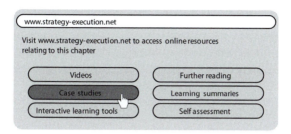

www.strategy-execution.net

Visit www.strategy-execution.net to access online resources relating to this chapter

Videos

Case studies

Interactive learning tools

Further reading

Learning summaries

Self assessment

Conclusion

We have too many high sounding words, and too few actions that correspond with them.

Abigail Adams

The challenge set

Strategy execution is one of the most significant challenges facing leaders in organizations today. Studies point to high levels of strategy execution failure, meaning investments in strategic planning are often wasted, important intentions not fulfilled, and stakeholders' needs and expectations not met.

Whether in business, the public sector, or the not-for-profit arena, organizations face more complex and demanding environments. Regulatory changes, increasing consumer power, technological innovation, and more-intense competition are placing organizations under pressure to get strategy execution right the first time. The same pressures are pushing organizations to manage greater internal complexity – and launch more sophisticated products, exploit new and more varied channels, and operate across different markets and geographies. The resulting internal complexity is making the strategy execution challenge even greater.

Strategy execution science is in its infancy – well behind where these organizations need it to be. We know far more about strategic planning and managing operations than we do about the critical linkage between them – strategy execution. Only a small amount of empirical research has provided evidence on how best to approach the challenge. Explicit guidance on the topic is still limited to a handful of books and educational programmes. Internal strategy execution experts remain rare, and very few external experts are knowledgeable in the area. Remarkably few people seem able to translate between the conceptual language of strategy and the gritty dialects of operations. It may be that abstract thinking powers and action orientation rarely reside in the same individual – yet that mixture of abilities is what organizations need to translate their long-term plans into concrete activities.

Despite these challenges, useful insights about how to tackle strategy execution can be gleaned from other areas, including the wider strategy field, organization theory, project management, organizational behaviour, and systems thinking. With these insights pulled together in fundamental and practical strategy execution models, organizations can secure advantage over competitors through selecting more executable strategies and implementing them more effectively.

The need for better retrospection

Perhaps the first step toward better strategy execution is to stop doing things – specifically, the wrong things. My own research shows how organizations readily slip into well-intentioned but symptom-focused problem solving as they tackle apparent performance constraints and pursue opportunities. Subtle but influential patterns are quickly reinforced and encourage quick fixes dealing only with surface problems. Without systematic diagnosis of apparent performance constraints, organizations repeatedly solve the wrong problems, waste time and resources, and introduce new problems.

One area in which research provides reasonable insights is into strategy execution barriers. It seems that a fairly consistent range of issues – about half of which are people-related – commonly act as barriers to successful strategy implementation. Knowledge of these is useful, but we need to go further. My research shows how these barriers are usually interrelated and, thus, need to be tackled on a more systemic basis. Leaders must interpret the unique characteristics of their organizations' particular situations and devise more-rounded responses. Chapter 4 introduced a systematic diagnosis framework to avoid symptom-focused problem solving and enable a more systemic analysis of performance constraints. Applying this process is not easy, but it need not necessarily be too time consuming and is critical if organizations are to cease perpetuating short-term illusory problem solving.

The need for better forward thinking

With the problems that really constrain performance properly uncovered, organizations have a more accurate picture of 'where they are' and how the systems created in the past really operate. However, leaders also need to be able to look forward, to plan and execute strategy in pursuit of organizational objectives.

The five Cs of strategy execution – causality, criticality, compatibility, continuity, and clarity – are principles reflecting the strategy execution challenge and what leaders have to do:

- Determine organizational objectives and the activities that will plausibly *cause* them to be achieved.
- Isolate *critical* activities, so that attention can be focused upon them so that they drive subsequent decisions.

- Ensure that these activities are *compatible*, so they do not pull organizations in different directions.
- Mesh these objectives and activities into organizational designs and systems to ensure *continuity* of their management over time and of the relationships between them.
- Ensure *clarity* to enhance a line of sight between individual responsibilities and organizational objectives and the commitment that stems from this.

These principles underpin the design of the inverted pyramid – the logically sequential decision-making framework that guides organizations through the:

- translation of conceptual overall objectives into critical activities
- alignment of organizational designs and systems, to ensure that critical activities are undertaken as intended and
- analysis of the internal and external environments, strategic performance measurement, and strategic risk management.

The inverted pyramid framework provides a detailed route-map for entire organizations and subunits within them, encouraging alignment between overall objectives, critical activities, and the organizational designs and systems that shape and drive action. This framework is inducted from my own case study research and draws upon prior strategy execution thinking and research to merge 'content' and 'process' approaches.

My research also revealed an important insight, heavily influencing the models developed in this book. There is a strong tendency, mirrored in some strategy execution theories, to leap from developing strategies straight to aligning organizational designs and systems. However, it is extremely difficult to align processes, structures, resource allocation systems, responsibilities, and so on with strategies. Instead, strategies need to be translated into concrete activities. When critical activities that will plausibly achieve overall objectives are identified, it is feasible to align organizational designs and systems with them. My own research showed that organizations are generally ill equipped to translate strategies into actions and need better ways to do this.

Strategy execution maps detail a systematic way to translate organizations' overall objectives into critical activities that will plausibly cause them to be achieved. Strategy execution maps are not easy to create – my research uncovered various pitfalls into which teams tend to fall when translating objectives into action, and these are outlined to help managers avoid them. However, developing strategy execution maps enables a thorough analysis of strategic choices and strategy execution options. It also provides ample opportunities to involve and engage those upon whom successful execution relies. Once choices are made and articulated, polished strategy execution maps are an effective method of communicating these. The examples of strategies and execution models adopted by IKEA and Apple show how their critical elements can be conveyed on a single page. They also show how strategy execution maps can be used to explore the fit between activities and associated trade-offs, highlighting the role of strategy execution in developing and securing competitive advantage. Strategy execution maps can also be used to help develop strategic performance measurement frameworks and identify strategic risks.

Not all legitimate activities are developed through top-down planning. Alignment between actions and objectives can nevertheless be tested and developed bottom-up using causal chains. Based on the same logic as strategy execution maps, these are useful for articulating, communicating, and exploring alignment between the products of projects (or other activities/initiatives) and organizations' overall objectives. They are also essential for identifying risks that can arise after the successful delivery of projects, preventing the achievement of overall objectives or creating negative unintended effects. Finally, they support the development of detailed performance measures and associated cost-benefit models for projecting and tracking actual benefits from projects and initiatives – including those that deliver 'soft' changes conventionally difficult to link with ultimate organizational objectives.

The need for better design

With these methods established for ensuring that the right concrete activities have been identified and articulated, attention can turn to how organizational designs and systems drive actual delivery of these activities. All the elements in phase 2 of the inverted pyramid framework can be shaped to ensure that critical activities happen. Project management systems and processes can be designed to maximize the chances of critical activities being delivered as intended. Equally, organization structure should reflect the best fit for critical activities. Resource allocation systems and the active management of subunit interfaces, along with projects and processes, are the things that can make these structures work well.

Successful strategy execution also requires leaders to pay attention to the individual perspective and how roles and responsibilities can be shaped – again with critical activities being the dominant driver. The quest for strong accountability can seriously conflict with the need for balanced performance measurement, demanding fine balance in decisions and signalling about these. The many risks of using crude techniques such as forced ranking for individual performance assessment can and should be avoided, especially in the absence of any evidence that these approaches deliver the benefits sometimes claimed.

Managing capacity, commitment, and capability are operational and human resources challenges – but ones important to strategy execution. These three performance variables are tightly associated, with their effects difficult to tease apart both when diagnosing performance constraints and planning strategy execution. In terms of causality, they lie far back from overall objectives and critical activities, so are inherently difficult to align with these. Paying close attention to them is thus important, not least because of the potency of any reward systems used to manage commitment. Despite its huge popularity, individual performance-related pay remains a highly risky practice, insufficiently supported by sound empirical research and evidence that it drives intended results. Similar risks exist even where extrinsic rewards are not on offer, but performance measures or targets draw attention toward excessively narrowly framed outcomes. Dysfunctional performance measures, targets, and reward systems are major causes of strategy execution failure. To implement strategies successfully, most large and complex organizations need to adopt more-rounded and sustainable methods to assess and manage individual performance.

Challenges for practitioners and researchers

Summarizing the main themes and thrusts of this book highlights the scale of the strategy execution challenge. Authors, consultants, and many others tend to make grand claims about the impact their ideas can make. Hopefully, the approaches outlined in this book will make a difference – but let me be clear about the shape of my hopes. We are taking early steps venturing into a management challenge that has proven elusive and awkward for the several decades it has been discussed. In tackling it, organizational leaders will need to keep their wits about them and not be tempted by intellectual shortcuts and oversimplified or unsupported ideas. History suggests it is easy to dream up nifty models – but they usually don't work. In my view, thoughtful attention paid to the unique circumstances of individual organizations and situations will pay dividends.

Similarly, more academics need to get away from their desks and take their research work deeply into complex organizations. We need more systematic empirical studies of strategy execution – preferably beginning with more multi-method, multi-source, extended, real-time, longitudinal, inductive research that builds the fundamental theoretical frameworks upon which more specific deductive studies can be built. As I mentioned in the Introduction, I sincerely hope a much closer partnership between those in practice, research, and teaching can evolve, as without it I doubt serious progress will be made in understanding the subject.

A final request

In closing, I wish you success in your continuing exploration of strategy execution – whether as a student of the subject or as a leader with responsibility for executing strategy in an organization. I hope this book helps you tackle this difficult but hugely important challenge.

As I have said, strategy execution is an emerging science, with much more work needing to be done to grow our understanding of it. Many of the ideas and frameworks presented in the book will need to be further developed and refined as further systematic research throws up new insights. I encourage all interested readers to contribute to and be part of that process. I warmly welcome comments on this book, suggestions for future editions, and other feedback from all readers at the companion website at www.strategy-execution.net. I hope this website will become a useful forum for discussion and development in the field of strategy execution.

Alternatively, I can be contacted directly at www.strategy-execution.co.uk/contact and welcome hearing from anyone interested in or facing the challenge of strategy execution.

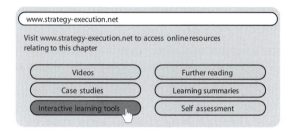

Appendices

Research methodology

This book reports a number of findings from my own research. A summary is provided here of the research methodology used in the studies producing these findings.

Building theory through longitudinal case studies

The strategy execution literature is limited by its weak theoretical and empirical underpinnings. There are few systematic empirical studies, and many of these are prematurely narrow studies, testing hypotheses in the absence of well-developed subject foundations that give context to such testing. The absence of clear definitions of the terms *strategy implementation* and *strategy execution* are evidence of this problem. Similarly, Larry Hrebiniak makes the point that managers know more about strategy formulation than implementation.[1] It is, thus, risky to assume that practitioners are knowledgeable and articulate about strategy execution, making research instruments such as surveys an unsatisfactory choice for exploring many strategy execution issues.

For these reasons, my research adopted an exploratory and qualitative approach to examine some of the fundamental issues in the field.[2] A grounded-theory approach was used to guide a series of case studies. Kathleen Eisenhardt's model for building theory from case studies was adopted.[3] Three major case studies were developed along with some additional vignettes. Each of the longitudinal case studies was conducted in real time. Two of the main cases were studied over a period of six years, and the third was studied over five years. There is substantial support for conducting studies of this sort.[4] Longitudinal studies overcome serious problems with cross-sectional studies, such as invalid assumptions about cause and effect relationships, ignorance of time lag effects, and limited triangulation.[5]

Sampling

Each of the cases was selected using a theoretical sampling model.[6] The study initially examined two cases in an organization that was large, long-established, performing well, and seeking to execute new strategies, on the basis that *if* organizations executing strategy have generally discovered effective strategy execution methods, then scale and learning-curve theories suggest this organization would have done so.[7] During the study, a third case with one contrasting characteristic was added – it was significantly smaller than the organization from which the first two cases were drawn. It was theorized that some of the phenomena observed in the first two cases *may* have been attributable, at least in part, to the *size* and corresponding *complexity* of the organization studied.[8]

The definition of the units of analysis (and thus boundaries) for the case studies was made in light of the organizations/subunits being examined, the relevant activities in which they were involved, and the research objectives.[9] The first two cases were drawn from two functions within a large service sector company. The third case focused upon an entire, but much smaller, public sector organization.

Data collection

The study design ensured high levels of triangulation.[10] Data source triangulation was ensured via collecting data at multiple levels in organizational hierarchies (to avoid 'elite bias'[11]) and a wide range of subunits and through prolonged engagement in the field. The level of methodological triangulation was high, with the following data collection methods being employed:

- archival sources and document review
- passive observation
- face-to-face interviews
- participant observation[12]
- action research[13]

As the study progressed in each subject organization, the level of participation was increased. This tactic was structured to enable the early collection of data pertaining to a relatively 'uncontaminated' field. As saturation was reached using each method and little incremental gain was being made with one data collection method, a more participative technique was adopted to facilitate deeper engagement with subjects and exploit a more constructivist approach to theory building.

Data analysis

Data from the cases were examined via a systematic process incorporating the following key phases:

- initial sorting and memos/remarks
- isolation of critical incidents[14]
- sequential analysis

- actor feedback
- open, axial, and selective coding[15]
- peer review and debriefing

A database was developed to allow integration and sophisticated analysis and to maintain an audit trail from raw data through to conclusions.

Key limitations

It is important to acknowledge the limitations of the study. Although modest generalizations can be made through theoretical sampling and strong replication of findings across the three cases, there are limitations on how far these generalizations can be extended. Further studies should build upon and test the theory inducted, isolating legitimately narrow phenomena related to which studies of statistically representative samples can be carried out usefully.

Analysis of strategy definitions

Table A1 provides an analysis of various definitions of strategy proposed by a selection of leading theorists. It demonstrates the range of views held but also helps to convey the meaning of the term.

Summary of strategy execution barriers research

Table A2 summarizes strategy execution barriers identified in a range of empirical studies. It categorizes the barriers discovered into 11 groups using appropriately re-stated descriptions of barriers if two or more studies cited barriers that were clearly the same. The barriers have been categorized to aid interpretation; however, it is important to note that such categorizations are problematic and subjective, because of the variation of ways in which implementation problems can be framed. See Chapter 4 for a discussion of these barriers.

Major strategy execution content models

Table A3 summarizes and compares the elements of the main 'content school' strategy execution models already developed.

Table A1 Analysis of various strategy definitions

Element	Chandler (1962)[1]	Andrews (1971)[2]	Hofer & Schendel (1978)[3]	Quinn (1980)[4]	Thompson & Strickland (1981)[5]	Johnson & Scholes (2002)[6]
Basic/fundamental framework/pattern of decisions/moves	✓	✓	✓	✓	✓	
Defining the business		✓				
Long-term perspective	✓					✓
Determination of mission/objective/goal	✓	✓				
Determination of major policies/plans to achieve goals	✓	✓	✓		✓	
Determination of courses of activities	✓					
Determination of direction						✓
Determination of scope						✓
Planned deployment/allocation of resources	✓		✓			✓
Planned interactions with environment/market/stakeholders			✓			✓
Integration of goals, policies and actions				✓		

1 Chandler, A. D. (1962) *Strategy and structure*. Cambridge, MA: MIT Press.
2 Andrews, K. R. (1971) *The concept of corporate strategy*. Homewood, IL: Dow Jones-Irwin.
3 Hofer, C. W. & Schendel, D. E. (1978) *Strategy formulation analytical concepts*. St Paul, MN: West Publishing Co.
4 Quinn, J. B. (1980) *Strategies for change: Logical incrementalism*. Homewood, IL: Irwin.
5 Thompson, A. A. & Strickland, A. J. (1981) *Strategy formulation and implementation: Tasks of the general manager*. Dallas TX: Business Publications.
6 Johnson, G., & Scholes, K. (2002) *Exploring corporate strategy*. (Sixth edition.) Harlow: Financial Times Prentice Hall.

Table A2 Barriers to strategy implementation identified in empirical studies

Key concept	Alexander (1985)[1]	Wessel (1993)[2]	McGrath et al (1995)[3]	Sandelands (1994)[4]	Al-Ghamdi (1998)[5]	Wernham (1984)[6]	Corboy & O'Corrbui (1999)[7]	Economist Intelligence Unit (2004)[8]	Hrebiniak (2005)[9]
Problems with strategy content									
Strategy not worth implementing							✓		
Inadequate 'market validity'						✓			
Inadequate 'technical validity'						✓			
Insufficient understanding of how strategy creation affects its execution									✓
Inadequate 'organizational validity'						✓			
Insufficient clarity of how the strategy will be implemented							✓		
Problems with implementation planning									
Implementation took longer than allocated	✓				✓				
Unanticipated problems	✓				✓				
No model to guide execution									✓
Insufficient recognition of blockers							✓		
Insufficient involvement of staff/inclusion of their recommendations								✓	
Problems with coordination of activities									
Ineffective budgeting								✓	✓
Ineffective organizational structures for fostering information sharing, coordination, and clear accountability								✓	✓
Lack of information/timing						✓			
Ineffective coordination of activities	✓				✓				
Key implementation tasks and activities insufficiently well defined	✓				✓				
Unclear individual responsibilities for implementing changes							✓		
Problems with feedback and control									
Inadequate information systems for effective monitoring	✓				✓				
Inadequate metrics, reports and consensus around these								✓	
Ineffective controls and feedback mechanisms									✓
Problems requiring top management interventions not escalated quickly enough					✓				

Key concept	Alexander (1985)[1]	Wessel (1993)[2]	McGrath et al (1995)[3]	Sandelands (1994)[4]	Al-Ghamdi (1998)[5]	Wernham (1984)[6]	Corboy & O'Corrbui (1999)[7]	Economist Intelligence Unit (2004)[8]	Hrebiniak (2005)[9]
Socio-political problems									
Ineffective top team functioning		✓							
Political turbulence			✓						
Inter-functional conflicts		✓							
Insufficient understanding and use of power and influence									✓
History/confidence						✓			
Leadership/management problems									
Excessively top-down management style		✓							
Inadequate management development		✓							
Insufficient chief executive/senior manager involvement in implementation							✓		
Leadership and direction from departmental managers insufficient	✓				✓				
Insufficiently execution-biased leadership									✓
Communication problems									
Poor vertical communications		✓						✓	
Customers and staff do not fully understand the strategy							✓		
Prioritization problems									
Too many priorities		✓							
Conflicting priorities		✓				✓			
Competing activities created distractions	✓				✓				
Conflicting goals						✓			
Resource problems									
Inadequate resources (money, people, materials)						✓		✓	

Table A2 continued ...

Key concept	Alexander (1985)[1]	Wessel (1993)[2]	McGrath et al (1995)[3]	Sandelands (1994)[4]	Al-Ghamdi (1998)[5]	Wernham (1984)[6]	Corboy & O'Corrbui (1999)[7]	Economist Intelligence Unit (2004)[8]	Hrebiniak (2005)[9]
Capability problems									
Excessive organizational inertia				✓					
Employee capabilities insufficient	✓								
Inadequate training/instruction for junior employees	✓								
Other problems									
Implementation delays						✓			
Normal business suffers during change									
Ineffective management of change (including cultural change)							✓		
Failure to create an execution-supportive culture									✓
Uncontrollable factors in external environment	✓				✓				✓
Failure to engage suppliers and/or customers								✓	

1 Alexander, L. D. (1985) 'Successfully implementing strategic decisions', *Long Range Planning*, 18, 91–7 surveyed 93 CEOs running Strategic Business Units in large firms, using a (highly structured) questionnaire testing perceptions about strategy implementation barriers and implementation success in each firm. This was followed up with 21 telephone interviews to examine the barriers in greater depth. Limited details of the methodology are provided but a risk of elite bias produced by CEOs' lack of knowledgeability of the reasons for strategy implementation failure is a likely limitation.

2 Wessel, J. (1993) 'The strategic human resource management process in practice', *Planning Review*, 21, 37–8.

3 McGrath, R. G., MacMillan, I. C., & Venkataraman, S. (1995) 'Defining and developing competence: A strategic process paradigm', *Strategic Management Journal*, 16, 251–75.

4 Sandelands, L. E. (1994) 'All talk and no action? Perish the thought', *Management Decision*, 32, 10–11.

5 Al-Ghamdi, S. M. (1998) 'Obstacles to successful implementation of strategic decisions: The British experience', *European Business Review*, 98, 322–7 to some extent replicated Alexander's study, mailing a slightly further developed (highly structured) survey questionnaire to 100 business in the Bradford area of the UK (the rationale for using this sample is not provided). 24 usable responses were apparently collected, precluding any validation of their knowledgeability about the phenomena under investigation.

6 Wernham, R. (1985) 'Obstacles to strategy implementation in a nationalized industry', *The Journal of Management Studies*, 22, 632–49 reports the examination of several projects being implemented in a single organization (British Telecommunications plc). The interviewee sample of 64 was sizable, but included only relatively senior personnel, introducing the possibility of elite bias. The study was limited to a single organization and apparently used single data method, limiting triangulation.

7 Corboy, M. & O'Corrbui, D. (1999) 'The seven deadly sins of strategy', *Management Accounting*, 77, 29–30 report findings based on a series of annual surveys consultancy firm Prospectus conducted in the financial services sector during the 1990s. The sector-specific survey may limit the extent to which its findings can be generalized. Limited methodological details are provided.

8 Economist Intelligence Unit (2004) *Strategy execution: Achieving operational excellence*. London: The Economist Intelligence Unit.

9 Hrebiniak, L. G. (2005) *Making strategy work: Leading effective execution and change*. Upper Saddle River, NJ: Pearson Education.

Table A3 Comparison of the main strategy implementation 'content school' framework

Model element	Galbraith & Nathanson (1978)[1]	Stonich (1982)[2]	Hrebiniak & Joyce (1984)[3]	Galbraith & Kazanjian (1986)[4]	Hrebiniak (2005)[5]
Strategy formulation	• Product/market strategy	• Strategy formulation	• Strategy formulation	• Product/market strategy	• Corporate strategy • Business strategy [and short-term operating objectives]
Organizational culture		• Culture			• Organizational culture
Organizational structure	• Structure	• Organization structure	• Primary structure	• Structure	• Corporate structure/integration • Business structure integration
Operating objectives		• Management processes: planning • Management processes: programming	• Operating level objectives		• Business strategy [and short-term operating objectives]
Information processes	• Information and decision processes			• Information and decision processes	
Operating structures			• Operating structure		• Business structure [/integration]
Integration of parts	• Integration mechanisms			• Integration mechanisms	• [Corporate structure/] integration • [Business structure/] integration
Performance measurement and rewards	• Reward system	• Management processes: measurement and reward systems	• Incentives and controls	• Reward system	• Incentives and controls • Human resources
Human resources	• People			• People	
Resource allocation system	• Resource allocation processes	• Management processes: budgeting		• Resource allocation processes	
Managing change		• Making strategy happen	• Strategic change	• Strategic adaption	• Change management
Organizational politics					• Power and influence
Leadership					• Leadership

1 Galbraith, J. R. & Nathanson, D. (1978) Strategy implementation: The role of structure and process. St Paul, MN: West Publishing Co.
2 Stonich, P. J. (1982) Implementing strategy. Cambridge, MA: Ballinger.
3 Hrebiniak, L. G. & Joyce, W. F. (1984) Implementing strategy. New York: Macmillan.
4 Galbraith, J. R. & Kazanjian, R. K. (1986) Strategy implementation: Structure, systems and process. St Paul, MN: West Publishing Co.
5 Hrebiniak, L. G. (2005) Making strategy work: Leading effective execution and change. Upper Saddle River, NJ: Pearson Education.

Notes

I INTRODUCTION

1 Economist Intelligence Unit (2004) *Strategy execution: Achieving operational excellence.* London: Economist Intelligence Unit. This study of executives reported that "only 43% rate their companies as having been successful or very successful at executing strategic initiatives over the past three years" (2004: 2) and that "forty-five per cent of executives say their company's or business unit's strategic initiatives have performed below plan" (2004: 5). Findings are based on a survey of 276 senior operations executives in the United States and Canada in eight mature industries. The companies involved had a wide range of annual turnovers (from less than $10 million to more than $10 billion). Surveying a wide range of respondents from board members to middle managers reduced risks of elite bias. Respondent knowledgability was confirmed via high self-reported involvement in both developing and executing strategic objectives.

2 See Mankins, M. C. & Steele, R. (2005) 'Turning great strategy into great performance', *Harvard Business Review,* January, 64–72. This finding is based on a survey of senior executives in 197 companies, who attributed an average 37 per cent "performance loss" (2005: 68) to 11 problems, most of which relate to strategy execution. The study examined the extent to which strategy implementation attempts are followed by anticipated performance increases. Few details of the research methodology are provided, but some potential limitations do exist. Most notably: the survey was the only source of data (precluding triangulation); it is not clear how the respondents assessed (accurately) the performance variations from plans (Mankins and Steele observe that "fewer than 15% of companies make it a regular practice to go back and compare the business's results with the performance forecast for each unit in its prior years' strategic plans" (2005: 66); the survey was only of "senior executives" (2005:66) and thus is likely to be affected by senior bias; and it is questionable whether the respondents would have had sufficient knowledge to attribute (with performance loss quantifications) strategy execution failures to specific problems, particularly given Mankins and Steele's separate observation that executives have "no way of knowing whether critical actions were carried out as expected, resources were deployed on schedule, competitors responded as anticipated, and so on" (2005: 68). Interestingly, no performance losses are attributed to external environmental factors at all, which one might expect.

3 Charan, R. & Colvin, G. (1999) 'Why CEOs fail' *Fortune,* June 21, 69–78.

4 Nutt, P. C. (1999) 'Surprising but true: Half the decisions in organizations fail', *Academy of Management Executive, 13,* 75–90.

5 See, for example, Corboy, M. & O'Corrbui, D. (1999) 'The seven deadly sins of strategy', *Management Accounting, 77,* 29–30, who report research findings that 70 per cent of strategies fail. The finding was based on a series of annual surveys by

consultancy firm *Prospectus* conducted in the financial services sector during the 1990s. The sector-specific survey may limit the extent to which its findings can be generalized. The reporting of perceived levels of strategy failure is also liable to various biases, including under-reporting by managers seeking to appear more successful than they were and limitations whereby managers without sufficient knowledgability of the phenomena investigated were surveyed.

6   Search conducted at http://www.google.com conducted on 3 December 2009.

7   Rajagopalan, N. & Spreitzer, G. M. (1997) 'Toward a theory of strategic change: A multi-lens perspective and integrative framework', *Academy of Management Review*, *22*, 48–80; Bougon, M. G. & Komocar, J. (1990) 'Directing strategic change: A dynamic wholistic approach'. In Huff, A. S. (Ed.), *Mapping strategic thought* (pp. 136–63). Chichester: Wiley.

8   For example, see Bossidy, L., Charan, R. & Burch, C. (2002) *Execution: The discipline of getting things done*. London: Random House Business Books; Hartman, A. (2004) *Ruthless execution: What business leaders do when their company hits the wall*. Englewood Cliffs, NJ: Prentice Hall.

9   See, for example, Bigler, W. R. Jr. & Norris, M. (2004) *The new science of strategy execution: How established firms become fast, sleek wealth creators*. Westport, CT: Praeger Publishers; Wall, S. J. (2004) *On the fly: Executing strategy in a changing world*. Hoboken, NJ: John Wiley & Sons; Hrebiniak, L. G. (2005) *Making strategy work: Leading effective execution and change*. Upper Saddle River, NJ: Pearson Education.

10   For an exploration of management tools and techniques and how they are used, see, for example, Ashkenas, R. N. & Shaffer, R. H. (1994) 'Beyond the fads: How leaders drive change with results', *Human Resource Planning, 17* (2), 25–44; Staw, B. M. & Epstein, L. D. (2000) 'What bandwagons bring: Effects of popular management techniques on corporate performance, reputation, and CEO pay', *Administrative Science Quarterly, 45,* 523–56; Rigby, D. & Bilodeau, B. (2009) *Management Tools,* Boston, MA: Bain & Company.

2   WHAT IS STRATEGY EXECUTION?

1   For any given organization, other forms of interactions with the environment will matter to different extents. For example, paying tax may be crippling for a business in a particular jurisdiction at a point in time. A merger is another example of a hugely significant interaction. However, market interactions matter greatly for all organizations. Interacting with customers or their equivalent (e.g. citizens, beneficiaries) via some form of product or service and through some form of channel is invariably central to achieving objectives.

2   See, for example, Mintzberg, H., Ahlstrand, B. & Lampal, J. (1998) *Strategy safari: The complete guide through the wilds of strategic management*. London: Prentice Hall.

3   In this context, overall objective means the highest-level or most fundamental objective and organization is intended generally enough to apply to entire organizations or indeed subunits within them that have clear purposes.

4   Rigby, D. & Bilodeau, B. (2009) *Management tools,* Boston, MA: Bain & Company.

5   Stonich, P. J. (1982) *Implementing strategy*. Cambridge, MA: Ballinger.

6   Eccles, T. (1994) *Succeeding with change: Implementing action-driven strategies*. London: McGraw-Hill, p. 10.

7   Ibid (p. 14, emphasis original).

8 Porter, M. E. (1994) 'Toward a dynamic theory of strategy'. In Rumelt, R. P., Schendel, D. E. & Teece, D. J. (Eds.) *Fundamental issues in strategy: A research agenda* (pp. 423–61). Boston, MA: Harvard Business School Press.

9 Andrews, K. R. (1960) *The concept of corporate strategy*. Homewood, IL: Irwin.

10 Galbraith, J. R. & Nathanson, D. (1978) *Strategy implementation: The role of structure and process*. St Paul, MN: West Publishing Co.; Stonich, op. cit.; Hrebiniak, L., & Joyce, W. (1984) *Implementing strategy,* New York: Macmillan; Galbraith, J. R. & Kazanjian, R. K. (1986) *Strategy implementation: Structure, systems and process*. St Paul, MN: West Publishing Co.

11 This point was made by Hrebiniak and Joyce, op. cit. in 1984 and remains true.

3   THE STRATEGY EXECUTION CHALLENGE

1 This quotation has also been attributed to Yogi Berra, Manfred Eigen, and Eigen's editor, Chuck Reid.

2 Charan, R. & Colvin, G. (1999) 'Why CEOs fail' *Fortune,* June 21, 69–78.

3 Aspesi, C. & Vardham, V. (1999) 'Brilliant strategy, but can you execute?', *The McKinsey Quarterly,* Winter, 59–99.

4 Charan & Colvin, op. cit.

5 See, for example, The BOC Group and London Business School (1994) *Building global excellence*. London: The BOC Group and London Business School; Guth, W. D. & MacMillan, I. C. (1986) 'Strategy implementation versus middle management self interest', *Strategic Management Journal, 7,* 313–27.

6 Hrebiniak, L. G. (2005) *Making strategy work: Leading effective execution and change*. Upper Saddle River, NJ: Pearson Education; Roberts, A. & MacLennan, A. F. (2003) *Making strategies work*. Harlow: Pearson.

7 Hrebiniak, op. cit.

8 These were the findings of a BBC *Panorama* documentary, broadcast in the United Kingdom in March 2001.

9 This revelation was aired on the BBC's *Question Time* programme, broadcast in the United Kingdom on 28 April 2005, just ahead of the United Kingdom's General Election on 5 May 2005. Tony Blair was returned to power with a much-reduced majority in the House of Commons.

10 Audit Commission (2007) *Public interest report. Response Times. Great Western Ambulance Service NHS Trust in respect of the former Wiltshire Ambulance Service NHS Trust. Audit 2005–2006*. 30 March. Online. Available at: http://www.audit-commission.gov.uk/SiteCollectionDocuments/PublicInterestReports/pir07greatwestern.pdf. (Accessed on 10 January 2010).

4   DIAGNOSING STRATEGY EXECUTION PROBLEMS

1 Search at http://www.google.com conducted on 3 July 2009.

2 See, for example, Rigby, D. & Bilodeau, B. (2009) *Management tools*. Boston, MA: Bain & Company.

3 Dreilinger, C. (1994) 'Why management fads fizzle', *Business Horizons, 37*(6), 11–15.

4 See, for example, Ansoff, H. I. (1965) *Corporate strategy: An analytical approach to business policy for growth and expansion*. New York: McGraw-Hill.

5 Tversky, A. & Kahneman, D. (1981) 'The framing of decisions and psychology of choice', *Science, 211,* 453–58.

6 See, for example, MacLennan, A. & Lee, G. (2007) 'Challenging customers: 10 tactics every HR business partner should know', *HR Network (Scotland), 2*(3), 28–30.

7 Argyris, C. and Schön, D. (1978) *Organizational learning: A theory of action perspective.* Reading, MA: Addison Wesley.

8 Call abandon rate is the proportion of calls abandoned by customers, usually because they have been waiting so long that they 'give up'.

5 A FRAMEWORK FOR STRATEGY EXECUTION

1 The idea of using causality in the strategic planning arena can be traced back at least to Sackman, H. (1971) *Mass information utilities and social excellence.* New York: Auerback. He suggested that the problems of prescriptive planning in uncertain environments might be overcome by conceiving plans as hypotheses, subject to rigorous empirical testing. Hrebiniak, L. G. & Joyce, W. F. (1984) *Implementing strategy.* New York: Macmillan, suggest that strategic decision making could be seen as a series of means-ends decisions linking long-term goals with shorter-term actions necessary to obtain these goals, though they do not elaborate on how this is done. In the field of managerial and organizational cognition (MOC), there has been wide use of causal mapping for exploring strategic logic. See, for example, Huff, A. S. (1990) (Ed.), *Mapping strategic thought.* Chichester: Wiley; Eden, C. & Ackermann, F. (1998) *Making strategy: The journey of strategic management.* London: Sage. In the field of performance measurement, Kaplan and Norton (e.g. Kaplan, R. S., & Norton, D. P. (1996) *The balanced scorecard: Translating strategy into action.* Boston, MA: Harvard Business School Press; Kaplan, R. S. & Norton, D. P. (2001) *The strategy focused organization: How balanced scorecard companies thrive in the new business environment.* Boston, MA: Harvard Business School Press) suggested that strategies are sets of cause and effect hypotheses and have loosely applied the notion of causality in the development of the balanced scorecard and later, strategy maps. Simons, R. (2000) *Performance measurement and control systems for implementing strategy: Text and cases.* Englewood Cliffs, NJ: Prentice Hall, also briefly discusses cause-and-effect thinking in relation to strategic planning, performance measurement, and control systems. The original inspiration for the use of causality here for strategy execution came from Kirkpatrick, D. L. (1959) 'Techniques for evaluation training programs', *Journal of American Society for Training Directors, 13,* 28–32. Although Kirkpatrick's application of causality was for training evaluation, it closely mirrors the kind of thinking useful to formulate and test assumptions for strategy execution.

2 Child, J. (1977) *Organization: A guide for managers and administrators.* New York: Harper & Row, proposed that consistency between management practices, structure, processes, and people was important.

3 This is known as the principal-agent problem. Managers (principals) must rely upon others (agents) to act on their behalf and must, therefore, seek to match the objectives of agents with those of the organization.

4 Some practitioners reject the idea that you can decide 'where you want to get to' because they recognize that the environment changes unpredictably and quickly. Hence, the argument goes, there is no point in defining a long-term, high-level objective. I don't particularly value this argument (which is part of a wider, rather polemic debate stimulated more by academics than practitioners), because such views are based on a fixed notion of how an overall objective should be constructed. The environment should influence the shape of the overall objective, and it should usually be broader and more process-oriented if the environment is highly unpredictable. For example, it might specify the intention to generate profit but not a narrowly defined industry in which this will be done. Additionally, 'long-term' should always be seen as relative to the environment. In very fast-moving environments, overall objectives need to be revisited more frequently than in very stable settings. In other words, you should

always be as specific as you can reasonably be under whatever circumstances you operate in. Furthermore, it is always necessary to have some conception of high-level objectives, even if this is only generated when evaluating an emergent opportunity. Otherwise, completely random activities would be as attractive as any others. Chapter 7 explores how to think about strategy execution 'bottom-up'.

5　This is a condition often applied to the notion of critical success factors. See, for example, Hardaker, M. & Ward, B. K. (1987) 'Getting things done', *Harvard Business Review, 65*(6), 112–20.

6　This element of the framework reflects the notion that, though many different analytical tools may be used to analyse the environment, the implications of these are best summarized as barriers/risks and enablers/opportunities specific to the organization's overall objective.

7　The principle of using leading and lagging indicators, though long-established, has been widely popularized by Kaplan and Norton, op. cit.

8　Other authors have proposed equivalent models (though these have mainly not been based on empirical research) that have been simpler but, in my view, too simplistic. For example, some academics have suggested that managers should move directly from considering business strategy and operating objectives to incentives and controls. The framework outlined here suggests such a move would ignore elements such as activities, roles and responsibilities, and commitment.

6　TRANSLATING STRATEGY INTO ACTION

1　Rigby, D. & Bilodeau, B. (2009) *Management tools.* Boston, MA: Bain & Company.

2　Herold, D. M. (1972) 'Long-range planning and organizational performance: A cross-validation study', *Academy of Management Journal, 15*(1), 91–102; Armstrong, J. S. (1982) 'The value of formal planning for strategic decisions: Review of empirical research', *Strategic Management Journal, 3*, 197–211; Boyd, B. K. (1991) 'Strategic planning and financial performance: A meta-analytical review', *Journal of Management Studies, 28*(4), 353–74; Camillus, J. C. (1975) 'Evaluating the benefits of formal planning systems', *Long Range Planning, 8*(3), 33–40; Fulmer, R. M., & Rue, L. W. (1974) 'The practice and profitability of long range planning', *Managerial Planning, 22*(6), May–June, 1–7.

3　Galbraith, J. R. & Nathanson, D. (1978) *Strategy implementation: The role of structure and process.* St Paul, MN: West Publishing Co.; Galbraith, J. R. & Kazanjian, R. K. (1986) *Strategy implementation: Structure, systems and process.* St Paul, MN: West Publishing Co.; Hrebiniak, L. & Joyce, W. (1984) *Implementing strategy,* New York: Macmillan; Stonich, P. J. (1982) *Implementing strategy.* Cambridge, MA: Ballinger.

4　Grady, M. W. (1991) 'Performance measurement: Implementing strategy', *Management Accounting, 72,* 49–54; Reed, R. & Buckley, M. R. (1988) 'Strategy in action: Techniques for implementing strategy', *Long Range Planning, 21,* 67–74; Roberts, A. & Pitt, S. (1990) 'Strategy implementation: A dynamic process guide', Working paper, London Business School; Roberts, A. & MacLennan, A. F. (2003) *Making strategies work.* Harlow: Pearson.

5　For example, see Grady, op. cit.; Roberts & Pitt, op. cit.; Roberts & MacLennan, op. cit. These authors' 'process school' models draw upon the notion of criticality. For discussions of criticality, see, for example, Daniel, D. R. (1961) 'Management information crisis', *Harvard Business Review,* September–October, 111–21; Rockart, J. F. (1979) 'Chief executives define their own data needs', *Harvard Business Review,* March–April, 238–41; Hardaker, M. & Ward, B. K. (1987) 'Getting things done', *Harvard Business Review, 65*(6), 112–20; Anthony, R. N., Deardon, J. & Vancil, R. F. (1972) *Management control systems,* Homewood, IL: Irwin; Leidecker, J. K. & Bruno,

A. V. (1984) 'Identifying and using critical success factors', *Long Range Planning, 17,* 23–32; Hofer, C. W. & Schendel, D. E. (1978) *Strategy formulation analytical concepts.* St Paul, MN: West Publishing Co.; Munro, M. C., & Wheeler, B. R. (1980) 'Planning, critical success factors, and management's information requirements', *MIS Quarterly,* December, 27–38; Boynton, A. C. & Zmud, R. W. (1984) 'An assessment of critical success factors', *Sloan Management Review,* 17–27; Jenster, P. V. (1987) 'Using critical success factors in planning', *Long Range Planning, 20,* 102–9.

6 See, for example, Eden, C., Ackermann, F. & Cropper, S. (1992) 'The analysis of cause maps', *Journal of Management Studies, 29,* 309–24; Eden, C. (1992) 'On the nature of cognitive maps', *Journal of Management Studies, 29,* 261–65; Eden, C. & Ackermann, F. (1998) *Making strategy: The journey of strategic management.* London: Sage; Kaplan, R. S. & Norton, D. P. (1996) *The balanced scorecard: Translating strategy into action.* Boston, MA: Harvard Business School Press; Kaplan, R. S. & Norton, D. P. (2001) *The strategy focused organization: How balanced scorecard companies thrive in the new business environment.* Boston, MA.: Harvard Business School Press; Neely, A., Adams, C. & Kennerley, M. (2002) *The performance prism: The scorecard for measuring and managing business success.* Harlow: Pearson Education.

7 Starbucks Corporation. *Our Starbucks mission.* Online. Available at: http://www. starbucks.com/mission/default.asp. (Accessed: 6 January 2010).

8 Starbucks Corporation Fiscal 2008 Annual Report Online. Starbucks Corporation (2008) Available at: http://investor.starbucks.com/phoenix.zhtml?c = 99518&p = irol-reportsAnnual. (Accessed: 23 November 2009).

9 Boswell, W. R. (2000) *Aligning employees with the organization's strategic objectives: Out of "line of sight", out of mind.* Unpublished PhD Thesis, Cornell University, Ithaca, NY.

10 The use of Key Environmental Indicators is widespread, and was specifically suggested for strategy execution by Roberts & Pitt, op. cit.

11 I described this technique in Roberts & MacLennan, op. cit. after several years of development in the field.

12 Argyris, C. and Schön, D. (1978) *Organizational learning: A theory of action perspective.* Reading, MA: Addison Wesley.

13 Argyris, C. (1989) 'Strategy implementation: an experience in learning', *Organizational Dynamics, 18*(2), 4–15.

14 Miller, G. A. (1956) The magic number seven plus or minus two: Some limits on our capacity for processing information. *Psychological Review, 64,* 81–97.

15 Tversky, A. & Kahneman, D. (1974) Judgement under uncertainty: Heuristics and biases. *Science, 185,* 1124–31; Schwenk, C. (1986) 'Information, cognitive biases, and commitment to a course of action', *Academy of Management Review, 11,* 298–310.

16 Taylor, S. E. & Fiske, S. T. (1975) 'Point of view and perception of causality', *Journal of Personality and Social Psychology, 32,* 439–45.

17 Nisbett, R.E. & Ross, L. (1980) *Human Inference: Strategies and Shortcomings of Social Judgment.* Englewood Cliffs, NJ: Prentice Hall.

18 Kahneman, D. & Tversky, A. (1973) 'On the psychology of prediction', *Psychological Review, 80,* 237–51.

19 Miller, N. & Campbell, D. T. (1959) 'Recency and primacy in persuasion as a function of the timing of speeches and measurements', *Journal of Abnormal and Social Psychology, 59,* 1–9.

20 Ward, W. C. & Jenkins, H. H. (1965) 'The display of information and judgement of contingency', *Canadian Journal of Psychology, 19,* 231–41. Kahneman & Tversky, op. cit. have demonstrated, for example, the tendency to ignore base rates, such as

evaluating a predictive accuracy without knowledge of how accurate random decisions would be.

21 Eihorn, H. J. & Hogarth, R. M. (1978) 'Confidence in judgement: Persistence of the illusion of validity', *Psychological Review, 85,* 395–416.

22 Nisbett & Ross, op. cit.

23 Fombrun, C. J. (1994) 'Taking on strategy, 1-2-3'. In Baum, J.A.C. & Singh, J. V. (Eds.), *Evolutionary dynamics of organizations* (pp. 199–204). New York: Oxford University Press.

24 Einhorn and Hogarth, op. cit. have shown that managers (including statisticians) tend to rely solely on 'positive hits' when validating hypotheses. In other words, they seek confirmatory evidence, even although this is a very poor validation of causality.

25 Miles, M. B. & Huberman, A. M. (1994) *Qualitative data analysis: An expanded sourcebook.* (Second edition) Thousand Oaks, CA: Sage.

26 Hischhoff, B. (1975) 'Hindsight does not equal foresight: The effect of outcome knowledge on judgement under uncertainty', *Journal of Experimental Psychology: Human Perception and Performance, 1,* 288–99.

27 Kahneman, D. & Tversky, A. (1979) 'Prospect Theory: An analysis of decision under risk', *Econometrica, 47,* 263–91.

28 See, for example, Wright, J. C. (1962) 'Consistency and complexity of response sequences as a function of schedules of noncontingent reward', *Journal of Experimental Psychology, 63,* 601–9.

29 Simon, H. A. (1947) *Administrative behavior: A study of decision-making processes in administrative organization.* New York: Macmillan.

30 See, for example, Hrebiniak, L. G. & Joyce, W. F. (2001) 'Implementing strategy: An appraisal and agenda for future research'. In Hitt, M. A., Freeman, R. E. & Harrison, J. S. (Eds.), *Handbook of strategic management* (pp. 602–26). Malden, MA: Blackwell Business.

31 Alexander, L. D. (1985) 'Successfully implementing strategic decisions', *Long Range Planning, 18,* 91–97; Al-Ghamdi, S. M. (1998) 'Obstacles to successful implementation of strategic decisions: The British experience', *European Business Review, 98,* 322–27. Both note that strategies are not broken down sufficiently. Allio says "[a]n important first step is to break down the basic logic of how a broader strategy is to be implemented into shorter-term actions, with a defined start, middle, and end" (2005: 15). However, he does not explain how to do this.

32 Arguably, it might even be worth specifying that it would increase average awareness/ perceived value of the product which would in turn increase average desire to purchase the product which would increase the attraction of new customers. This is a good example of the problems balancing the level of detail and technical accuracy with the limitations of managers' cognitive capabilities and practical requirements. It is also a good example of where specific contextual information such as the nature of the product, market, scope of promotional potential, and so on is very helpful in informing an appropriate level of detail.

33 Heskett, J. L., Jones, T. O., Loveman, G. W., Sasser, W. E. & Schlesinger, L. A. (1994) 'Putting the service profit chain to work', *Harvard Business Review,* March–April, 164–74; Reichheld, F. F. (1993) 'Loyalty-based management', *Harvard Business Review,* March, 64–73.

34 Some authors have recognized problems with ambiguous language in strategy development. For example, Allio, op. cit., who also notes the importance of establishing a common language for successful strategy implementation. Wunder, T. (2005) 'New strategy alignment in multinational corporations', *Strategic Finance,* November, 35–41 notes similar concerns. Eden, C. & Ackermann, F. (1998) *Making*

strategy: The journey of strategic management. London: Sage, also advise against ambiguity and imprecision of terminology in developing strategy maps.

35 This problem has been identified, at a high level, by Brache, A. P. & Bodley-Scott, S. (2007) *Implementation: How to transform strategic initiatives into blockbuster results.* New York: McGraw-Hill, who warn against limiting the prioritization of initiatives to only those necessary for initiatives that are required to execute your strategy.

36 Porter, M. E. (1996) 'What is strategy?', *Harvard Business Review*, November–December, 61–78.

37 Anonymous (2006) 'IKEA: Flat pack accounting', *The Economist*, 11 May.

38 Forbes (2009) '*The world's billionaires: #5 Ingvar Kamprad & family'*, Online. 3 November. Available at: http://www.forbes.com/lists/2009/10/billionaires-2009-richest-people_Ingvar-Kamprad-family_BWQ7.html. (Accessed: 30 November 2009).

39 Apple, Mac, iPod, iPhone, iTunes, iWeb, MobileMe, iDisk, iLife, iWork, iMac, AirPort, Apple TV, MacBook Air and MagSafe are all trade marks used/owned by Apple Inc.

40 Wilcox, J. (2009) '*Apple has 91% of market for $1,000+ PCs, says NPD'*, Online. Betanews. (22 July) Available at: http://www.betanews.com/joewilcox/article/Apple-has-91-of-market-for-1000-PCs-says-NPD/1248313624. (Accessed: 30 November 2009).

41 Spektor, A (2009) '*Apple becomes world's most profitable handset vendor in Q3 2009'*, Online. Strategy Analytics. (10 November) Available at: http://strategyanalytics. com/default.aspx?mod=ReportAbstractViewer&a0=5118. (Accessed: 30 November 2009).

42 Apple Inc. (2009) '*10-K for fiscal year ended September 26, 2009'*, Online. Available at: http://www.apple.com/investor. (Accessed: 30 November 2009).

43 Industries are groups of similar organizations (in terms of resources utilized and products and services created) that potentially compete for the same customers. Industries can usefully be defined in terms of both products offered and their functions, and by examining future pressures and existing ones.

44 See, for instance, Porter, M. E. (1980) *Competitive strategy: Techniques for analysing industries and competitors.* New York: Free Press; Porter, M. E. (1985) *Competitive advantage: Creating and sustaining superior performance.* New York: Free Press; Porter, M. E. (1998). *On competition.* Boston, MA: Harvard Business School Press.

45 Porter, M. E. (1980) *Competitive strategy: Techniques for analysing industries and competitors.* New York: Free Press, p. 35.

46 See for example, Hill, C. W. L. (1988) 'Differentiation versus low cost of differentiation and low cost: A contingency framework', *Academy of Management Review, 13*(3), 401–12.

47 Hope, C. (2009) 'Ikea to open 10 stores in assault on town centres', *Daily Telegraph.* Online. Available at: http://www.telegraph.co.uk/finance/2929769/Ikea-to-open-10-stores-in-assault-on-town-centres.html. (Accessed: 1 December 2009).

48 See, for example, Prahalad, C. K., & Hamel, G. (1990) 'The core competence of the corporation', *Harvard Business Review,* May–June, 79–91; Mahoney, J.T. & Pandian, J. R. (1992) 'The resource-based view within the conversation of strategic management', *Strategic Management Journal, 13*, 363–80; Peteraf, M. A. (1993) 'The cornerstones of competitive advantage: A resource-based view', *Strategic Management Journal, 14*, 179–91; Wernerfelt, B. (1984) 'A resource-based view of the firm', *Strategic Management Journal, 5*, 171–80; Wernerfelt, B. (1995) 'The resource-based view of the firm: Ten years on', *Strategic Management Journal, 16*, 171–4.

49 See Selznick, P. (1957) *Leadership in administration: A sociological interpretation.* New York: Harper & Row.

51 This logic chimes with Eccles, T. (1994) *Succeeding with change: Implementing action-driven strategies.* London: McGraw-Hill, who says, "If the managers of two competing companies have the same intended and sensible strategy and one firm can implement its intentions better, faster and with less cost than its rival, then it can win the competitive battle by virtue of those superior implementation skills" (1994: 23).

51 Nutt, P. C. (2001) 'Strategic decision making'. In Hitt, M. A., Freeman, R. E. & Harrison, J. S. (Eds.) *The Blackwell handbook of strategic management* (pp. 35–69). Oxford: Blackwell; Bardach, E. (1977) *The implementation game.* Cambridge, MA: MIT Press.

52 Nutt, P.C. (1987) 'Identifying and appraising how managers install strategy', *Strategic Management Journal, 8,* 1–14.

7 ALIGNING ACTION WITH STRATEGY

1 For example, Igor Ansoff and Michael Porter.

2 For example, Charles Linbloom and Henry Mintzberg.

3 Herold, D. M. (1972) 'Long-range planning and organizational performance: A cross-validation study', *Academy of Management Journal,* March, 91–102; Armstrong, J. S. (1982) 'The value of formal planning for strategic decisions: Review of empirical research', *Strategic Management Journal, 3,* 197–211; Boyd, B. K. (1991) 'Strategic planning and financial performance: A meta-analytical review', *Journal of Management Studies, 28*(4), 353–74; Camillus, J. C. (1975) 'Evaluating the benefits of formal planning systems', *Long Range Planning, 8*(3), 33–40; Fulmer, R. M., & Rue, L. W. (1974) 'The practice and profitability of long range planning', *Managerial Planning, 22,* (6) May–June, 1–7.

4 See, for example, Leontiades, M., & Tezel, A. (1980) 'Planning perceptions and planning results', *Strategic Management Journal, 1,* 65–75.

5 This is consistent with findings from research into attribution theory, which shows that individuals tend to overestimate their influence over their environments. See, for example, Heider, F. (1958) *The psychology of interpersonal relations.* New York: Wiley; Jones, E. E. & Harris, V. A. (1967) 'The attribution of attitudes', *Journal of Experimental Social Psychology, 3,* 1–24; Ross, L. (1977) 'The intuitive psychologist and his shortcomings: Distortions in the attribution process'. In Berkowitz, L. (Ed.), *Advances in experimental social psychology,* 173–220. New York: Academic Press.

6 I reported this finding in Roberts, A. & MacLennan, A. F. (2003) *Making strategies work.* Harlow: Pearson.

7 I reported this finding in Roberts & MacLennan (Ibid.).

8 Limited retrospective confidence about the causal relationships toward the effect end of a causal chain are compounded by the abstract nature of concepts such as profitability in large and complex organizations. Reported profits, for example, can look like the results of definitive calculations but in reality can represent a crude snapshot indication of underlying and sustainable profitability. Consider, for example, how many years of enormous profits reported by some of the world's largest banks were wiped out by shattering losses over only a few months in the 2008/2009 'credit crisis'.

8   ALIGNING ORGANIZATIONAL DESIGNS & SYSTEMS

1   See, for example, Slack, N. & Lewis, M. (2008) *Operations strategy.* (Second edition.) Harlow: FT Prentice Hall; Slack, N., Chambers, S. & Johnston, R. (2007) *Operations management.* (Fifth edition.) Harlow: FT Prentice Hall.

2   Kates, A. & Galbraith, J. R. (2007) *Designing your organization: Using the star model to solve 5 critical design challenges.* San Francisco, CA: Jossey-Bass.

3   W. L. Gore & Associates, Inc. Online. Available at: http://www.gore.com. (Accessed: 3 January 2010)

4   W. L. Gore & Associates, Inc. W. L. Gore & Associates: *Bringing Dreams to Reality.* Online. Available at: http://www.gore.com/en_xx/aboutus/timeline/index.html. (Accessed 3 January 2010).

5   For the purposes of this discussion, we need not distinguish resources from assets, as might be done for accounting purposes.

6   See Mendelow, A. (1981) 'Environmental Scanning: The Impact of Stakeholder Concept'. In *Proceedings of the Second International Conference on Information Systems* (pp. 299–308), Cambridge, MA. Medelow's approach has been popularized by various others, notably Johnson, G., & Scholes, K. (2002) *Exploring corporate strategy.* (Sixth edition.) Harlow: Financial Times Prentice Hall.

7   Boswell, W. R. (2000) *Aligning employees with the organization's strategic objectives: Out of "line of sight", out of mind.* Unpublished PhD Thesis,. Cornell University, Ithaca, NY.

8   See Melcher, R. (1969) 'Roles and relationships: Clarifying the manager's job', *Personnel,* May–June, 34–41; Galbraith, J. (1973) *Designing complex organizations.* Reading, MA: Addison-Wesley; Beckhard, R. & Harris, D. (1977) *Organization transitions: Managing complex change.* Reading, MA: Addison-Wesley; Gilmore, T. (1979) 'Managing collaborative relationships in complex organizations', *Administration in Social Work, 3*(2) 167_80; McCann, J. E. & Gilmore, T. N. (1983) 'Diagnosing organizational decision making through responsibility charting', *Sloan Management Review, 24*(2), 3–15.

9   Project managers will be familiar with using a work breakdown structure for this purpose.

10 Welch, J. (2001) *Jack: Straight from the gut.* New York: Warner Books.

11 See, for example, Michaels, E., Handfield-Jones, H. & Axelrod, B. (2001) *The war for talent.* Boston, MA: Harvard Business School Press.

12 Houldsworth, E. & Jirasinghe, D. (2006) *Managing and measuring employee performance.* London: Kogan Page.

13 Lawler, L. E. (2002) 'The folly of forced ranking', *Strategy & Business, 28,* 28–32.

14 Osborne, T. & McCann, L.A. (2004) 'Forced ranking and age-related employment discrimination', Spring, *Human Rights Magazine.*

15 Novations Group, Inc. (2004) *Uncovering the growing disenchantment with forced ranking performance management systems.* Boston, MA: Novations Group, Inc.

16 Lawler, L. E. (2003) 'Reward practices and performance management system effectiveness', *Organization Dynamics, 32,* 396–404.

17 See Grote, R. (2005) *Forced ranking: Making performance management work.* HBS Working Knowledge. Online. Available at: http://hbswk.hbs.edu/archive/5091. html. (Accessed 9 January 2010). Grote cites a study that suggests forced rankings and automatic dismissals may produce a 16 per cent improvement in "workforce potential" after two years (Scullen, S., Bergey, P. & Aiman-Smith, L. (2005) 'Forced distribution rating systems and the improvement of workforce potential: A baseline simulation', *Personnel Psychology, 58*(1): 1–32. Grote says it shows "the basic hypothesis underlying the forced ranking, rank-and-yank methodology is solid", and *Business Week* described the study as providing "hard data" to support

the use of forced rankings (see Anonymous. (2006) 'The struggle to measure performance', *Business Week,* 9 January). However, the study was actually an entirely theoretical simulation built upon numerous untested assumptions and no real world observations. The researchers themselves carefully caveat, "Like all simulations, ours is an incomplete representation of reality" and "important effects (e.g. on morale, productivity, or profitability) are largely outside the scope." They clearly state they were not seeking to inform whether forced distribution ranking systems were good or bad for organizations.

18   Indeed, Scullen, Bergey & Aiman-Smith's (cp. cit.) simulation suggested that the 16 per cent improvement would fall to only two per cent after six years.

19   See, for example, Heider, F. (1958) *The psychology of interpersonal relations.* New York: Wiley; Jones, E. E. & Harris, V. A. (1967) 'The attribution of attitudes', *Journal of Experimental Social Psychology, 3,* 1–24; Ross, L. (1977) 'The intuitive psychologist and his shortcomings: Distortions in the attribution process'. In Berkowitz, L. (Ed.), *Advances in experimental social psychology,* 173–220. New York: Academic Press.

20   Grote, R., op. cit.

21   Asch, S. E. (1946) 'Forming impressions of personality', *Journal of Abnormal and Social Psychology, 41,* 258–90; Avery, R. D. & Campion, J. E. (1982) 'The employment interview: A summary and review of research', *Personnel Psychology, 35,* 281–322; Cardy, R. L. & Dobbins, G. H. (1986) 'Affect and appraisal accuracy: Liking as an integral dimension in evaluating performance', *Journal of Applied Psychology, 71,* 672–78; Lefkowitz, J. (2000) 'The role of interpersonal affective regard in supervisory performance ratings: A literature review and proposed causal model', *Journal of Occupational and Organizational Psychology, 73,* 67–85; Miller, N. & Campbell, D. T. (1959) 'Recency and primacy in persuasion as a function of the timing of speeches and measurements', *Journal of Abnormal and Social Psychology, 59,* 1–9; Schoorman, F. D. (1998) 'Escalation bias in performance appraisals: An unintended consequence of supervisor participation in hiring decisions', *Journal of Applied Psychology, 73,* 58–62.

22   McBriatry, M. A. (1984) 'Performance appraisal: Some unintended consequences', *Public Personnel Management, 17,* 421–34.

23   See, for example, Livingston, J. S. (1969) 'Pygmalion in management', *Harvard Business Review, 47,* 81–89.

24   Anonymous, op. cit.

25   See, for example, Slack, N., Chambers, S. & Johnston, R. (2007) *Operations management.* (Fifth edition.) Harlow: FT Prentice Hall; Slack, N. & Lewis, M. (2008) *Operations strategy.* (Second edition.) Harlow: FT Prentice Hall.

26   Chartered Institute of Personnel & Development (2006) *Reward Annual Management Survey,* London: Chartered Institute of Personnel & Development.

27   Mercer HR (2006) *UK executive pay survey.* 7 March, London: Mercer HR.

28   Greenbury, R. (1995) *Directors' remuneration: Report of a study group chaired by Sir Richard Greenbury.* London: Gee Publishing: Hampel, R. (1998) *Committee on Corporate Governance.* London: Gee Publishing.

29   Benito, A. & Conyon, M. (1999) 'The Governance of Directors' Pay from UK companies', *Journal of Management and Governance, 3,* 117–36; Conyon, M., Gregg, P. & Machin, S. (1995) 'Taking care of business: Executive compensation in the United Kingdom', *Economic Journal, 105,* 704–14; Conyon, M. (1997) 'Corporate Governance and Executive Compensation', *International Journal of Industrial Organization, 15,* 493–509; Jensen, M. & Murphy, K. (1990) 'Performance pay and top management incentives', *Journal of Political Economy, 98,* 225–64; Main, B. G. M., Bruce, A. & Buck, T. (1996) 'Total board remuneration and company performance', *Economic Journal, 106,* 1627–44.

30 Conyon, M. & Murphy, K. (2000) 'The prince and the pauper? CEO pay in the United States and United Kingdom', *Economic Journal, 110,* 640–71.

31 Buck, T., Bruce, A., Main, B. G. M. & Udueni, H. (2003) 'Long term incentive plans, executive pay and U.K. company performance', *Journal of Management Studies, 40,* 1709–27.

32 Porac, J. F., Wade, J. B. & Pollock, T. G. (1999) 'Industry categorizations and the politics of the comparable firm in CEO compensation', *Administrative Science Quarterly, 44,* 112–44; Pass, C. (2003) 'Long-term incentive schemes, executive remuneration and corporate performance: An empirical study', *Corporate Governance, 3,* 18–27.

33 Philip, J. (1998) *Do strategic share repurchase programs create long-run firm value?* PhD Thesis, University of Illinois at Urbana-Champaign, Illinois.

34 Christine, J. (1995) *The growth of performance-based managerial pay: Implications for corporate finance, regulatory policy, and corporate governance.* PhD Thesis, Massachusetts Institute of Technology, Cambridge, MA; Rahavan, K. R. (2004) *The effects of stock repurchases on long-term operating performance in banking firms: An empirical study.* DBA Thesis, Cleveland State University, Cleveland, OH.

35 Locke, E. A. & Latham, G. P. (1990) *A theory of goal setting and task performance.* Englewood Cliffs, NJ: Prentice Hall.

36 Lee, T. W., Locke, E. A., & Phan, S. H. (1997) 'Explaining the assigned goal-incentive interaction: The role of self-efficacy and personal goals', *Journal of Management, 23,* 541–59.

37 Kohn, A. (1993) 'Why incentive plans cannot work', *Harvard Business Review,* September–October, 54–63.

38 Pfeffer, J. (1998) *The human equation: Building profits by putting people first.* Boston, MA: Harvard Business School Press.

9 APPENDICES

1 Hrebiniak, L. G. (2005) *Making strategy work: Leading effective execution and change.* Upper Saddle River, NJ: Pearson Education.

2 The adoption of a qualitative research mode is consistent with the growing recognition of its value in this field of study. See Hoskisson, R. E., Hitt, M. A., Wan, W. P. & Yu, D. (1999) 'Theory and research in strategic management: Swings of pendulum', *Journal of Management, 25,* 417–45, who note the increasing use of qualitative approaches to examine strategic management issues in particular. Also see Miles, M. B. & Huberman, A. M. (1994) *Qualitative data analysis: An expanded sourcebook.* (Second edition.) Thousand Oaks, CA: Sage.

3 See Glaser, B. G. & Strauss, A. L. (1967) *The discovery of grounded theory: Strategies for qualitative research.* London: Weidenfeld and Nicolson; Strauss, A. L. & Corbin, J. (1998) *Basics of qualitative research: Techniques and procedures for developing grounded theory.* (Second edition.) Thousand Oaks, CA: Sage; Eisenhardt, K. M. (1989) 'Building theories from case study research', *Academy of Management Review, 14*(4), 532–50. Also see Porter, M. E. (1994) 'Toward a dynamic theory of strategy'. In Rumelt, R. P., Schendel, D. E. & Teece, D. J. (Eds.) *Fundamental issues in strategy: A research agenda* (pp. 423–61). Boston, MA: Harvard Business School Press, who is clear about the need for the use of case studies in the strategy field, saying, "Academic journals have traditionally not accepted or encouraged the deep examination of case studies, but the nature of strategy requires it. The greater use of case studies in both books and articles will be necessary for real progress at this stage in the field's development" (1994: 431).

4 See, for example, Hall, R. I. (1984) 'The natural logic of management policy making: Its implications for the survival of an organization', *Management Science, 8,* 927;

Hrebiniak, L. G. & Joyce, W. F. (2001) 'Implementing strategy: An appraisal and agenda for future research.' In Hitt, M. A, Freeman, R. E. & Harrison, J. S. (Eds.), *Handbook of strategic management* (pp. 602–26), Oxford: Blackwell Business; Pettigrew, A. M. (1990) 'Longitudinal field research on change: Theory and practice', *Organization Science, 1,* 267–92. Hrebiniak and Joyce argue that because strategy implementation activities occur over extended timeframes and typically involve many actors and enormous task complexity, researchers should ideally maintain access to subjects for long periods. Pettigrew notes, "[t]here are remarkably few studies of change that actually allow the change process to reveal itself in any kind of substantially temporal or contextual manner" (1990: 269) and suggests, "[t]ruth is the daughter of time" (1990: 271).

5 Miles & Huberman, op. cit.

6 Yin, R. K. (1994) *Case study research: Design and methods.* (2nd edition) Thousand Oaks, CA: Sage.; Eisenhardt, op. cit.; Pettigrew, op. cit.; Miles & Huberman, op. cit. Though the primary goal of case study research is to build, rather than test, theory, modest generalizations can be drawn from small non-random samples and applied to theory rather than populations, especially when this theory is replicated across cases.

7 Keat, P. & Young, P. (1992) *Managerial economics.* New York: Macmillan; Porter, M. E. (1980) *Competitive strategy: Techniques for analysing industries and competitors.* New York: Free Press; Porter, M. E. (1985). *Competitive advantage: Creating and sustaining superior performance.* New York: Free Press.

8 Altering the methodology in this way is recognized as being a valuable research in cases where empirically generated insights justify it (Yin, op. cit.; Miles & Huberman, op. cit.; Pettigrew, op. cit.).

9 Yin, op. cit.

10 Triangulation verifies data and makes findings more credible if multiple data logically lead to the same conclusions. See Creswell, J. W. (1998) *Qualitative inquiry and research design: Choosing among five traditions.* Thousand Oaks, CA: Sage; Lincoln, Y. S. & Guba, E. G. (1985) *Naturalistic inquiry.* Beverly Hills, CA: Sage; Miles & Huberman, op. cit.; Patton, M. Q. (1987) *How to use qualitative methods in evaluation.* Newbury Park, CA: Sage; Stake, R. E. (1995) *The art of case study research.* Thousand Oaks, CA: Sage; Yin, op. cit.

11 Miles & Huberman, op. cit.

12 Burrell, G. & Morgan, G. (1979) *Sociological paradigms and organizational analysis: Elements of the sociology of corporate life.* London: Heinemann Educational Books; Denzin, N. K. (1989) *The research act.* Englewood Cliffs, NJ: Prentice Hall; Lincoln & Guba, op. cit.; Spradley, J. P. (1980) *Participant observation.* London: Thomson Learning.

13 Argyris, C., Putnam, R., & McLain Smith, D. M. (1985) *Action science: Concepts, methods, and skills for research and intervention.* San Francisco, CA: Jossey-Bass; Cooperrider, D. L. & Srivastra, R. (1987) 'Appreciative inquiry in organizational life'. In Woodman, R. W. & Pasmore, W. A. (Eds.), *Research in organizational change and development* (pp. 169). Stamford, CT: JAI Press; Harmon, M. M. (1981) *Action theory for public administration.* New York: Longman; Johnson, G., Melin, L. & Whittington, R. (2003) 'Guest editors' introduction. Micro strategy and strategizing: Towards an activity-based view', *Journal of Management Studies, 40,* 3–22.

14 Campbell, J., Dunnette, M., Lawler, E., & Weick, K. E. (1970) *Managerial behaviour, performance and effectiveness.* New York: McGraw-Hill; Flanagan, J. (1954) 'The critical incident technique', *Psychological Bulletin, 51,* 327–58.

15 Strauss, A. L. & Corbin, J. (1998) *Basics of qualitative research: Techniques and procedures for developing grounded theory.* (Second edition) Thousand Oaks, CA: Sage.

References

Al-Ghamdi, S. M. (1998) 'Obstacles to successful implementation of strategic decisions: The British experience', *European Business Review, 98,* 322–7.

Alexander, L. D. (1985) 'Successfully implementing strategic decisions', *Long Range Planning, 18,* 91–97.

Andrews, K. R. (1960) *The concept of corporate strategy.* Homewood, IL: Irwin.

—— (1971) *The concept of corporate strategy.* Homewood, IL: Dow Jones-Irwin.

Anonymous (2006) 'IKEA: Flat pack accounting', *The Economist,* 11 May.

Ansoff, H. I. (1965) *Corporate strategy: An analytical approach to business policy for growth and expansion.* New York: McGraw-Hill.

Argyris, C. (1989) 'Strategy implementation: An experience in learning', *Organizational Dynamics, 18* (2), 4–15.

Argyris, C. and Schön, D. (1978) *Organizational learning: A theory of action perspective.* Reading, MA: Addison Wesley.

Argyris, C., Putnam, R., & McLain Smith, D. M. (1985) *Action science: Concepts, methods, and skills for research and intervention.* San Francisco: Jossey-Bass.

Armstrong, J. S. (1982) 'The value of formal planning for strategic decisions: Review of empirical research', *Strategic Management Journal, 3,* 197–211.

Asch, S. E. (1946) 'Forming impressions of personality', *Journal of Abnormal and Social Psychology, 41,* 258–90.

Ashkenas, R. N. & Shaffer, R. H. (1994) 'Beyond the fads: How leaders drive change with results', *Human Resource Planning, 17* (2), 25–44.

Aspesi, C. & Vardham, V. (1999) 'Brilliant strategy, but can you execute?', *The McKinsey Quarterly,* Winter, 89–99.

Avery, R. D. & Campion, J. E. (1982) 'The employment interview: a summary and review of research', *Personnel Psychology, 35,* 281–322.

Bardach, E. (1977) *The implementation game.* Cambridge, MA: MIT Press.

Beckhard, R. & Harris, D. (1977) *Organization transitions: managing complex change.* Reading, MA: Addison-Wesley.

Benito, A. & Conyon, M. (1999) 'The governance of Directors' Pay from UK Companies', *Journal of Management and Governance, 3,* 117–36.

Bigler, W. R. Jr. & Norris, M. (2004) *The new science of strategy execution: How established firms become fast, sleek wealth creators.* Westport, CT: Praeger Publishers.

Bossidy, L., Charan, R., & Burch, C. (2002) *Execution: The discipline of getting things done.* London: Random House Business Books.

Boswell, W. R. (2000) *Aligning employees with the organization's strategic objectives: Out of "line of sight", out of mind.* Unpublished PhD Thesis. Cornell University.

Bougon, M. G. & Komocar, J. (1990) 'Directing strategic change: A dynamic wholistic approach'. In Huff, A. S. (Ed.) *Mapping strategic thought* (pp. 136–63). Chichester: Wiley.

Boyd, B. K. (1991) 'Strategic planning and financial performance: A meta-analytical review', *Journal of Management Studies, 28*(4), 353–74.

Boynton, A. C. & Zmud, R. W. (1984) 'An assessment of critical success factors', *Sloan Management Review,* 17–27.

Brache, A. P. & Bodley-Scott, S. (2007) *Implementation: How to transform strategic initiatives into blockbuster results.* New York: McGraw-Hill.

Buck, T., Bruce, A., Main, B. G. M. & Udueni, H. (2003) 'Long term incentive plans, executive pay and U.K. company performance', *Journal of Management Studies, 40,* 1709–27.

Burrell, G. & Morgan, G. (1979) *Sociological paradigms and organizational analysis: Elements of the sociology of corporate life.* London: Heinemann Educational Books.

Camillus, J. C. (1975) 'Evaluating the benefits of formal planning systems', *Long range planning, 8*(3), 33–40.

Campbell, J., Dunnette, M., Lawler, E., & Weick, K. E. (1970) *Managerial behaviour, performance and effectiveness.* New York: McGraw-Hill.

Cardy, R. L. & Dobbins, G. H. (1986) 'Affect and appraisal accuracy: Liking as an integral dimension in evaluating performance', *Journal of Applied Psychology, 71,* 672–78.

Chandler, A. D. (1962) *Strategy and structure.* Cambridge, MA: MIT Press.

Charan, R. & Colvin, G. (1999) 'Why CEOs fail' *Fortune,* June 21, 69–78.

Chartered Institute of Personnel & Development (2006) *Reward Annual Management Survey,* London: Chartered Institute of Personnel & Development.

Child, J. (1977) *Organization: A guide for managers and administrators.* New York: Harper & Row.

Christine, J. (1995) *The growth of performance-based managerial pay: Implications for corporate finance, regulatory policy, and corporate governance.* PhD thesis, Massachusetts Institute of Technology, Cambridge, MA.

Conyon, M. (1997) 'Corporate governance and executive compensation', *International Journal of Industrial Organization, 15,* 493–509.

Conyon, M. & Murphy, K. (2000) 'The prince and the pauper? CEO pay in the United States and United Kingdom', *Economic Journal, 110,* 640–71.

Conyon, M., Gregg, P. & Machin, S. (1995) 'Taking care of business: Executive compensation in the United Kingdom' *Economic Journal, 105,* 704–14.

Cooperrider, D. L. & Srivastra, R. (1987) 'Appreciative inquiry in organizational life'. In Woodman, R. W. & Pasmore, W. A. (Eds.) *Research in organizational change and development* (p. 169). Stamford, CT: JAI Press.

Corboy, M. & O'Corrbui, D. (1999) 'The seven deadly sins of strategy', *Management Accounting, 77,* 29–30.

Creswell, J. W. (1998) *Qualitative inquiry and research design: Choosing among five traditions.* Thousand Oaks, CA: Sage.

Daniel, D. R. (1961) 'Management information crisis', *Harvard Business Review,* September–October, 111–21.

Deardon, J., & Vancil, R. F. (1972) *Management control systems.* Homewood, IL: Irwin.

Denzin, N. K. (1989) *The research act.* Englewood Cliffs, NJ: Prentice Hall.

Dreilinger, C. (1994) 'Why management fads fizzle', *Business Horizons, 37*(6), 11–15.

Eccles, T. (1994) *Succeeding with change: Implementing action-driven strategies.* London: McGraw-Hill.

Economist Intelligence Unit (2004) *Strategy execution: Achieving operational excellence.* London: The Economist Intelligence Unit.

Eden, C. (1992) 'On the nature of cognitive maps', *Journal of Management Studies, 29,* 261–65.

Eden, C. & Ackermann, F. (1998) *Making strategy: The journey of strategic management.* London: Sage.

Eden, C., Ackermann, F. & Cropper, S. (1992) 'The analysis of cause maps', *Journal of Management Studies, 29,* 309–24.

Eihorn, H. J. & Hogarth, R. M. (1978) 'Confidence in judgement: Persistence of the illusion of validity', *Psychological Review, 85,* 395–416.

Eisenhardt, K. M. (1989) 'Building theories from case study research', *Academy of Management Review, 14*(4), 532–50.

Flanagan, J. (1954) 'The critical incident technique', *Psychological Bulletin, 51,* 327–58.

Fombrun, C. J. (1994) 'Taking on strategy, 1-2-3' In Baum, J. A. C. & Singh, J. V. (Eds.). *Evolutionary dynamics of organizations* (pp. 199–204). New York: Oxford University Press.

Fulmer, R. M. & Rue, L. W. (1974) 'The practice and profitability of long range planning', *Managerial Planning, 22*(6), May–June, 1–7.

Galbraith, J. (1973) *Designing complex organizations.* Reading, MA: Addison-Wesley

Galbraith, J. R. & Kazanjian, R. K. (1986) *Strategy implementation: Structure, systems and process.* St Paul, MN: West Publishing Co.

Galbraith, J. R. & Nathanson, D. (1978) *Strategy implementation: The role of structure and process.* St Paul, MN: West Publishing Co.

Gilmore, T. (1979) 'Managing collaborative relationships in complex organizations', *Administration in Social Work, 3*(2) 167–80.

Glaser, B. G. & Strauss, A. L. (1967). *The discovery of grounded theory: Strategies for qualitative research.* London: Weidenfeld and Nicolson.

Grady, M. W. (1991) 'Performance measurement: Implementing strategy', *Management Accounting, 72,* 49–54.

Greenbury, R. (1995) *Directors' remuneration: Report of a study group chaired by Sir Richard Greenbury.* London: Gee Publishing.

Grote, R. (2005) *Forced ranking: Making performance management work.* HBS Working Knowledge. Online. Available at: http://hbswk.hbs.edu/archive/5091.html. (Accessed 9 January 2010).

Guth, W. D. & MacMillan, I. C. (1986) 'Strategy implementation versus middle management self interest', *Strategic Management Journal, 7,* 313–27.

Hall, R. I. (1984) 'The natural logic of management policy making: Its implications for the survival of an organization', *Management Science, 8,* 927.

Hampel, R. (1998) *Committee on Corporate Governance.* London: Gee Publishing.

Hardaker, M. & Ward, B. K. (1987) 'Getting things done', *Harvard Business Review, 65*(6), 112–20.

Harmon, M. M. (1981) *Action theory for public administration.* New York: Longman.

Hartman, A. (2004) *Ruthless execution: What business leaders do when their company hits the wall.* Upper Saddle River, NJ: Prentice Hall.

Heider, F. (1958) *The psychology of interpersonal relations.* New York: Wiley.

Herold, D. M. (1972) 'Long-range planning and organizational performance: A cross-validation study', *Academy of Management Journal, 15*(1), 91–102.

Heskett, J. L., Jones, T. O., Loveman, G. W., Sasser, W. E. & Schlesinger, L. A. (1994) 'Putting the service profit chain to work', *Harvard Business Review,* March–April, 164–74.

Hill, C. W. L. (1988) 'Differentiation versus low cost of differentiation and low cost: A contingency framework', *Academy of Management Review, 13*(3), 401–12.

Hischhoff, B. (1975) 'Hindsight does not equal foresight: The effect of outcome knowledge on judgement under uncertainty', *Journal of Experimental Psychology: Human Perception and Performance, 1,* 288–99.

Hofer, C. W. & Schendel, D. E. (1978) *Strategy formulation analytical concepts.* St Paul, MN: West Publishing Co.

Hoskisson, R. E., Hitt, M. A., Wan, W. P. & Yu, D. (1999) 'Theory and research in strategic management: Swings of pendulum', *Journal of Management, 25,* 417–45.

Houldsworth, E. & Jirasinghe, D. (2006) *Managing and measuring employee performance.* London: Kogan Page.

Hrebiniak, L. G. (2005) *Making strategy work: Leading effective execution and change.* Upper Saddle River, NJ: Pearson Education.

Hrebiniak, L. G. & Joyce, W. F. (1984) *Implementing strategy.* New York: Macmillan.

—— (2001) 'Implementing strategy: An appraisal and agenda for future research'. In Hitt, M. A, Freeman, R. E. & Harrison, J. S. (Eds.) *Handbook of strategic management* (pp. 602–26), Oxford: Blackwell Business.

Huff, A. S. (1990) (Ed.) *Mapping strategic thought.* Chichester, UK: Wiley.

Jensen, M. & Murphy, K. (1990) 'Performance pay and top management incentives', *Journal of Political Economy, 98,* 225–64.

Jenster, P. V. (1987) 'Using critical success factors in planning', *Long Range Planning, 20,* 102–9.

Johnson, G. & Scholes, K. (2002) *Exploring corporate strategy.* (Sixth edition.) Harlow: Financial Times Prentice Hall.

Johnson, G., Melin, L. & Whittington, R. (2003) 'Guest editors' introduction. Micro strategy and strategizing: Towards an activity-based view', *Journal of Management Studies, 40,* 3–22.

Jones, E. E. & Harris, V. A. (1967) 'The attribution of attitudes', *Journal of Experimental Social Psychology, 3,* 1–24.

—— (1967) 'The attribution of attitudes', *Journal of Experimental Social Psychology, 3,* 1–24.

Kahneman, D. & Tversky, A. (1973) 'On the psychology of prediction', *Psychological Review, 80,* 237–51.

—— (1979) 'Prospect theory: An analysis of decision under risk', *Econometrica, 47,* 263–91.

Kaplan, R. S (1996) *The balanced scorecard: Translating strategy into action.* Boston, MA: Harvard Business School Press.

—— & Norton, D. P. (2001) *The strategy focused organization: How balanced scorecard companies thrive in the new business environment.* Boston, MA.: Harvard Business School Press.

Kates, A. & Galbraith, J. R. (2007) *Designing your organization: Using the star model to solve 5 critical design challenges.* San Francisco, CA: Jossey-Bass.

Keat, P. & Young, P. (1992) *Managerial economics.* New York: Macmillan.

Kirkpatrick, D. L. (1959) 'Techniques for evaluation training programs', *Journal of American Society for Training Directors, 13,* 28–32.

Kohn, A. (1993) 'Why incentive plans cannot work', *Harvard Business Review,* September–October, 54–63.

Lawler, L. E. (2002) 'The folly of forced ranking', *Strategy & Business, 28,* 28–32.

—— (2003) 'Reward practices and performance management system effectiveness', *Organization Dynamics, 32,* 396–404.

Lee, T. W., Locke, E. A. & Phan, S. H. (1997) 'Explaining the assigned goal-incentive interaction: The role of self-efficacy and personal goals', *Journal of Management, 23,* 541–59.

Lefkowitz, J. (2000) 'The role of interpersonal affective regard in supervisory performance ratings: A literature review and proposed causal model', *Journal of Occupational and Organizational Psychology, 73,* 67–85.

Leidecker, J. K. & Bruno, A. V. (1984) 'Identifying and using critical success factors', *Long Range Planning, 17,* 23–32.

Leontiades, M. & Tezel, A. (1980) 'Planning perceptions and planning results', *Strategic Management Journal, 1*, 65–75.

Lincoln, Y. S. & Guba, E. G. (1985) *Naturalistic inquiry.* Beverly Hills, CA: Sage.

Livingston, J. S. (1969) 'Pygmalion in management', *Harvard Business Review, 47,* 81–89.

Locke, E. A. & Latham, G. P. (1990) *A theory of goal setting and task performance.* Englewood Cliffs, NJ: Prentice Hall.

McBriatry, M. A. (1984) 'Performance appraisal: Some unintended consequences', *Public Personnel Management, 17,* 421–34.

McCann, J. E. & Gilmore, T. N. (1983) 'Diagnosing organizational decision making through responsibility charting', *Sloan Management Review, 24*(2), 3–15.

McGrath, R. G., MacMillan, I. C. & Venkataraman, S. (1995) 'Defining and developing competence: A strategic process paradigm', *Strategic Management Journal, 16,* 251–75.

MacLennan, A. & Lee, G. (2007) 'Challenging customers: 10 tactics every HR business partner should know', *HR Network (Scotland), 2*(3), 28–30.

Mahoney, J. T. & Pandian, J.R. (1992) 'The resource-based view within the conversation of strategic management', *Strategic Management Journal, 13*, 363–80.

Main, B. G. M., Bruce, A. & Buck, T. (1996) 'Total board remuneration and company performance', *Economic Journal, 106*, 1627–44.

Mankins, M. C. & Steele, R. (2005) 'Turning great strategy into great performance', *Harvard Business Review,* January, 64–72.

Melcher, R. (1969) 'Roles and relationships: Clarifying the manager's job', *Personnel,* May–June, 34–41.

Mendelow, A. (1981) 'Environmental Scanning: The Impact of Stakeholder Concept'. In *Proceedings of the Second International Conference on Information Systems* (pp. 299–308), Cambridge, MA.

Mercer HR (2006) *UK executive pay survey.* 7 March, London: Mercer HR.

Michaels, E., Handfield-Jones, H. & Axelrod, B. (2001) *The war for talent.* Boston, MA: Harvard Business School Press.

Miles, M. B. & Huberman, A. M. (1994) *Qualitative data analysis: An expanded sourcebook.* (Second edition) Thousand Oaks, CA: Sage.

Miller, G. A. (1956) The magic number seven plus or minus two: Some limits on our capacity for processing information. *Psychological Review, 64,* 81–97.

Miller, N. & Campbell, D. T. (1959) 'Recency and primacy in persuasion as a function of the timing of speeches and measurements', *Journal of Abnormal and Social Psychology, 59,* 1–9.

Mintzberg, H., Ahlstrand, B. & Lampal, J. (1998) *Strategy safari: The complete guide through the wilds of strategic management.* London: Prentice Hall.

Munro, M. C. & Wheeler, B. R. (1980) 'Planning, critical success factors, and management's information requirements', *MIS Quarterly,* December, 27–38.

Neely, A., Adams, C. & Kennerley, M. (2002) *The performance prism: The scorecard for measuring and managing business success.* Harlow: Pearson Education.

Nisbett, R. E. & Ross, L. (1980) *Human inference: Strategies and shortcomings of social judgment.* Englewood Cliffs, NJ: Prentice Hall.

Novations Group, Inc. (2004) *Uncovering the growing disenchantment with forced ranking performance management systems.* Boston, MA: Novations Group, Inc.

Nutt, P. C. (1987) 'Identifying and appraising how managers install strategy', *Strategic Management Journal, 8,* 1–14.

—— (1999) 'Surprising but true: Half the decisions in organizations fail', *Academy of Management Executive, 13,* 75–90.

—— (2001) 'Strategic decision making'. In Hitt, M.A., Freeman, R.E. & Harrison, J.S. (Eds.) *The Blackwell handbook of strategic management* (pp. 35–69). Oxford: Blackwell

Osborne, T. & McCann, L. A. (2004) 'Forced ranking and age-related employment discrimination', Spring, *Human Rights Magazine*.

Pass, C. (2003) 'Long-term incentive schemes, executive remuneration and corporate performance: An empirical study', *Corporate Governance, 3,* 18–27.

Patton, M. Q. (1987) *How to use qualitative methods in evaluation*. Newbury Park, CA: Sage.

Peteraf, M. A. (1993) 'The cornerstones of competitive advantage: A resource-based view', *Strategic Management Journal, 14,* 179–91.

Pettigrew, A. M. (1990) 'Longitudinal field research on change: Theory and practice', *Organization Science, 1,* 267–92.

Pfeffer, J. (1998) *The human equation: Building profits by putting people first.* Boston, MA: Harvard Business School Press.

Philip, J. (1998) *Do strategic share repurchase programs create long-run firm value?* PhD thesis, University of Illinois at Urbana-Champaign, Illinois.

Porac, J. F., Wade, J. B. & Pollock, T. G. (1999) 'Industry categorizations and the politics of the comparable firm in CEO compensation', *Administrative Science Quarterly, 44,* 112–44.

Porter, M. E. (1980) *Competitive strategy: Techniques for analysing industries and competitors*. New York: Free Press.

—— (1985) *Competitive advantage: Creating and sustaining superior performance*. New York: Free Press.

—— (1994) 'Toward a dynamic theory of strategy'. In Rumelt, R. P., Schendel, D. E. & Teece, D. J. (Eds.) *Fundamental issues in strategy: A research agenda* (pp. 423–61). Boston, MA: Harvard Business School Press.

—— (1996) 'What is strategy?', *Harvard Business Review*, November–December, 61–78.

—— (1998) *On competition*. Boston, MA: Harvard Business School Press.

Prahalad, C. K. & Hamel, G. (1990) 'The core competence of the corporation', *Harvard Business Review,* May–June, 79–91.

Quinn, J. B. (1980) *Strategies for change: Logical incrementalism*. Homewood, IL: Irwin.

Rahavan, K. R. (2004) *The effects of stock repurchases on long-term operating performance in banking firms: An empirical study.* DBA thesis, Cleveland State University, OH.

Rajagopalan, N. & Spreitzer, G. M. (1997) 'Toward a theory of strategic change: A multi-lens perspective and integrative framework', *Academy of Management Review, 22,* 48–80.

Reed, R. & Buckley, M. R. (1988) 'Strategy in action: Techniques for implementing strategy', *Long Range Planning, 21,* 67–74.

Reichheld, F. F. (1993) 'Loyalty-based management', *Harvard Business Review,* March, 64–73.

Rigby, D. & Bilodeau, B. (2009) *Management Tools,* Boston, MA: Bain & Company.

Roberts, A. & MacLennan, A. F. (2003) *Making strategies work.* Harlow: Pearson.

Roberts, A., & Pitt, S. (1990) 'Strategy implementation: A dynamic process guide', Working paper, London Business School.

Rockart, J. F. (1979) 'Chief executives define their own data needs', *Harvard Business Review,* March–April, 238–41.

Ross, L. (1977) 'The intuitive psychologist and his shortcomings: Distortions in the attribution process'. In Berkowitz, L. (Ed.) *Advances in experimental social psychology, 10,* 173–220. New York: Academic Press.

Sackman, H. (1971) *Mass information utilities and social excellence*. New York: Auerback.

Sandelands, L. E. (1994) 'All talk and no action? Perish the thought', *Management Decision, 32,* 10–11.

Schoorman, F. D. (1998) 'Escalation bias in performance appraisals: an unintended consequence of supervisor participation in hiring decisions', *Journal of Applied Psychology, 73,* 58–62.

Schwenk, C. (1986) 'Information, cognitive biases, and commitment to a course of action', *Academy of Management Review, 11*, 298–310.

Scullen, S., Bergey, P. & Aiman-Smith, L. (2005) 'Forced distribution rating systems and the improvement of workforce potential: A baseline simulation', *Personnel Psychology, 58*(1): 1–32.

Selznick, P. (1957) *Leadership in administration: A sociological interpretation.* New York: Harper & Row.

Simon, H. A. (1947) *Administrative behavior: A study of decision-making processes in administrative organization.* New York: Macmillan.

Simons, R. (2000) *Performance measurement and control systems for implementing strategy: Text and cases.* Englewood Cliffs, NJ: Prentice Hall.

Slack, N. & Lewis, M. (2008) *Operations strategy.* (Second edition.) Harlow: FT Prentice Hall.

Slack, N., Chambers, S. & Johnston, R. (2007) *Operations Management.* (Fifth edition.) Harlow: FT Prentice Hall.

Spradley, J. P. (1980) *Participant observation.* London: Thomson Learning.

Stake, R. E. (1995) *The art of case study research.* Thousand Oaks, CA: Sage.

Staw, B. M. & Epstein, L. D. (2000) 'What bandwagons bring: Effects of popular management techniques on corporate performance, reputation, and CEO pay', *Administrative Science Quarterly, 45,* 523–56.

Stonich, P. J. (1982) *Implementing strategy.* Cambridge, MA: Ballinger.

Strauss, A. L. & Corbin, J. (1998) *Basics of qualitative research: Techniques and procedures for developing grounded theory.* (Second edition) Thousand Oaks, CA: Sage.

Taylor, S. E. & Fiske, S. T. (1975) 'Point of view and perception of causality', *Journal of Personality and Social Psychology, 32,* 439–45.

The BOC Group and London Business School (1994) *Building global excellence.* London: The BOC Group and London Business School.

Thompson, A. A. & Strickland, A. J. (1981) *Strategy formulation and implementation: Tasks of the general manager.* Dallas, TX: Business Publications.

Tversky, A. & Kahneman, D. (1974) Judgement under uncertainty: Heuristics and biases. *Science, 185,* 1124–31.

—— (1981) 'The framing of decisions and psychology of choice', *Science, 211,* 453–58.

Wall, S. J. (2004) *On the fly: Executing strategy in a changing world.* Hoboken, NJ: John Wiley & Sons.

Ward, W. C. & Jenkins, H. H. (1965) 'The display of information and judgement of contingency', *Canadian Journal of Psychology, 19,* 231–41.

Welch, J. (2001) *Jack: Straight from the gut.* New York: Warner Books.

Wernerfelt, B. (1984) 'A resource-based view of the firm', *Strategic Management Journal, 5,* 171–80.

—— (1995) 'The resource-based view of the firm: Ten years on', *Strategic Management Journal, 16,* 171–74.

Wernham, R. (1985) 'Obstacles to strategy implementation in a nationalized industry', *The Journal of Management Studies, 22,* 632–49.

Wessel, J. (1993) 'The strategic human resource management process in practice', *Planning Review, 21,* 37–38.

Wright, J. C. (1962) 'Consistency and complexity of response sequences as a function of schedules of noncontingent reward', *Journal of Experimental Psychology, 63,* 601–9.

Wunder, T. (2005) 'New strategy alignment in multinational corporations', *Strategic Finance,* November, 35–41.

Yin, R. K. (1994) *Case study research: Design and methods.* (2nd edition) Thousand Oaks, CA: Sage.

Index

assessment 180–3; key implications
185; misaligned measures 183–5,
185; need for 180; performance
measurement: detailed design of
139–42; feedforward effects 183;
framework 64; strategic *see* strategic
performance measurement; use of
causal chains to identify 139
performance-related pay (PRP) 187–91,
192–3
PEST 76
Picasso, Pablo 193–7
pitfalls: with causal chains 126–8; with
causality 85–92; in translating strategy
into action 92–8
planned strategy 10–11, **12**
polished maps 98–111
Porter, Michael 99, 105–8, 110
post-implementation risks 131, **132**, 133
practitioners, challenges for 204
predictive modelling 143
principal-agent problem 12, 190, 217n3
prioritisation: resource allocation 165
problems: diagnosis of 39–40; with
projects 157; strategy execution 29–51
process design, integrating 160
process models 72
processes 61; aligning organizational
designs and systems, 158–61; design
and improvement 159–60; feedback
from 161; feedback in HR example
161; integrating design 160; low-cost
airline example 158; mapping 159–60;
mobile network failure example **159**;
resource allocation 166–7; role of
158–9
processing failure **88**
project management: and bottom-up causal
chains 117–24; diagnosis in **156**;
processes 155, **156**; strategic 155; and
strategic risk management 129–30
projects 60–1; absenteeism example 157;
aligning organizational designs and
systems 153–8; definition **154**; doing
the right 155; embedding products
157; handling at right level 155–6;
problems with 157; resource allocation
166–7; strategic alignment in 156–7;
value of to strategy execution 153–5
public sector agency example **43**, 44–5,
168–70

RACI matrix *see* responsibility charting
rank and yank systems 181–3
RASCI matrix *see* responsibility charting
regulation, government 17–18
reporting: interface management 173, 175
research, challenges for 204
research methodology 206–8
resource allocation: aligning organizational
designs and systems, 165–8;
framework 61; natural selection
167–8; prioritisation 165; projects and
processes 166–7; sharing resources
168; strategic commissioning **168–70**;
time horizons 166
resource-based view 110
resource interaction, pattern of 8–10
resource sharing 168
responsibilities: individual 62
responsibility charting 177–9
retail banking example 83
retailer sales management training *see*
sales management training example
retrospection, importance of 201
reward management: incentivising
people specifically to do right 190–3;
incentivising senior executives 188–9;
intrinsic motivators 193; potency
of 187–8; motivation through PRP
189–90
risk definitions **129**
risk management: processes 160; strategic
129–36, 196
roles and responsibilities: aligning
organizational designs and systems,
175–9; conventional definition 175–7;
framework 62; responsibility charting
177–9
RoyalSunAlliance example **21**

sales management training example 30,
40, 41–2, 144, **145–6**; causal chain
123, **124**, 139, **140**, 194
sequential task dependency 128
sequential thinking 66
seven step diagnostic process 38–50
share schemes 188–9
solution-orientation: test **32–3**
staff inflexibility: mini case study **45–8**
staff motivation 74
stakeholder management 171–3, **174**
stakeholders 73–4; alignment analysis
matrix 172–3, **174**; definition 172;